Praise for *Metadata in the Digital Library*

'Gartner's latest book is written with his characteristic clarity and authority. He defines the concepts of metadata in an engaging and natural way and his book bridges the gap between theory and practice by using examples from his own work at the Warburg Institute Library. He has taken a fresh approach to explaining how XML works, as well as widely used metadata standards such as Dublin Core and METS. The chapters on Metadata Management (Chapter 3) and the Semantic Web (Chapter 10) are particularly informative. This quality of writing comes from a deep understanding of the subject coupled with direct experience of day-to-day management and use of metadata. *Metadata in the Digital Library* will be a valuable resource for postgraduate students studying information and knowledge organisation at our University.'

Dr David Haynes, *School of Computing, Edinburgh Napier University*

'This book is a fantastic blend of technical detail, disciplinary expertise and introductory information. A general description and discussion about metadata contextualises more detailed analyses of good practice guidelines for creating interoperable metadata. While the book is most relevant to digital libraries, the concepts and standards discussed are relevant across the GLAM sector. Readers new to the adventures of metadata for digital collections will feel challenged (in the best possible way) and experts will have an authoritative reference they can use to support their work. I thoroughly enjoyed reading this book and plan on adding it to my modules' core reading lists.'

Kristen Schuster, *Lecturer in Digital Curation, King's College London*

Metadata in the Digital Library

Metadata in the Digital Library

Building an Integrated Strategy with XML

Richard Gartner

Published by Facet Publishing
7 Ridgmount Street, London WC1E 7AE
www.facetpublishing.co.uk

Facet Publishing is wholly owned by CILIP: the Library and Information Association.

British Library Cataloguing in Publication Data
A catalogue record for this book is available from the British Library.

ISBN 978-1-78330-484-4 (paperback)
ISBN 978-1-78330-485-1 (hardback)
ISBN 978-1-78330-486-8 (PDF)
ISBN 978-1-78330-532-2 (EPUB)

First published 2021

Text printed on FSC accredited material.

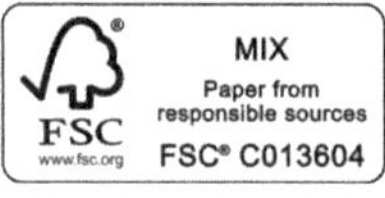

Typeset from author's files in 10.5/13 pt Revival 565 and Frutiger by Flagholme Publishing Services.
Printed and made in Great Britain by CPI Group (UK) Ltd, Croydon, CR0 4YY.

Contents

Figures and Tables

Figures

Tables

Acknowledgements

I would like to acknowledge my friends and colleagues at the Warburg Institute, King's College London, Dr Williams's Library and the Bodleian Library who have provided me with such support and guidance over many years. The same thanks are due to many other colleagues here and abroad, including my friends on the METS Editorial Board with whom I have had the pleasure of working for almost 20 years.

I would also like to thank Pete Baker and Michelle Lau at Facet for their help in developing this book and the effortless way that they steered me through to its completion.

Abbreviations

AACR2	Anglo-American Cataloging Rules, Second Edition
AIP	Archival Information Package
AVI	Audio Video Interleave
CIDOC-CRM	CIDOC (International Council of Museums International Committee for Documentation) Conceptual Reference Model
DACS	Describing Archives: A Content Standard
DC	Dublin Core
DCC	Digital Curation Centre
DCMI	Dublin Core Metadata Initiative
DIDL	Digital Item Declaration Language
DIP	Dissemination Information Package
FRBR	Functional Requirements for Bibliographic Records
ID	identifier
IPR	intellectual property rights
ISAD(G)	General International Standard Archival Description
ISO	International Organization for Standardization
JPEG	Joint Photographic Experts Group
LCNAF	Library of Congress Name Authority File
LCSH	Library of Congress Subject Headings
MADS	Metadata Authority Description Schema
MARC	MAchine Readable Cataloguing
METS	Metadata Encoding and Transmission Standard
MIX	NISO Metadata for Images in XML Schema
MODS	Metadata Object Description Schema
MP3	Moving Pictures 3 (audio format) MPEG (Motion Picture Experts Group) Layer-3
MPEG	Moving Picture Experts Group
OAI-PMH	Open Archives Initiative Protocol for Metadata Harvesting

OAIS	Open Archival Information System
ODL	Oxford Digital Library
PREMIS	PREservation Metadata: Implementation Strategies
RDA	Resource Description and Access
RDF	Resource Description Framework
SGML	Standard Generalised Markup Language
SIP	Submission Information Package
TIFF	Tagged Image File Format
URI	Uniform Resource Identifier
URL	Uniform Resource Locator
XML	eXtensible Markup Language
XPath	XML Path Language
XSLT	eXtensible Stylesheet Language Transformations
W3C	World Wide Web Consortium
WAV	Waveform Audio File Format
WDL	Warburg Digital Library
W3C	World Wide Web Consortium
WMV	Windows Media Video
XML	eXtensible Markup Language
XPath	XML Path Language
XSLT	eXtensible Stylesheet Language Transformations

1

Introduction, Aims and Definitions

1.1 Origins

For as long as libraries, museums or archives have existed their curators have been compiling information to assist in organising the collections that they house and making their contents accessible. We can look back thousands of years to see this in action: we may go, for instance, to the ancient city of Ur, whose princess, Ennigaldi-Nanna, compiled inventories of her private museum of antiquities on clay cylinders, or to the biographical registers of authors compiled by Kallimachos of Cyrene for works held in the Royal Library of Alexandria. We can trace from these distant times an almost unbroken line of developments in the ways in which this information has been compiled and the forms that it takes, until we reach the distant descendants of these ancient pioneers in such contemporary achievements as WorldCat, a union catalogue of 2.8 billion works in 18,000 libraries.

The term universally applied to this information, which supports, refers to or acts as an auxiliary to our collections, is *metadata*. This word, derived etymologically from both Greek and Latin, literally means 'data about data', and it is with this concise definition that it is usually introduced. Although metadata has been created for millennia, the term itself made its first appearance only in the late 1960s, when the computer scientist Phillip Bagley defined it as:

> the ability to associate explicitly with a data element a second data element which represents data 'about' the first data element. This second data element we might term a 'metadata element'.
>
> (Bagley 1968, 26)

This concept rapidly became common parlance in computer science and even inspired an animated film, entitled *Metadata*, that was produced by the National Film Board of Canada in 1971 (Foldès 1971). It is now ubiquitous in information science to refer to the relationship between an item of data and the information by which it is described or referenced.

1.2 From information science to libraries

The concept of metadata translates very easily, by analogy, to the processes by which libraries and librarians have long been creating and employing information to assist in the discovery and management of their collections. It takes no stretch of the imagination to label the contents of collections as 'data' and the catalogues that are compiled to guide users to these as 'metadata'. In addition to these publicly visible forms of library metadata, we can also add the mass of administrative information – anything from acquisition ledgers to loan records – which libraries use to acquire their holdings and make them available to their readers.

When we move from traditional, paper-based libraries to their digital counterparts (and what exactly is a digital library will be discussed shortly) the metadata/data model fits even more closely. In a similar way to what we could call 'analogue' libraries, the digital library consists of the data files or digital assets which form its collections and the associated metadata which allows these to be managed, discovered, retrieved, disseminated and preserved. There are obvious analogies between the form and function of metadata in analogue and digital libraries, but also important differences which will be explored later in this chapter.

At this point it would be helpful to clarify what is meant by a 'digital library' and why this term is used throughout the book instead of such expressions as 'digital collections' or 'digital repositories', to which it is often seen as equivalent. Early definitions tended to emphasise the 'digital' rather than the 'library'; for instance, in an influential article from 1995, William Saffady described it as:

> a library that maintains all, or a substantial part, of its collections in computer-processible form as an alternative, supplement or complement to the conventional printed and microform collections that currently dominate library collections.
>
> (Saffady 1995, 221)

The reference to microform collections certainly dates this article, but many would still see its emphasis on the digital format of materials and their institutional setting (as part of a 'library', itself undefined in the quote) as the key factors that define a 'digital library'.

This does not assist us in determining what makes such a collection of digital objects a library. The essential ingredient that allows us to make this move is the concept of *curation*. This word derives from the Latin *curare*, meaning 'to care for' or 'to nurture', which in the broadest sense encapsulates what a librarian attempts to do for their collections. Curation is essential for the preservation of a culture, and also its evolution over time; beyond preservation itself, often seen as its core function, it also involves selecting the definitive features of a culture, describing them and putting them into context in order to make them comprehensible when accessed or disseminated.

This, of course, is what librarians have been doing for as long as there have been libraries. Shirley Baker, for many years Dean of Washington University Libraries, expressed it succinctly many years ago:

> Librarians do four things: we select and acquire, we classify, we provide equitable access, and we preserve.
>
> (quoted in Gartner 2004, 191–208)

All of these are key to what makes a digital collection a true digital library. Such a library selects its holdings using a coherent acquisition policy which aims to create a balanced collection that is relevant to its users' needs. It classifies and describes them so that they can be found easily and assessed for their relevance. It provides access on an equitable basis to its user community. It preserves them for future use so that they, and the knowledge that they contain, do not disappear into the digital ether.

If we move from *what* the 'analogue' and 'digital' do to *why* they are doing it, it may be appropriate to quote the words of S. R. Ranganathan, the Indian librarian often considered the father of library science. His often-repeated 'Five Laws of Library Science', first laid out in his monograph of the same name in 1931, are concise and highly focused statements of what libraries of all types should be about:

> Books are for use.
> Every reader his or her book.
> Every book its reader.
> Save the time of the reader.
> The library must be a growing organism.
>
> (Ranganathan 1931)

If we make some appropriate substitutions to broaden the scope of these principles to other media, we still have an apposite set of principles by which a digital collection could be regarded as a digital library. Such a library is in the business of matching its holdings to users so that nothing lies dormant, everyone has access to the resources they require and every one of these can find its way to whoever needs it, saving their time in the process. Such a library will also be a growing organism, unlikely to stand still for long if it is to thrive and develop.

For these reasons, it is appropriate to call a curated digital collection or repository a digital library. Although the preceding paragraphs have stressed the continuity of a digital library's processes and functions with those of its analogue predecessors, there are many ways in which the curation of such a library is more complex and requires additional skills. The relative fragility of the digital file, its dependence on the medium on which it is stored, the opacity of this medium which requires the decoding of data before it can be read, its tractability (the ease with which it can be changed and manipulated) and the simple ways in which it can be copied and disseminated all present additional challenges to its curators which the custodians of paper collections did not and do not have to face.

1.3 The central place of metadata

The ubiquity of metadata in the work of librarians for centuries highlights its pivotal role in curation. It has an essential place in the selection of the key facets of a culture, their description, their placement into context as an aid to comprehension and their dissemination. It also has a central place in the processes by which a culture, analogue or digital, is preserved for future generations. Without metadata we would have no curation, and hence no culture.

Ranganathan's five laws would also be unachievable without metadata. Without it books (or their digital equivalents) would, if not unusable per se, be difficult to find in anything but a random way and so would spend their time accumulating dust (real or virtual) on their analogue or digital shelves. We could not match every book (or its digital counterpart) to its reader and every reader to their book without metadata and without it saving their time, that would indeed be a forlorn hope. The library as a growing organism would soon wither away without metadata to support it, ending up as an inchoate morass of objects in whose murk the user would soon lose their way if they dared to approach it at all in the hope of finding what they needed.

Essential though it is, producing metadata is a complex, potentially time-consuming and often expensive business. For these reasons it is important that its creation and application are carried out in the context of a coherent, overall strategy. Such a strategy needs to take into account both the current and future contexts within which the digital library will operate: not only must metadata support the day-to-day operations of the library, including the delivery of its collections and their administration, but it must also look to the future, aiming to ensure the preservation of the digital objects to which it is an essential counterpart.

To design and implement a coherent metadata strategy requires a grasp of the essentials of metadata theory and how it may be applied in the context of the requirements of a specific digital library. If at all possible, ad hoc approaches should be avoided; instead, a strategy should be rooted in the extensive body of work which has gone into the creation of metadata *standards*. Applying these inevitably imposes some constraints on what we can do and how we do it, but these need not be so rigid as to dictate matters to the extent that a digital library loses its *raison d'être*: metadata should be at the service of the collection and its users, not vice versa. The challenge is to implement a strategy which is rooted in standards but flexible enough to enable a library's requirements to be met in full.

The problem with metadata standards is, as the computer scientist Andrew Tannenbaum so memorably put it, 'that you have so many to choose from; furthermore, if you do not like any of them, you can just wait for next year's model' (Tannenbaum 2003, 254). Standards are, to say the least, plentiful and always proliferating: every sector that relies on metadata, including most obviously libraries, museums, archives, information technology and publishing, has its own set of standards which are not necessarily designed to communicate readily with those originating from outside its domain. Within each sector there are usually multiple standards, each of which is designed for a specific set of functions and all of which add further to the metadata jungle.

The upshot of this messy state of affairs is that there is no single standard which will meet all of the needs of a digital library. A metadata strategy requires the implementation of multiple standards which may not be designed to co-exist without friction. The challenge is to meld several of these into a single coherent architecture which should be logical and easy to implement in a working environment. The overall aim should be to create something that allows a digital library to operate day to day but is also easy to share with others, independent of a single software platform and capable of preservation in the long term.

The aim of the following chapters is to map out a strategic approach of this kind by introducing the basic principles of metadata theory and providing a practical guide to their implementation in the context of the digital library. Because the systems used to host such a library are inevitably transient and are likely to become obsolete well before the contents of its collections, the emphasis in the strategy expounded here will be on creating a 'canonical' metadata record for a digital object; this is one which is independent of these systems but which can be used to populate them as they are now, and their successors in the future. For this reason, much of the model on which the strategy is based is derived from the discipline of digital preservation.

Throughout the book reference is made to the metadata standards discussed, their accompanying documentation and other resources which may be of use when implementing them. These are listed in the appendix

'Standards and Resources' towards the end of the volume, where each is assigned an identifier by which it is referenced with a superscript in the main text, for example, 'the Anglo-American Cataloging Rules (AACR2)[S1] ...'.

1.4 The book in outline

Chapter 2 introduces the concept of metadata in the context of analogue and digital libraries, demonstrating their areas of congruence but also the additional complexity of digital library metadata. It introduces the three types into which metadata is usually divided: descriptive, administrative and structural. It then describes the three core components of which metadata is composed – semantics, content rules and syntax – and explains what is meant by a metadata standard.

Chapter 3 lays out the basic principles that should underlie any metadata strategy for the digital library. The most crucial among these are that it should be capable of supporting all stages of a digital object's lifecycle, that it can meet the needs of preservation in the long term and that it should be standards based whenever possible. The chapter will introduce the Open Archival Information System[C3.4] architecture, the model with which this book's metadata strategy is designed to integrate. The chapter also explains the importance of interoperability and the ready transferability of metadata.

Chapter 4 will move from the theory of metadata to explaining how one may begin to apply these basic principles in practice. Three approaches are discussed. The first is the direct application of existing models and standards from the digital library community. The second is the design of conceptual models based on the needs of a given application and their translation into these standards. The third is to design a bespoke metadata scheme from scratch. The chapter then examines the role of a logical system of identifiers, internal and external, in underpinning a metadata architecture and suggests a scheme for these which can be applied to all of the data and metadata in a digital library.

Chapter 5 discusses syntax, the mechanism by which metadata is encoded to build up structures that extend beyond its basic semantic elements. It introduces eXtensible Markup Language (XML), the interoperable format which is recommended for housing metadata record. The chapter demonstrates the advantages of XML, including its value for preservation, its platform and software independence and its ready interoperability. It explains how XML may be created, edited and transformed into other formats. This final feature is key to making it a primary choice for recording the canonical version of a metadata record, which is the kernel of this metadata strategy.

Chapter 6 outlines the architectural underpinnings of this metadata strategy in the form of the Metadata Encoding and Transmission Standard

(METS)[S.17]. This is an XML schema which provides a logically structured envelope for holding all of the descriptive, administrative and structural metadata associated with a digital object. The overall shape of a METS file is explained here, as well as the mechanisms by which it embeds metadata from other schemas and how it handles structural metadata of any degree of complexity.

Chapter 7 covers descriptive metadata, the type which is most visible to the end-user of a digital library and the most important for enabling its collections to be discovered. Three core standards are introduced in some detail, Metadata Object Description Schema (MODS)[S.18], Dublin Core[S.13] and MARCXML[S.15], and it is demonstrated how these may be integrated into the METS framework. Other important subject-specific schemas are also introduced more briefly.

Chapter 8 moves the discussion on to the use of content rules to enhance the value of descriptive metadata. It introduces the concept of cataloguing rules and explains how they may be applied within a digital library, either by the implementation of existing sets or by devising local guidelines. It then examines the use of thesauri for subject access and authority files for such semantic components as personal or geographic names. Key cataloguing rules, thesauri and name authorities are introduced and their incorporation into descriptive metadata schemas is explained. The chapter also examines the Metadata Authority Description Schema (MADS)[S.16], a standard for the encoding and exchange of taxonomies, classifications and authority lists, which may be useful when local supplements to, or replacements for, pre-existing equivalents are constructed.

Chapter 9 introduces the complex area of administrative and preservation metadata, the strain that is not immediately visible to an end-user but which fulfils the vital functions of supporting the management of a digital library and ensuring that its collections are preserved. This metadata is much more complex than that required for a traditional, analogue library: it includes in its remit technical information on the library's digital objects, details of intellectual property rights (IPR) and metadata that is orientated towards preservation, such as an audit trail of all actions performed on a digital object from its initial creation onwards. The chapter introduces the preservation standard PREservation Metadata: Implementation Strategies (PREMIS)[S.23] as the primary receptacle for this type, supplemented by additional schemas where more detailed and specific technical and rights metadata is required.

Chapter 10 concentrates on interoperability and what can be done to ensure that metadata can be easily shared with others and transferred between systems with minimum effort. The chapter covers a number of methods to enable this, which include the exchange of METS records and the definition of METS Profiles which formally document them, the use of metadata harvesting protocols and the adoption of the Resource Description Framework (RDF)[C10.10] to enable integration with the Semantic Web.

Chapter 11 demonstrates how the strategy described in this book may be implemented in real-world settings by describing two case studies in which it is applied. In the first, the strategy underlies a library of digitised books which uses as its foundation bibliographic records downloaded from a university library catalogue. In the second, a metadata scheme for a collection of digital photographs is created from scratch and translated into the standards that form the basis of this strategy.

Chapter 12 summarises the multiple strands of this strategy and concludes by demonstrating its pivotal role in making a digital collection a 'library'.

The chapters are followed by the list of standards and resources mentioned earlier and a short set of recommended further readings which supply background and contextual information on the standards and methods touched upon throughout the book.

The bridge between theory and practice that the book aims to establish is key to a successful metadata strategy. Without the former it is not possible to produce metadata with an overall coherence and long-term potential for reuse and preservation. Without the latter the digital librarian will achieve little in a working environment. Without a conjunction of theory and practice it is too easy to create messy metadata environments which store up problems in the long term, something that any librarian (digital or otherwise) would wish to avoid. The author hopes that this book will equip the librarian with both and demonstrate how their synthesis will place their digital collections on a solid foundation.

2

Metadata Basics

2.1 Introduction

In the opening chapter of this book the concept of metadata was introduced in terms of its etymology ('data about data') and Bagley's first definition ('a second data element which represents data "about" [a] first data element'). Both point out that at its centre is the idea of a conjunction between two elements: metadata always refers to something else, the data which is its referent. The nature of this relationship in many ways determines the form that the metadata will take and the relationship itself is dictated by the purpose for which it is compiled.

This immediately brings us to an important but sometimes forgotten feature of metadata: that it is constructed for a purpose; it is an artificial creation, not something that is found in the world itself. The purpose for which any metadata is compiled inevitably dictates everything about it, from the terms that it employs to describe its referent data to the way in which it is organised. The most significant impact that the purpose behind metadata can have is in determining what it encompasses and what it chooses to omit; it is inherently selective in its remit and can never claim to be universal.

Metadata should also never be seen as inherently objective: it is making a statement about the world, and this statement is a subjective one. This may seem obvious in the case of something as clearly human-created as a classification scheme; but it is also true of automatically compiled metadata such as logs of user access to web pages, where the choice of what to record is selective and so, to some extent at least, subjective.

All of the standards that will be covered in this book (and what exactly constitutes a metadata standard will be discussed shortly) have been constructed for a given purpose and with a circumscribed remit; they therefore inevitably exhibit these features of selectivity and constraint. This does allow them to be focused and so able to perform the functions for which they have been devised, but it does mean that no single one can encompass all of the metadata requirements for a digital library. The strategy that will be outlined in the coming chapters will, therefore, aim to integrate several standards into something coherent, usable and with long-term viability.

2.2 Three types of metadata

Metadata as it has been defined so far is quite a broad concept and so at this point it would be useful to refine it to something more specific. This is best done by dividing it into one of three categories defined by the functions that they are designed to fulfil, which are commonly termed *descriptive*, *administrative* and *structural*. As will be seen in the following pages, all three must usually be present in a digital library if it is to operate effectively.

2.2.1 Descriptive metadata

Descriptive metadata is the type with which users of libraries – analogue or digital – are most familiar as it is the most visible of the three. This is the information which enables them to determine the existence of an item and locate it within a collection. For these reasons it is often called *finding* metadata, and it usually presents itself to the user in the form of a catalogue record (Figures 2.1 and 2.2).These two images, one of a traditional catalogue card and one a screenshot of an entry in an online catalogue, show the type of descriptive metadata that we would expect to find in any library; they include such standard bibliographic elements as the names of authors, titles and publication details (usually the place of publication, publisher and date of publication). All of this is useful for someone who is looking for a specific

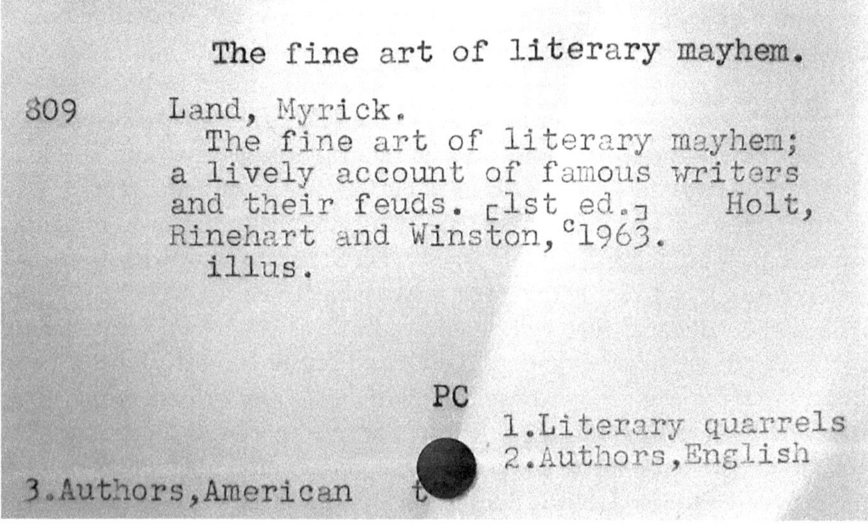

The fine art of literary mayhem.

809 Land, Myrick.
The fine art of literary mayhem; a lively account of famous writers and their feuds. [1st ed.] Holt, Rinehart and Winston, c1963.
illus.

PC

1.Literary quarrels
2.Authors,English
3.Authors,American

Figure 2.1 *Descriptive metadata in a standard catalogue card* (Image by Wikimedia Commons user 'ScottishTShirt' – CC BY-SA 4.0)

Author	Müller, Johannes von.
Title	**Metadata : how to relate to images : ein Ausblick auf eine mögliche Zukunft der Ikonologie / Johannes von Müller.**
Imprint	Bonn : Max Weber Stiftung - Deutsche Geisteswissenschaftliche Institute im Ausland.
Descript.	p. 33 : ill. ; 30 cm.

LOCATION	CLASSMARK	STATUS
Warburg Archive	NBM 80	APPLY TO STAFF

Series	Weltweit vor Ort ; 2016, 2
Note	In: Weltweit vor Ort. -- vol. 2 (2016).
Subject	Warburg, Aby, 1866-1929. Mnemosyne.

Figure 2.2 *Descriptive metadata in an online catalogue* (Warburg Institute, University of London)

book for which they already have such details as its author or title, or if they are searching for more works by a given writer. More specific information such as the note that a volume is a first edition (in the card catalogue entry) or part of a series (in the online record) can be useful in helping them to ensure that they find the exact edition they are looking for (in the first example) or perhaps to expand their search to other works in the same series (in the second).

These records also contain a further essential component of descriptive metadata, an indication of the subjects covered by the work that it describes. On the catalogue card the number 809 is the code for what a cataloguer has judged to be the subject of the book according to the widely used Dewey Decimal Classification, in this case 'History, description, critical appraisal of more than two literatures'. At the bottom of the card some more subject information is given in the form of short phrases taken from a list of subject terms compiled for use in the library where this volume is housed. In the online catalogue a similar subject indicator, also taken from a list of allowed terms, is shown at the bottom of the entry.

As these examples are taken from library catalogues whose collections consist primarily of printed texts, the components of descriptive metadata shown derive from traditional bibliography and utilise the terms that it has evolved over time to describe this class of materials. Other digital collections may present a very different array of elements that reflect the characteristics of their contents and the distinctive requirements of their users. Figure 2.3 (on the next page), a screenshot from an archive of photographs of works of art, for instance, has a less generic set of metadata attached to it.

Here the emphasis is on the iconography of the image, the subject of the work of art depicted, which is often described in minute detail. In this case the legend from Greek mythology of Daphne and her transformation into a laurel tree is specified down to the level of which of her limbs have

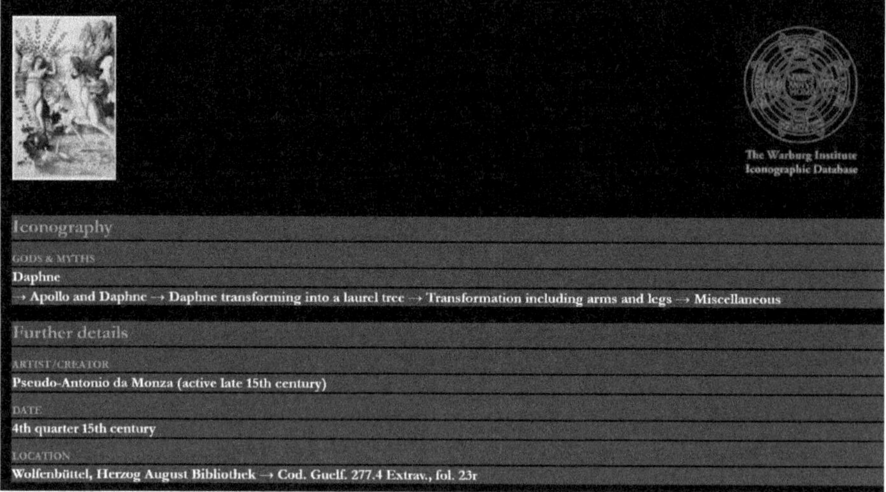

Figure 2.3 *Descriptive metadata in the Warburg Institute's Iconographic Database* (Warburg Institute, University of London)

metamorphosed into leaves. The metadata takes this form because it belongs to a highly specialised collection, the Iconographic Database of the Warburg Institute in London[C11.5], which is primarily a scholarly resource of iconographic subjects and so gives priority to these over artists' names or the titles of works which most image archives prefer. It therefore goes into great detail annotating these subjects and is less interested in the information that would typically be found in a standard library catalogue or more generic photographic archive.

If we move from the academic to the commercial sector, a very different array of descriptive metadata is likely to be provided. Figure 2.4 (opposite), a screenshot from the commercial video streaming service MUBI[C2.2], demonstrates the type of information that would assist its audience in finding a film to watch.

MUBI's audience is primarily orientated towards arthouse cinema and so it presents a carefully curated selection from outside the mainstream fare that would be found at a multiplex. In addition to information required to identify the film (its original German-language title, its director, country of origin and the date of its initial release), we also see its genre (horror), its running time and that it is a silent film. We are also given a brief synopsis, a rating based on reviews from the service's subscribers and 'Our Take', an informal summary that explains its likely attraction to MUBI's viewers. We might also consider the still image underlying the text as a form of descriptive metadata designed to give an idea of the overall atmosphere invoked by the film.

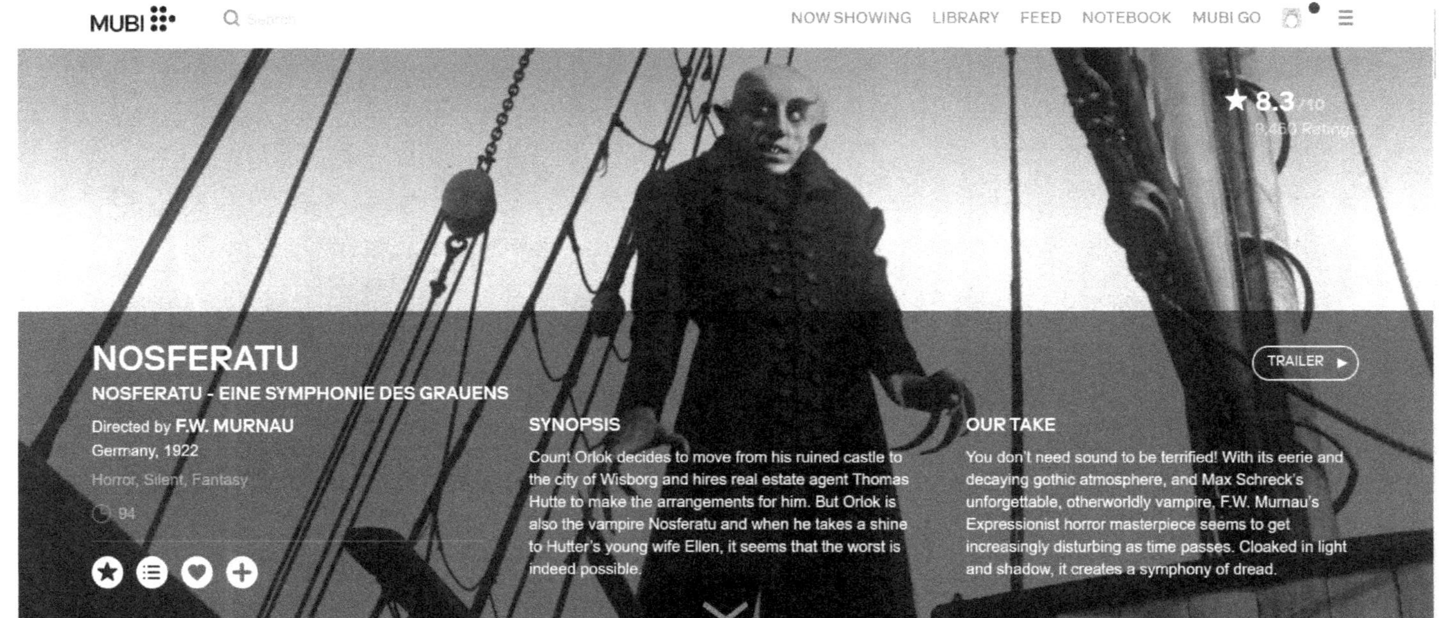

Figure 2.4 *Descriptive metadata from the video streaming service MUBI* (Image © MUBI)

These examples should demonstrate the diversity of descriptive metadata and how it is shaped by the requirements of its intended audience in order to be effective. This diversity inevitably gives rise to a profusion of standards, the key ones of which will be highlighted in Chapters 7 and 8. Different sectors, such as libraries, archives, publishing or commerce, have developed their own standards which tend to predominate among their practitioners. Conversely some, such as Dublin Core (DC)[S.13], are designed to be generic and applicable across multiple domains.

The choice of a descriptive metadata standard may therefore well be influenced by the community in which a digital library operates: a collection of digitised books, for instance, will often choose one which originates in the practices and procedures that predominate in the wider profession of librarianship. The selection of a standard should, however, be based on whether it will meet the needs of a given application and its intended audience, regardless of its provenance.

2.2.2 Administrative metadata

Descriptive metadata may be the form that is most visible to end-users, but in a digital library it is often dwarfed in scale and complexity by its administrative counterpart. Libraries and archives have always kept records to carry out the tasks required for the maintenance of their collections; these include lists of acquisitions, financial accounts, conservation records and details of items borrowed and returned by users. These can be extensive and time consuming to maintain in traditional, analogue collections, but in the digital library they must be supplemented by a range of metadata that specifically supports the administration of the items that make up its holdings.

The reason for this extra layer of metadata derives from the nature of the digital object itself. The fact that a digital file needs decoding by software in order to be usable requires technical details of its make-up to be accessible in some form; for instance, the encoding format of a still image file must be known before it can be displayed. The ease with which digital files can be copied and transmitted requires information to protect the intellectual property invested in them and to control by whom and in what circumstances they may be accessed. The ease with which they can be altered and manipulated and the fragility of the media on which they are stored require yet more documentation, aimed specifically at ensuring their long-term preservation. If the digital object is derived from an analogue original (for instance a digitised book), details of the latter need to be recorded as well.

The broad category of 'administrative' metadata is usually broken down into subdivisions; the four most commonly defined of these, which are designed to meet the requirements laid out in the previous paragraph, are known respectively as *technical*, *rights*, *preservation* and *source* metadata.

2.2.2.1 Technical metadata

A digital file in the form in which it is stored is, in essence, nothing more than a stream of binary digits and so is opaque to humans. It therefore needs some degree of decoding to make it understandable; for instance, a still image of a page of a book requires this to make it readable in a way that an analogue page on paper does not. Some information is required by the software that performs this decoding so as to understand the parameters within which it must operate; this will vary according to the format of the digital file itself.

For a still image the software needs to know the encoding format (for instance, Tagged Image File Format (TIFF) or Joint Photographic Experts Group (JPEG)), the size of its dimensions in pixels, its colour depth, whether it has been compressed, the algorithms used to perform this if it has been and so on. Moving images require much the same information with the addition of such details as frame rates and the codecs used for compression and decompression. Even text, one of the easiest formats to interpret, requires information on encoding, character sets, markup and even page sequencing (right-to-left for Hebrew or Arabic, for instance).

Much of this information can probably be derived automatically by the software that decodes a file and presents it to a user; we cannot, however, count on this happening reliably and with full accuracy in the future, as file formats and encoding mechanisms may well change and render current ones obsolete. For this reason it is usually advisable to record technical metadata explicitly and include it when a digital object is stored.

A number of metadata standards to do this have been compiled by practitioners in the curation of digital collections. Each type of digital file – still image, moving image, text, audio and so on – has one or two well-established standards which have become firmly embedded in their user communities and so are safe choices for holding this essential technical metadata. The pre-eminent among these for the objects that usually populate a digital library will be introduced in Chapter 9.

2.2.2.2 Rights metadata

The second major subdivision of administrative metadata is the information required to manage the IPR of the materials held in a digital library's collections. It is no secret that piracy is rife on the internet as a result of the ease with which digital objects can be copied, altered and moved around. The majority of digital libraries make their collections freely available to any interested user through such initiatives as Creative Commons[C2.1], a set of licences designed to allow the legal sharing and reuse of creative works. Some libraries and many other (particularly commercial) collections will need to protect the intellectual property of their works as part of their business models. Whether collections are made freely available or not, some rights metadata will be needed to make clear the IPR status of their contents and administer access to them.

Rights metadata requires three essential components to ensure its viability. The first of these is a declaration of the IPR status of the digital object, including whether or not it is in copyright and, if it is, the terms under which it is made available. It is here, for instance, that a work released under Creative Commons will state this fact and the conditions attached to it under the licence granted. The second, a necessary adjunct to the first, is a statement of who the rights holders are if it is not in the public domain.

The final component of rights metadata is the information needed to allow the library's delivery mechanism to administer access to the digital object. Its users may well have a variety of disparate rights which govern the ways in which they can interact with the items in a collection; for instance, some may be allowed to view low-resolution versions of images only, others (perhaps subscribers to a commercial service such as a picture library) may have access to their higher-quality equivalents, perhaps with the ability to download them. Some online newspapers, such as *The Independent* in the UK, categorise their articles as either freely available to all or 'premium' and so limited to paying subscribers only: rights metadata is necessary to control these multiple levels of access.

This is another integral area of administrative metadata for which a number of standards exist: they are also discussed in Chapter 9.

2.2.2.3 Preservation metadata

Another significant branch of administrative metadata is the set required to ensure the preservation of a digital library's content in the long term. Digital preservation is a complex discipline in its own right with a set of protocols which have been established by practitioners in the field to ensure the longevity of collections well into the future. When it comes to ensuring its long-term survival, a digital file presents all manner of challenges which are less pressing for its traditional analogue counterparts. Most of these derive from its dependence on storage media which inevitably deteriorate over time. To counteract this, elaborate procedures must be set up to ensure, at the very least, a well-managed regime of checking files for deterioration and periodically refreshing them to new media.

To enable digital preservation to be carried out effectively requires an array of specialised metadata which, in the words of a report from the Digital

Preservation Coalition '[maintains] the availability, identity, persistence, renderability, understandability and authenticity of digital objects over long periods of time' (Lavoie and Gartner 2013, 2). A core function of this metadata is to provide *contextual* information for a digital object which, it is hoped, will make it comprehensible to delivery systems in the distant future, and their curators confident in its authenticity.

Technical metadata of the type discussed above is clearly an important part of this, but preservation metadata will supplement it by including a wider range of information to place a digital object in context. An important part of this will be details of its provenance, which should include a meticulous audit trail of its history, including its creation, what has been done to it thereafter (in terms of reformatting or copying to new media, for instance) and who has been responsible for its custodianship and the performance of these actions. It is also essential to provide some assurance that the object is what it purports to be and has not been manipulated in any way. This can be done by recording 'fixity' information in the form of 'checksums', strings generated from the binary digits of a file which change if it is altered.

Preservation metadata and the key standard for recording it, PREservation Metadata: Implementation Strategies[S.23], are discussed in detail in Chapter 9.

2.2.2.4 Source metadata

When an item in a digital library is not born digital but generated by the digitisation of an analogue, usually paper-based, original it is important to separate the metadata for this pre-existing object from that of its digital surrogate. For its descriptive metadata, the standards that are used to describe the digital object (covered in Chapter 7) will usually suffice to perform the same function here: they merely require to be identified as referring to the source instead of the surrogate, either by tagging them as such explicitly or by placing them within a part of the overall metadata structure where they can be readily identified as belonging to this type.

Technical metadata that relates to the physical object that has been digitised should also be recorded here; this will vary according to the media on which it is held. For a recording taken from an audio cassette, for instance, we may wish to record the number of tracks on the tape, their configuration and the speed at which it should be played. For a vinyl disc it could be useful to know the type of grooves embedded on it, its playback speed and possibly the type of stylus needed. Fortunately, many of the technical metadata standards discussed later in this book are designed to accommodate analogue originals as well as their digital derivatives. Only very rarely will it be necessary to devise an ad hoc scheme to record this type of metadata.

Source metadata will be discussed in more detail in Chapters 6, 7 and 9.

2.2.3 Structural metadata

The third type of metadata is one that is generally inherent (and so invisible) in an analogue library object but usually needs to be explicitly stated for its digital counterpart. This is metadata which describes its internal structure, the way in which its constituent components are ordered with respect to each other in order to create the complete object as we recognise it. It is this which, in the analogue world, turns a set of pages into a book or a sequence of frames on a strip of celluloid into a film.

In a physical book this metadata is encoded in the physical arrangement of the leaves that make it up; their ordering as they are glued into the spine provides this essential sequential structure which enables it to be read as intended. Additional structural metadata may also be recorded explicitly in the form of a table of contents, which divides the book's intellectual content up in ways that have a meaning for the author and reader; this may be a simple listing of chapters or it may impose some degree of hierarchy by dividing these into sub-chapters or shorter passages.

A digitised book may consist of several hundred image files which also require to be viewed in sequence if they are to make any sense – the image for page one must come immediately before the image for page two and so on. Without the benefit of a physical medium to establish this sequence, explicit metadata must be provided to ensure that these images are viewed in the correct order. As is the case for a physical book, it is also often useful to supplement this with tables of contents and other structural metadata which may assist in the navigation of the work as a whole.

In the case of a digitised film we do not need to record basic sequential metadata explicitly, as digital video formats automatically encode this to ensure that its frames are shown in the correct order. As is the case for a book, however, it is often useful to add structural metadata by segmenting a video in order to allow easier navigation; this, for instance, gives us the 'chapters' into which a DVD is often divided. Audio recordings can also benefit from this. An opera is one example where a sequential ordering of tracks is necessary to make sense of it as performed but which may also benefit from additional structural metadata in order to allow specific arias or choruses to be easily located.

The flexibility of the digital medium, which allows us to navigate digital objects more easily than is often possible with their analogue equivalents, can be greatly enhanced by including rich structural metadata. This can add a 'value-added' component to digitisation, enabling its potential to be better appreciated by the users of a digital library. For this reason alone it should be part of any metadata strategy.

Structural metadata and its implementation within the architecture of METS[S.17], the scheme at the centre of this metadata strategy, are discussed in Chapter 6.

2.3 The core components of metadata

The generic definition of metadata as 'data about data' is perhaps a little too nebulous to be of much use when it comes to its application in working systems. To clarify our thinking and allow us to pin down more precisely what it means in practice, it can be useful to separate this rather amorphous concept into its more focused sub-components, each of which requires careful consideration in its own right if we are to build a coherent overall strategy. Three of these are usually identified its core constituents, their nomenclature borrowed rather loosely from the vocabulary of linguistics: they are syntax, semantics and content rules.

2.3.1 Syntax

Syntax is defined in linguistics by the Oxford English Dictionary as 'the set of rules and principles in a language according to which words, phrases, and clauses are arranged to create well-formed sentences' (OED Online 2020b). By analogy it is used in information science to describe the ways in which metadata is encoded to build up meaningful structures from its basic components. Syntax functions in both as a means to allow interoperability and exchange – in the case of language the communication of thoughts and ideas, in metadata the transmission of the semantic elements that it encodes.

Syntax does this establishing a set of mutually accepted rules and structures which are understood by both parties to the interchange. Two speakers of the same language can understand the sentences that they exchange by virtue of their shared understanding of the syntactic conventions by which they are structured. Two systems can similarly make sense of each other's metadata only if they have a shared understanding of the ways in which it is encoded. Such an understanding is also needed if metadata is to be usable within the digital library itself: a delivery system which does not recognise the form of its encoding will find it impossible to handle.

Encoding mechanisms for metadata can take many forms, from text files to spreadsheets to database tables. For the sake of interoperability, text, which can be read by any system, is usually preferable to locking metadata in formats which require more complex, usually software-dependent, interpretation; for instance, a table in the relational database mySql requires this specific package if it is to be deciphered, whereas a text file can be read by multiple software applications. For this reason, most digital libraries employ a text-based syntax as the optimal medium for metadata.

Text may be a relatively uncomplicated format but this does not entail that the metadata it contains is crude or simplistic. Text files at their simplest may just be 'flat' label/content pairs but they can also include highly complex structures capable of recording relationships between metadata elements with great expressive potential. XML, the syntax introduced in detail in Chapter 5 and recommended in this book as the basis for a metadata strategy, has this strength. It is a tightly structured architecture, essentially hierarchical but with the potential to cut across its hierarchies if required; this ensures that nothing need be lost when it is used for metadata of any degree of complexity.

2.3.2 Semantics

The second sub-component of metadata to which careful consideration must be given is also borrowed by analogy from linguistics. Semantics in that discipline is the study of meaning, specifically as the Oxford English Dictionary defines it, 'the study of the meaning of signs, and of the relationship of sign vehicles to referents' (OED Online 2020a). The second part of this definition is especially relevant to the application of the term 'semantics' to metadata; here it is the relationship between a 'sign vehicle' (a field in a metadata scheme) and its 'referent' (the data that this field contains or references).

A less technical way of describing this is to say that semantics defines the meanings of the fields which metadata uses to refer to the data it describes and the labels that make these meanings clear. DC[S.13], for instance, a simple metadata scheme discussed in more detail in Chapter 6, defines 15 of these containers or fields with such labels as **Title**, **Creator** or **Date.** In addition to supplying these, DC also provides explanations as to what their meanings are which are (very slightly) more detailed than the single-word labels attached to them: **Title** for instance, is defined as 'a name given to a resource', **Creator** as 'an entity primarily responsible for making the resource' and **Date** as 'a point or period of time associated with an event in the lifecycle of the resource'.

One obvious characteristic of these labels is that they are essentially arbitrary: DC uses English-language terms for these but they could just as effectively use their equivalents in other languages or non-linguistic labels (for instance, the numeral **245** is used to mark a title in the library cataloguing standard MARC (MAchine Readable Cataloguing)). Another important feature to note is that the exact meaning of a label need not be the same in different metadata schemes, indeed this is very unlikely to be the case. A comparison of the definitions for what various schemes describe as a 'subject', for instance, shows the diversity of meanings attached to this concept (Table 2.1 opposite).

Table 2.1 *Definition of 'subject' in four metadata schemes*

Scheme	Definition of 'subject'
DC[S.13]	A topic of the resource
MODS[S.18]	A term or phrase representing the primary topic(s) on which a work is focused
PBCore (public broadcasting)[S.22]	Topic headings or keywords that portray the intellectual content of the asset
VRA Core (visual objects)[S.29]	Terms or phrases that describe, identify, or interpret the Work or Image and what it depicts or expresses

These four schemes, all of which will be discussed later, show a range of subtle but nonetheless distinct approaches to defining a subject. DC has perhaps the vaguest of these, much dependent on our understanding of the word 'of'. All of the others go into slightly more detail of the relationship between a topic and a resource, MODS defining it by its focus and PBCore by specifying that it is its intellectual content. VRA Core provides the most precise definition as is perhaps required for a scheme that is designed to describe visual rather than textual or verbal objects.

These definitions clearly attempt to describe the same concept in a general sense but differ in their approaches to how broadly or narrowly they draw their definitions. Varying degrees of semantic breadth of this kind can make it difficult to exchange metadata in a way that enables the meaning of its content to be understood without some degree of interpretation. They also mean that it is essential that a semantic definition in metadata acknowledges its provenance, the scheme in which it is defined. We need to know when we see the label 'Title' whether this is 'Title' as defined in DC, MODS or another scheme in order to understand what we are dealing with. We shall examine an efficient way of linking semantics to their provenance in the form of the Uniform Resource Identifier in Chapter 4.

2.3.3 Content rules

Semantics defines the containers in which metadata is held but it is also important to have some control over the content that is put into these. To do this we need to employ *content rules*, which prescribe what populates a metadata field and the form that it takes.

Without some control of this kind we would rapidly find that our metadata becomes very messy indeed. If, for instance, we do not regulate how we record people's names, we soon end up with unusable author indexes in which every variant vies for attention with every other. To take a simple example, we could look at the author of *The Adventures of Tom Sawyer*. His real name was Samuel Clemens but he also published under the pseudonyms

Louis de Conte and Quintus Curtius Snodgrass. He is best known, however, under the pen-name Mark Twain, but even this has 26 variants in other languages (such as Tuwen, Make or T u-wen, Ma-k o). Which should we use? The obvious path, and the one most often (but not always) taken, is to designate his best-known name as our preferred term, but we do need a rule to state this clearly. Other examples may be much less clear cut than this, and so unambiguous rules and their consistent application are both essential.

This example demonstrates the necessity of two functions for content rules. The first is to mandate *what* should be included in a metadata record. Which variant of Twain's name should we use? The second dictates the *format* of an entry. Should we list him simply as 'Twain, Mark' or should we add more information, such as his birth and death dates, 'Twain, Mark 1835–1910', to pin him down more precisely? This could be particularly important in the case of more common names (for instance, the thousands of authors named 'John Smith').

Content rules usually employ two approaches to addressing these issues. The first is to provide a set of instructions, usually known as *cataloguing rules*, which are designed to ensure consistency in the creation of metadata. The second is to employ lists of terms which conform to these rules and can be incorporated directly into metadata records.

Different sectors tend to create their own cataloguing rules which become established practice within their respective communities. In libraries AACR2[S.1], first published in 1967, and its intended successor Resource Description and Access (RDA)[S.24] are the predominant standards and form the basis of most online catalogues in use today. In the archives sector their counterpart is known as ISAD(G)[C8.5] (General International Standard Archival Description), a list of rules and elements which define conventions for the contents of archival finding aids. More specialised guidelines also exist for particular classes of materials such as rare books.

The lists that complement these cataloguing rules usually cover subject terms and names. The first of these are often called *subject headings*: these are preferred terms, usually formatted according to a prevailing set of rules such as AACR2, which are designed to ensure consistency for this potentially messy part of a metadata record. Subject headings are usually provided in a hierarchical arrangement known as a *thesaurus*, in which they are listed with terms which are broader or narrower than themselves as well as synonyms and alternatives for which they are the preferred term. By browsing up and down this hierarchy the cataloguer can select a term at the specific level of precision for the concept that they are recording and use the same term for the same subject in all of their records.

List of names are usually known as *authority files*; these are most commonly but not exclusively used for personal, geographic or corporate entities. A prime example is the Library of Congress Name Authority File[C8.7], an inventory of more than 10 million, covering persons, places and organisations, all formatted according to AACR2 conventions.

Chapter 8 covers the use of cataloguing rules, subject headings and name authority files and how they may be applied within a metadata strategy.

2.4 Metadata standards

The three essential constituents of metadata – syntax, semantics and content rules – form the basis of what we will frequently refer to in this book as 'metadata schemes'. We will also often supplement this term with its rather more formal counterpart, 'metadata standards'. The difference between these is that standards are metadata schemes which have been developed in user communities by formal processes governing their design and development, including the submission and approval of new features. A centralised authority is usually responsible for maintaining and developing a standard as well as disseminating it within its community and a team of experts in their field are responsible for overseeing these operations.

A basic definition of a metadata standard is one by Priscilla Caplan, author of the widely used textbook *Metadata Fundamentals for All Librarians*: 'a set of metadata elements and rules for their use which have been designed for a particular purpose' (Caplan 2003, 5). To fulfil its designated purpose a standard must specify at least one of the three core components listed above. DC, for instance, contents itself with defining semantics alone, the set of fields in which metadata is to be stored. It does not specify any syntax, such as XML, as a requirement for compliance with this standard. The descriptive metadata standard MODS, on the other hand, goes further than DC in specifying semantics and its preferred syntax (XML).

This book will recommend the use of established metadata standards wherever possible but will also demonstrate how they can be extended, adapted or supplemented if they do not fully meet the demands of a given application.

2.5 Conclusion

This chapter has introduced the core concepts of metadata, including its overarching tripartite division into descriptive, administrative and structural, and its three core components of syntax, semantics and content rules. To begin to apply these as the basis of a coherent metadata strategy it is now necessary to move away from what we might call the ontology of metadata, what it is made of, to consider the broader strategic rationale for employing it. In the next chapter we shall examine the aims of a metadata strategy and establish the basic principles that we should try to put into practice as we design and implement it.

3

Planning a Metadata Strategy: Basic Principles

3.1 Introduction

In this chapter we begin to move from what metadata is in the abstract towards its application in practice. It is at this point that we should begin to think at a relatively high level about the basic principles to follow when devising a metadata strategy; we will then attempt in the next chapter to translate these into the first steps towards their implementation. By starting our planning at this relatively abstract level we should be able to keep in mind a picture of how metadata fits into the workings of a digital library in both the short and long term.

3.2 Principle 1: Support all stages of the digital curation lifecycle

We saw in Chapter 1 that one of the key principles that makes a digital collection a digital library is the concept of *curation*. Digital curation shares many features with its analogue counterpart, including its emphasis on selection, description, the provision of access and preservation; it also presents the librarian with multiple additional challenges because of the nature of the digital medium itself. The digital object, whether it is a book, video, audio or image, is opaque to the user in its raw state, a stream of binary digits: it needs decoding to render its contents visible and accessible. It is stored on media which have nothing like the proven longevity of paper, and so requires a carefully designed and applied set of procedures, such as regular copying to new stock, to preserve it. It is easily copied and transformed in ways which may nullify its integrity, and so often requires some form of digital rights management to protect the intellectual property of its owners.

The complex requirements of digital curation make it essential to devise an overall framework for all of the processes required to carry it out. Several high-level conceptual models have been designed to map these and put them into a coherent and, hopefully, easily understood form. These form something of a template for the design of a working system and a checklist to ensure that no essential components are missing from it.

One of the best known of these is known as the DCC Curation Lifecycle Model[C3.1], so named after the UK's Digital Curation Centre, which originally devised it. Figure 3.1 shows the model expressed in graphical form.

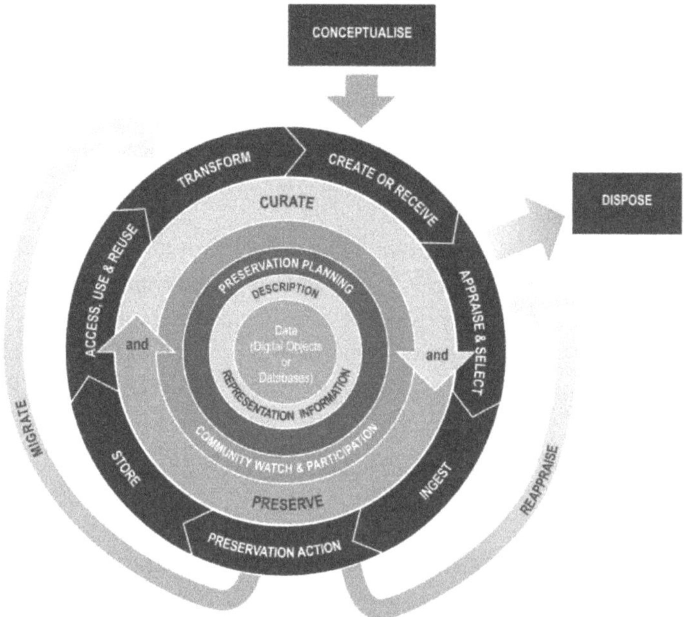

Figure 3.1 *DCC Curation Lifecycle Model* (Digital Curation Centre)

At the centre of the diagram are the digital objects (or possibly databases) which make up the core of a collection. Surrounding this are a number of concentric circles, the outermost of which contains the actions which must be undertaken sequentially if the curation and preservation work of a digital library is to be successful. They start at the top with the creation or receipt of the digital objects to be added to the library. This is followed by an appraisal of their worth and consequent selection or rejection and disposal; those that have passed this stage are then ingested into the collection. Once inside, further actions are needed to preserve and store them and then disseminate them to users so that they can be accessed, used and reused. The circle is then completed by the potential creation of new materials, derived from those which have undergone these processes and emerged from them in a form that makes this possible. The circular shape of the overall model emphasises the way in which the curation of digital collections feeds through into the creation of new works, and so new collections.

Two offshoots which bypass this circular sequence may arise during the preservation stage. The first of these is a reappraisal and possible rejection of ingested objects which fail validation tests, for instance it they are corrupt, which sends us back to the initial appraisal stage. The second is a migration to a new format if an object arrives in one which is unusable or has a poor potential for long-term preservation; in this case the storage and access stages are bypassed, the object is transformed to create a new variant and the whole process starts again.

These sequential activities are complemented by what the DCC calls 'full lifecycle actions', those which should operate continuously to prevent their counterparts from proceeding in a haphazard and unstructured way; these are 'Preservation Planning' and 'Community Watch and Participation', which includes keeping an eye open for new developments and practices. These are represented by the second concentric circle, surrounding the kernel of the diagram.

The prime position occupied by the first circle is 'Description and Representation Information', metadata by any other name. This is placed so centrally because all of the operations that surround it would be impossible if it were not present. As we shall see throughout this book, metadata is needed to support the creation of digital objects, their selection, ingestion, preservation, storage, access and transformation. We need to plan a strategy which embraces all of these, which inevitably entails the integration of a diverse range of descriptive, administrative and structural metadata into a coherent whole.

The lifecycle model will therefore provide a useful checklist to ensure that our metadata sustains the functions of a dynamic digital library in their entirety. We should aim to check always that the strategy we develop supports all of its stages.

3.3 Principle 2: Support the long-term preservation of the digital object

In the same way that it is useful to visualise the roles and activities that maintain a curated digital library in its day-to-day operation, it can also be helpful to do this to clarify the processes which are fundamental to the preservation of its collections in the long term. Metadata will once more have a key role here, and employing a template akin to the DCC Curation Lifecycle Model will enable us to see more clearly where it fits in to a digital preservation architecture and how it supports its purposes.

One of the most significant models of this type is known as the Open Archival Information System (OAIS)[C3.4]. As its name implies, this emphasises the objective of a digital library which aims to ensure the future longevity of its collections as well as providing a readily accessible route for its users to consult them in the present. Many significant practitioners in digital libraries, archives and repositories subscribe to the principles of OAIS and use it as a model for their operations; they include such bodies as the Library of Congress, the British Library and the Bibliothèque nationale de France.

As is the case for the DCC Digital Curation Lifecycle model, a diagram (Figure 3.2) is the most helpful way to grasp the essentials of an OAIS system.

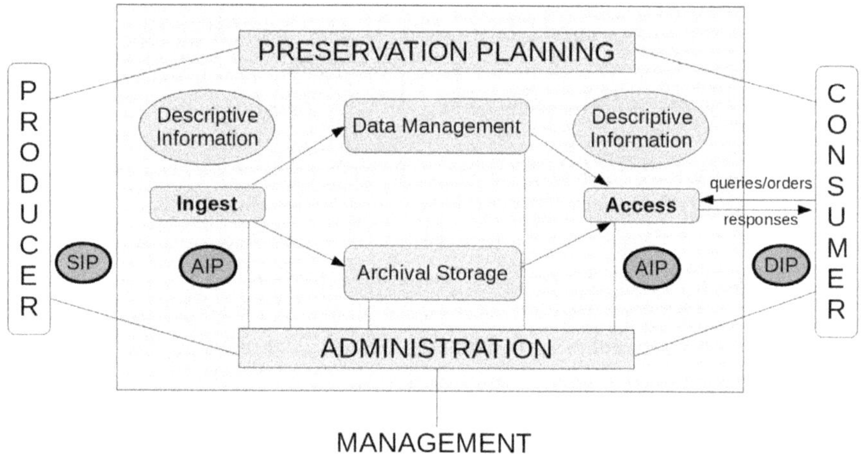

Figure 3.2 *Open Archival Information System model*

The diagram shows, from left to right, a linear view of how digital objects are created by the efforts of their producers, are ingested into an archive and are accessed by 'consumers' by sending queries and receiving responses. In the middle of the grey box which represents the archive itself two parallel streams follow on from the initial ingest. The first of these, labelled 'Data Management', consists of the activities needed to manage the data and metadata that supports its operations; the second, 'Archival Storage', represents those activities that handle the ingest, storage and dissemination of the objects themselves. These must operate in tandem to maintain a properly curated collection which allows for access by the consumers on the right of the diagram.

Lurking inside the diagram are three acronyms, SIP, AIP and DIP, which stand for, respectively, Submission Information Package, Archival Information Package and Dissemination Archival Package. As their names imply, these bundle a digital object with all the information needed to describe, store and preserve it. They are therefore intended to bring together data and metadata tied up in a neat and discrete package.

These information packages fulfil disparate roles within the overall architecture. The SIP brings together the data and metadata for a digital object as it is submitted to and ingested into the archive. The AIP does the same for the object as it is kept in storage and the DIP puts them into a form in which the object can be provided to the 'consumer'. These packages are not necessarily identical; it is likely, for instance, that the AIP will add to the metadata in the SIP with administrative information required by the archive to manage the digital object. It is probable that much of this will be omitted from the DIP presented to the end-user; this will instead concentrate on the descriptive metadata that users need to find the object and assess its relevance to their interests.

Although the OAIS architecture is designed with an archive in mind, it is also valid as a model for many of the operations of a working digital library. The processes that it outlines, such as ingestion, access, data management and storage, are also key to running such a library and the metadata requirements that it defines for enabling these are just as applicable. When designing a strategy, therefore, it is sound practice to base it on the principles of the OAIS information packages; doing so will ensure that, as well as serving the current needs of a digital library, it provides durable metadata which supports the future preservation of its collections.

We should aim, therefore, to create metadata that can function as an AIP as defined in the OAIS model. To do this, we should aim to bring together the various types of metadata needed to describe and manage a digital object into a discrete package with a coherent internal architecture in which all have a logical and clearly defined place. This will then form what we could call the 'canonical' statement of the metadata for a given object, which we will maintain as its definitive record. We will then translate this into any form required to meet the needs of the moment; we will, for instance, do this to transform it into the formats mandated by a delivery system or to exchange it with others if we wish to share it in this way. Conversely, we should also be able to generate this package from incoming metadata in any format commonly used within our professional community.

For these reasons, we will aim to devise a strategy centred on the creation of an OAIS AIP as the canonical statement of our metadata.

3.4 Principle 3: Ensure interoperability

A metadata strategy which is in any way forward looking should not constrain itself to serving only the digital library for which it is devised. Libraries have been sharing their metadata for a long time – for over four centuries, in the case of the Bodleian Library in Oxford, which published its first printed catalogue for others to consult in 1605. In the interconnected world that the internet has made possible the exchange of metadata is much easier and more commonly practised than ever before. This has brought about such exceptional resources as the monumental union catalogue WorldCat[C3.5], the Getty Research Portal[3.3] subject gateway for art history and the Europeana[3.2] web portal to collections in European museums.

If we wish to leave open the prospect of sharing our metadata with others either now or in the future we should aim to render it as interoperable as possible. Interoperability in its purest form is the ability to exchange metadata between systems without modification or manipulation (Taylor 2004), with little human intervention, preferably none, beyond that involved in its initial creation (Bauman 2011). This ideal may be difficult to attain, but to at least approach it requires two complementary types of interoperability, syntactic and semantic. 'Syntactic' entails that the metadata is presented in an encoding format that both donor and recipient can understand. 'Semantic' dictates that the meaning of its content should be intelligible to both parties so that it can be correctly interpreted when transferred.

We should ensure, therefore, that the canonical statement of metadata (or AIP) on which this strategy will be centred is interoperable both syntactically and semantically. To do this requires that we choose an encoding format which is readily transferable and metadata schemes which are widely understood within our intended community of users and, preferably, well beyond that.

3.5 Principle 4: Control metadata content wherever possible

To make any of our metadata fit for purpose we need to exercise some control over the content with which it is populated. This is particularly important for descriptive metadata, which is the primary mechanism by which users interact with collections. To do this entails employing and following content rules to ensure that there is consistency in what is found in any given field. It also requires us, as far as possible, to employ some degree of control over the formatting of this content.

Controlling content generally requires adopting two practices in tandem. The first is to adhere to a set of cataloguing rules which mandate the choice of content for each field and, usually, the form that it takes. The second, which acts as a supplement to the first, is to make use of lists of terms from which this content is chosen. For names, these take the form of extensive compilations formatted in accordance with the cataloguing rules that they complement and are usually known as *name authorities*. For subjects, hierarchical arrangements from broader to narrower are often employed to allow a choice of terms at the required degree of precision: these are known as *thesauri*, after the classic reference work devised by Peter Mark Roget in 1852.

The choice of which rules, name authorities and thesauri to implement may not be a straightforward one. It will often be dictated by the practices that predominate in the community within which the digital library is embedded and the types of objects that make up the bulk of its collections. A collection of digitised books, for instance, which forms part of an otherwise traditional academic library, would tend to employ rules and practices emanating from the principal custodians of practices within that sector, such as the AACR2[S.1]. Name authorities and subject terms may be taken from generic schemes intended to cover the scope of knowledge as a whole, such as the Library of Congress Name Authority File[C8.7] and Library of Congress Subject Headings[C8.9], or subject-specific resources like the Getty Research Institute's Union List of Artist Names[C8.13] and Art and Architecture Thesaurus[C8.1] for names and subjects in the visual arts.

The advice here is to employ cataloguing rules and authority control over metadata content *as far as possible*. This qualification is needed because the constraints that they impose may sometimes prove problematic. A specialised collection may, for instance, find some relevant names missing from published authority lists, or discover that established thesauri lack the subject terms which communicate adequately its intellectual contents. Standards may often be over rigid, slow to update and not reflect the diversity of a library's users and the ways in which they interact with its resources. A pragmatic approach to the implementation of content rules and authorities will be needed to deal with cases where they do not meet fully the requirements of a collection and its users, and will usually involve supplementing them with locally devised additions that are compatible with established standards. Some guidance on how this can be done will be provided in Chapter 8.

3.6 Principle 5: Ensure software independence

It should be clear from much of the discussion in this chapter, particularly those parts which emphasise the need to consider the long-term preservation of data and metadata, that it is important to ensure that it can exist independently of the technical infrastructures which house the digital library and archive its contents. The platforms employed today, and the software that enables them to run, will undoubtedly be obsolete well before the value of our collections has run its course. Our metadata must be in a form which will allow it to be incorporated into any system that will take over the hosting of our collections in the future.

The canonical statement of our metadata, in OAIS terms, the AIP which was introduced earlier in this chapter, must be constructed with this imperative in mind. It should not be tied to any software platform and must be an open, non-proprietary standard. It must also be malleable enough to allow us to generate metadata in any form required by the present and future systems in which our library will reside.

3.7 Principle 6: Impose a logical system of identifiers

A digital library of any size will rapidly expand to become a complex environment with many thousands of data objects and their associated metadata. This can easily become chaotic and hard to manage unless it is designed from the outset in a strictly organised way which ensures that every component has a logical place within its architecture and this place is clearly identifiable at all times. Without such an approach it is very easy for the contents of its collections and their constituent components, such as the image files in a digitised book, to become lost within the labyrinth.

For a metadata strategy this entails a coherent approach to attaching an identifier to every component which delineates unambiguously where it fits into the overall architecture. By 'component' here is meant every metadata record, all significant subsections within a record, every data object and every file of which it is composed. This is akin to the spine label on a book in a traditional library which indicates its place on the shelves; in a digital environment we need something much more complex, because, by analogy, every page requires a separate label in addition to the one that identifies the book itself.

A consistent system of identifiers which are internal to a digital library is vitally important, but if we wish our metadata to be interoperable beyond the confines of our collections we need to ensure that they can provide the same degree of unambiguous identification anywhere on the internet. This is best done by supplementing any internal identifier with another that is designed specifically for this purpose, the Uniform Resource Identifier (URI), which will be introduced in the next chapter.

3.8 Principle 7: Use standards whenever possible

A theme which underlies much of the discussion in this chapter is the importance of standards. These arise through the combined efforts of experts within their respective communities who create, develop and maintain them in an organised and strategic way. By employing an established standard we can be confident that we are using something that has been tried and tested to ensure its viability; there is no sense in reinventing the metadata wheel if others, possibly more expert than ourselves, have already set it rolling.

Two problems can arise, however, when it comes to embedding established standards within a metadata strategy. The first is deciding which ones to choose from the abundance that is available. Priscilla Caplan, whose definition of a standard was quoted in Chapter 2, notes 15 of these in use in educational or cultural institutions for descriptive metadata alone (Caplan 2003). Some stand out as primary choices to fill the slots in a digital library's metadata make-up; for others, the choice is not so clear cut. In the chapters that follow key standards for each type will be recommended, but alternatives will be pointed out where these are available; the overall strategy will remain valid even if the choice of standards for particular roles differs from these recommendations.

The other problem is the risk of shoehorning metadata into a standard which does not fully address our needs. This could happen for many reasons. It may be that its semantics do not adequately represent what we wish to express. It may be that its structure is too simple when more complexity is required, for instance if it is a 'flat' sequence of fields where a hierarchy would express better the relationships between parts. It may be over rigid, perhaps stipulating mandatory fields that are irrelevant to our needs. Employing a standard is inevitably a compromise, but there are ways of ensuring that its application is not a concession too far.

The standards recommended in this book should readily meet most metadata requirements for a wide variety of collections. Most are flexible enough to ensure that they do not impose unnecessary constraints in order to conform to them; many can also be supplemented should they not be rich enough in themselves to express everything required. In some cases, such as the MODS standard for descriptive metadata, they include mechanisms for adding extra semantics beyond their core set; in others, multiple standards may be used in conjunction to provide the semantic coverage required. It is, therefore, entirely possible to base a strategy on standards while retaining the option to introduce extra flexibility as required.

3.9 Principle 8: Ensure the integrity of the metadata itself

While the objects that constitute the collections in a digital library are justifiably considered its primary assets, the metadata that allows the library to operate and these objects to be accessed and preserved is a valuable resource in its own right. The creation of metadata can be time consuming and expensive, often accounting for the most significant portion of the cost of creating a digital collection after the digitisation itself (Stroeker and Vogels

2014, 39). For these reasons, metadata objects should be treated with the same care as their data counterparts, particularly in ensuring their long-term preservation and authenticity and that they can always be identified precisely.

To ensure the preservation of metadata records entails choosing encoding formats which are robust enough to be readable long into the future. To establish their authenticity we should record information on their provenance, creation and changes so that they can be trusted as reliable resources in their own right. As is the case for the digital objects of which they are counterparts, a coherent system of identifiers is also needed to ensure that they cannot become misplaced within the complex structures of a digital library and that they have an interoperable potential for sharing outside it.

3.10 Summary: the basic principles of a metadata strategy

To summarise this chapter, these are the principles which the strategy outlined in the remainder of this book aims to follow.

Principle 1: Support all stages of the digital curation lifecycle

We will design metadata which supports and enables the processes of selection, ingest, preservation, storage, access and transformation within the digital curation lifecycle. This will entail devising a metadata architecture that integrates all the descriptive, administrative (technical, preservation, rights and source) and structural metadata needed to do this.

Principle 2: Support the long-term preservation of the digital object

We will devise a metadata strategy which addresses the needs of a well-managed system for preservation in the long term by following the principles of the OAIS model. This entails centring the strategy on the creation of an OAIS AIP which will form the 'canonical' statement of our metadata into which ingested metadata (SIP) can be translated and from which any variety of metadata required for dissemination (DIP) can be generated.

Principle 3: Ensure interoperability

We will make our metadata as interoperable as possible, both syntactically and semantically, by ensuring that our AIP uses an encoding format which is readily transferable between systems and that the standards that we employ for metadata are widely used and firmly embedded within our target community of users.

Principle 4: Control metadata content wherever possible

We will enhance its interoperability further by ensuring that we apply content rules, name authorities and subject thesauri to control its content. Wherever possible these will be established resources maintained by authorities within their respective communities, but we will supplement them when necessary with localised additions.

Principle 5: Ensure software independence

We will ensure that our metadata is in a format which is not tied to any one software platform, by employing an open, non-proprietary encoding syntax for it.

Principle 6: Impose a logical system of identifiers

We will label every component of our collections and metadata with an unambiguous identifier that conforms to a coherent overall scheme. We will also ensure that these are viable outside our own library by complementing these internal identifiers with external URIs.

Principle 7: Use standards whenever possible

We will apply well-established standards for our metadata wherever possible. We will use standards that are extensible, should they not prove adequate to meet our requirements in full. If necessary, we will also use multiple standards for the same type of metadata.

Principle 8: Ensure the integrity of the metadata itself

We aim to curate our metadata with the same care as our data: we will do this by ensuring that it is in a format which safeguards its long-term preservation, that we record information on its creation and maintenance to verify its authenticity and that we employ a well-designed system of identifiers to maintain and share it.

The next chapter begins to elaborate on how these principles may be applied in practice. In doing so, it outlines the overall strategy that will be fleshed out throughout the remainder of this book.

4

Planning a Metadata Strategy: Applying the Basic Principles

4.1 Introduction

This chapter covers the initial steps required to implement the principles just defined in a metadata strategy capable of practical application. Putting these into practice entails mapping out a canonical statement of metadata, an OAIS AIP, based on established standards wherever possible. It should be software independent and interoperable; this should extend to its syntax, semantics and content. It will include as an integral component a coherent and pervasive system of identifiers and will ensure that its records are themselves carefully curated in terms of preservation, authenticity and identification. The strategy as a whole should be capable of supporting all stages of the digital curation lifecycle.

4.2 Initial steps: standards as a foundation

There has been much emphasis in the preceding discussion about the importance of standards, and so particular consideration should be given to their place within an overall strategy. The benefits of employing standards are manifold: they include embedding metadata within best practices, ensuring no repeat of mistakes that have been ironed out as standards have been developed and enhancing the interoperable potential of a digital library's collections. They do, however, have the potential sometimes to distort the environment that we construct by over-rigidity or a poor semantic fit with its requirements.

The initial question to be asked, therefore, is how to embed standards within a metadata strategy.

Three approaches are possible here:

- to take a metadata standard 'off the shelf' and apply it directly;
- to map out a metadata architecture and then translate or serialise it to an established standard;

- to devise a metadata scheme which is local to a digital library, possibly mapping it to established standards to make it easier to share with others.

4.2.1 'Off the shelf' standards

The simplest approach to employing an established standard is to implement it directly. This means, as a minimum, adopting its semantics, the fields that it defines, as the basic components on which a metadata strategy is built. DC[S.13], which will be discussed in detail in Chapter 7, is one which is widely used as a generic scheme for a diverse range of digital objects. Its 15 fields are broad enough to encompass most requirements and it is easy to learn – two factors which make it a good option for the semantics of a metadata architecture. Many digital libraries and repositories design their systems around it for these reasons; they include the online web-publishing platform Omeka[C4.1], the DC editing interface of which is shown in Figure 4.1.

Other standards are rather more complex than the simple flat-file approach of DC. The descriptive metadata standard MODS[S.18], for instance, has a hierarchical structure which requires more complicated input

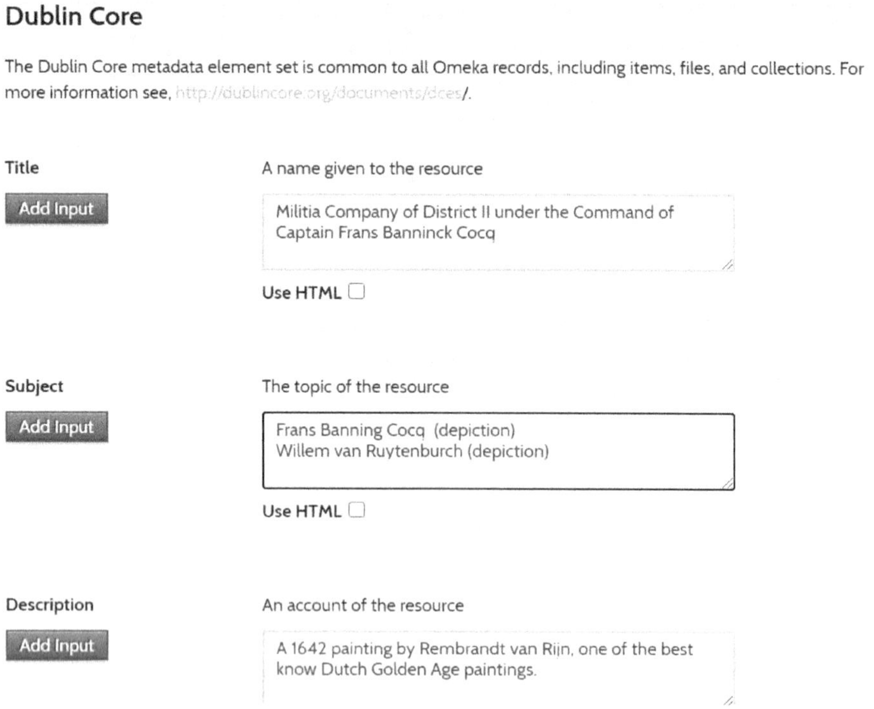

Dublin Core

The Dublin Core metadata element set is common to all Omeka records, including items, files, and collections. For more information see, http://dublincore.org/documents/dces/.

Title
Add Input
A name given to the resource
Militia Company of District II under the Command of Captain Frans Banninck Cocq
Use HTML

Subject
Add Input
The topic of the resource
Frans Banning Cocq (depiction)
Willem van Ruytenburch (depiction)
Use HTML

Description
Add Input
An account of the resource
A 1642 painting by Rembrandt van Rijn, one of the best know Dutch Golden Age paintings.

Figure 4.1 *Inputting Dublin Core metadata into Omeka* (screenshot reproduced by permission of Omeka)

interfaces, as is shown in the screenshot from the open-source digital library system Islandora[C11.3] in Figure 4.2.

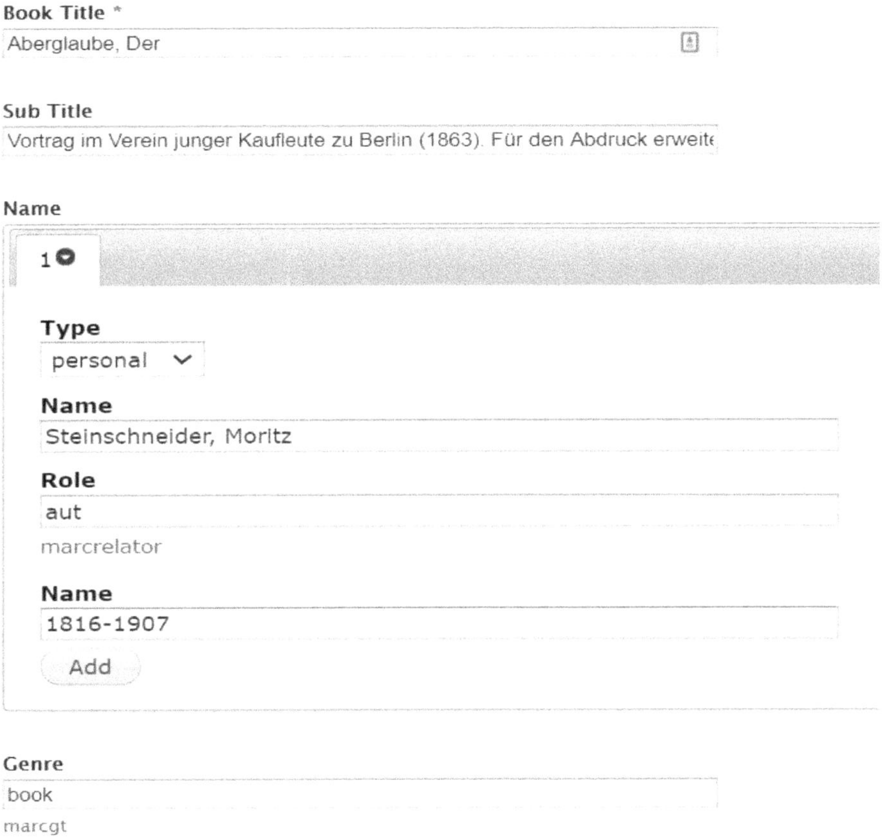

Book Title *

Aberglaube, Der

Sub Title

Vortrag im Verein junger Kaufleute zu Berlin (1863). Für den Abdruck erweit

Name

1

Type

personal

Name

Steinschneider, Moritz

Role

aut

marcrelator

Name

1816-1907

Add

Genre

book

marcgt

Figure 4.2 *Inputting MODS metadata into Islandora*

Even this interface produces relatively simple MODS files which do not make full use of its expressive potential. In most cases this will not be problematic because these records will be detailed enough for a digital library's users to find what they need, but it may sometimes be necessary to supplement what can be created in this way by employing other mechanisms.

One of these is to enhance these records or create new ones by converting metadata from pre-existing resources. One of the virtues of XML, the encoding syntax which is recommended in this book, is that it is highly malleable and can bring together metadata from a diverse set of sources into a single whole. An obvious example of this is often possible when compiling a collection of digitised books. If these are created from the holdings of a physical library they will almost certainly have corresponding records conforming to the MARC standard in the library's online catalogue. It is relatively straightforward to download and convert these to XML schemas such as MARCXML[S.15] or MODS using tools provided by their maintenance bodies. An approach of this kind will be demonstrated in Chapter 7 and the first case study in Chapter 11.

The preferred option, therefore, is to implement established standards, either by directly creating records conforming to them or by conversion from others. This should be relatively straightforward if a digital library and the items that it holds fit neatly into an established set of practices. A collection of digitised books, journals or other library materials can readily adopt the bibliographic descriptive metadata standards which have developed in libraries, supplementing them with technical, preservation and rights standards from the respective areas of professional practice. Collections of videos, audio files, broadcast radio programmes or visual art objects can similarly adopt standards which have been developed by practitioners within these fields.

4.2.2 Mapping out an architecture and serialising it into a standard

When there is not an obvious fit between a collection and a metadata standard an extra step may be required. It is better, if at all possible, to employ such a standard for the many reasons cited earlier, and so some reconciliation between the collection's requirements and the semantics of a standard may be needed to make this happen. This can be done by mapping out a metadata architecture and then translating it into the framework of an established standard; this translation is known as 'serialisation'.

The first stage of this process is to create a map of the overall metadata architecture that will meet our requirements. The easiest way to clarify our thoughts and produce a coherent map of this kind is to do so diagrammatically. We do this by listing the metadata components or fields that are needed and then noting how they relate to each other with arrows and simple semantic descriptions of their relationships. If, for instance, we have a digital image taken from an analogue photograph of a work of art we might draw up a very simple map of the kind shown in Figure 4.3 opposite.

This demonstrates that a description of the image necessitates four distinct components or entities, each of which requires its own subset of metadata. The top of the diagram shows basic information on the work of art depicted. Here we limit ourselves to just its title and the artist who created it. The image in which it is reproduced is where we record information on the iconographic subject that is portrayed; this element is associated with the

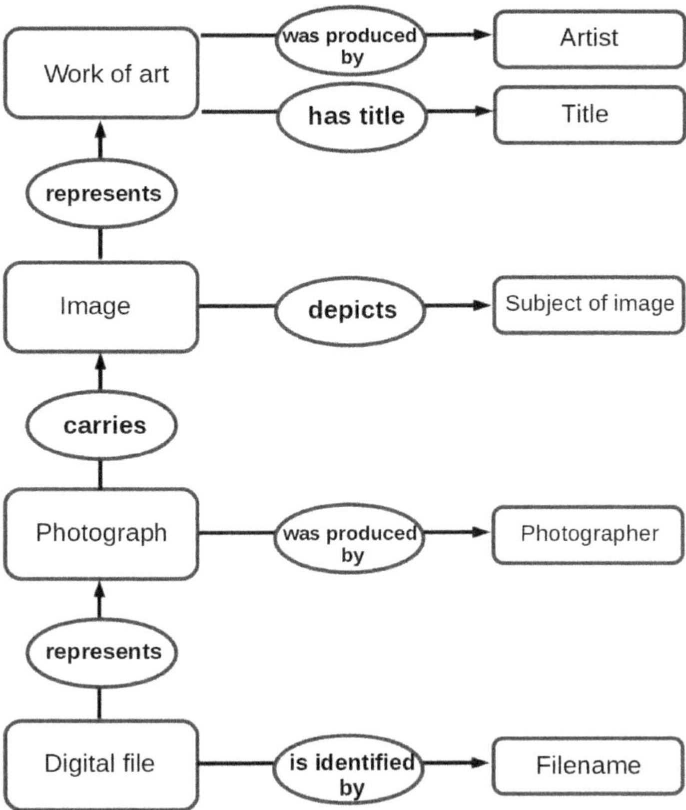

Figure 4.3 *Metadata map (highly simplified) for a digitised photograph of a work of art*

image rather than the work itself because different reproductions of the same object may have distinct subjects associated with them (for instance multiple images may be taken of a large painting, each of which highlights a different subject). For the analogue photograph which has been digitised we may wish to document the name of the photographer who took it, and for the digital file we need to note its filename so that it can be located and retrieved as required.

For an image of Michelangelo's *Pietà* in St Peter's Basilica in Rome, the metadata fields could be filled out as shown in Figure 4.4 on the next page.

Although it is quite feasible to draw up such a map from scratch, it is sensible to base it on existing practices if possible. This entails using an established conceptual model, akin to the DCC Digital Lifecycle or OAIS architecture, as the basis for the design. Models of this type are analogous to metadata standards in that they define core components and their

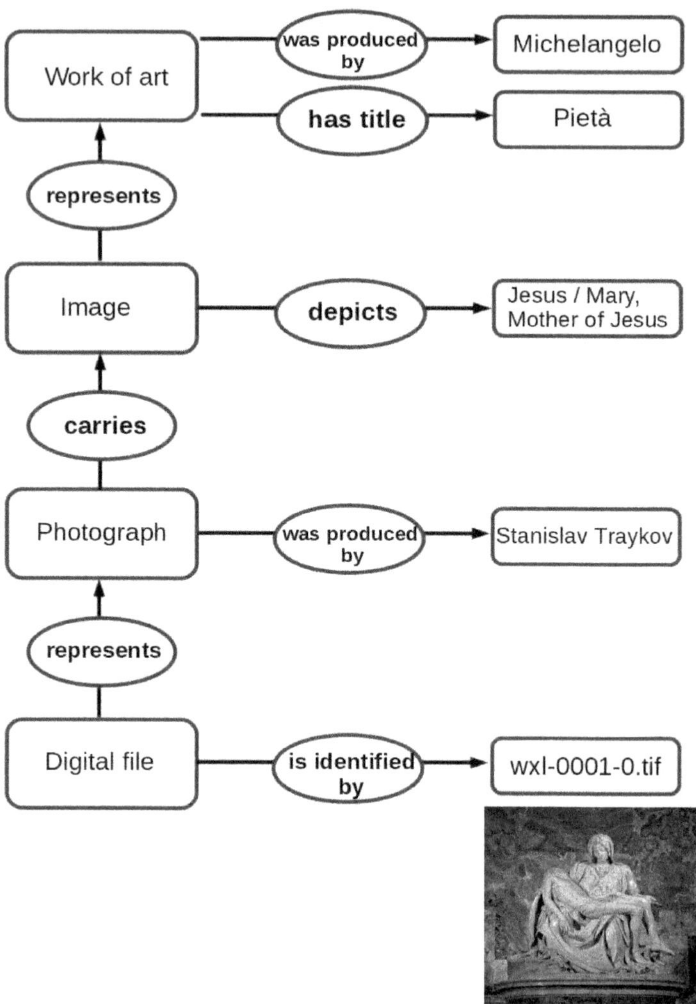

Figure 4.4 *Map in Figure 4.3 populated with metadata* (photograph by Stanislav Traykov)

interrelationships. They do this at a highly abstract level, concentrating on the basic, often broadly defined, concepts upon which more specific metadata schemes can be built.

A useful model of this kind, which is employed in the second case study in Chapter 11, is the CIDOC Conceptual Reference Model (CIDOC-CRM)[S.4]. This defines the essential concepts and relationships that underpin documentation in the cultural heritage sector, specifically galleries, libraries, archives and museums. It starts at a highly abstract level by dividing everything into four categories: **space-time** (eras, time periods and so on),

events (when things come into existence or leave it, and events involving people), **material things** and **immaterial things** (concepts or components of information). Under these are numerous classes of sub-concepts, such as **visual item** (for instance the **Image** in Figures 4.3 and 4.4), **human-made thing** (the **Work of Art** and **Photograph** in those figures) or **information object** (the **Digital File**). These are in turn supplemented by 'properties', the semantic linkages (such as **depicts** or **has title**) that express relationships between components. All of the links in Figures 4.3 and 4.4, which are represented by ovals in the middle of the arrows, are properties conforming to CIDOC-CRM.

This may all seem a little too abstract when one is faced with the practicalities of designing a working metadata scheme, but it is worth getting to know the basics of such a model for several reasons. Because this is such a long-established standard (first published in 1994) and is built on the knowledge and experience of experts in the field, it can be relied upon to represent a coherent example of best practice. As a result, it can save much time and effort when compared to beginning such a potentially daunting task as designing a metadata architecture from scratch. It also, perhaps most importantly, ensures some degree of interoperability at a high level with other collections which have employed the same model as the basis of their own metadata.

The next stage is to serialise this design by mapping its elements and their interrelationships into an existing standard. MODS, the schema recommended in Chapter 7, is an obvious candidate for this. It has a rich set of elements, over 70 in total, many of which can be qualified to make them more specific as required. It can accommodate complex linkages between these and express intricate networks of semantic relationships without difficulty. It is also extensible, allowing additions to be made to its core elements so as to incorporate semantics that they themselves lack, albeit at the cost of some loss of interoperability.

The simple model shown in Figures 4.3 and 4.4 translates readily into MODS: a sample file and an explanation of the mapping can be found in the Appendix towards the end of this volume. Most of the schemes recommended in the following chapters should be amenable to this approach, particularly if an established standard such as CIDOC-CRM underlies the model that we draw up. A more complex example of a real-world exercise of this type is given in the second case study in Chapter 11.

4.2.3 Devising a local metadata scheme

If our metadata requirements are so specialised that no standard will accommodate them and as a result it is impossible to draw up a model and serialise it to an established scheme, the last resort is to design our own. This has some obvious disadvantages in terms of reduced interoperability and potential isolation from the best practices that have evolved within a professional community, but sometimes the use of a pre-existing standard may require us to shoehorn our metadata to a degree that distorts its purpose and renders it unusable for its intended purpose.

The first stage of this process is identical to that employed in the last section, creating a map of an overall architecture that details the metadata components required and the semantic relationships that link them. This is best done diagrammatically as was shown in Figure 4.3. The next stage is to define the scheme itself.

We do this by documenting its metadata elements and their relationships. This is technically known as a *data dictionary*, 'a collection of metadata describing the contents, format, and structure of a database and the relationship between its elements, used for controlling access to and manipulation of the database', as the Oxford English Dictionary defines it (OED Online 2020c). This may consist in its most basic form of little more than the names of fields, their definitions, whether they are optional or mandatory and what type of content (text, numeric, etc.) each can contain. A more complex dictionary will document their interrelationships and mandate rules for populating their contents (for instance, specifying a particular thesaurus for a **subject** field).

One further decision to make is whether to specify a syntax for encoding the scheme. The recommended path here is to use the data dictionary to define an XML schema, a set of elements and rules for their interrelationships expressed in a formal language known, rather unimaginatively, as XML Schema. These schemas will be discussed in detail in the next chapter; the advantage of using one to define a local metadata scheme is that it will be in an interoperable syntax and so will integrate fully with the overall XML architecture that forms the basis of the strategy detailed in this book. If this syntax is employed, a locally defined XML schema can act in concert with other established schemas as far its semantics allow.

One further step which can mitigate the limited interoperability of an ad hoc scheme of this type is to attempt a mapping to an established standard. One obvious target is DC, the broad semantics of whose fields make at least partial mappings possible for most schemes, albeit at the cost of losing some precision when local elements are mapped to this more generic set of elements. Mapping to DC can be far from ideal, but it does allow some limited degree of interoperability to be grafted onto an otherwise isolated set of metadata. It may be a particularly good choice, as it is so widely used and forms the basis of other schemes devised specifically for the sharing and harvesting of metadata (such as the Open Archives Initiative Protocol for Metadata Harvesting[S.21] of which there will be more in Chapter 10).

4.2.4 How standards support the basic principles

The role of standards is central to applying many of the basic principles outlined in the previous chapter, including, of course, 'Use standards whenever possible' (Principle 7). Employing them enhances interoperability (Principle 3) and supports all stages of the digital curation lifecycle (Principle 1), as most have been designed to perform an integral role within it. They also have a crucial role to play in the operation of an OAIS-conformant archival system (Principle 2), particularly in the construction of a robust AIP to form the canonical version of the metadata which should occupy a central place in a metadata strategy. Appropriate standards also ensure the effective control of metadata content (Principle 4), which is important for enhanced interoperability.

4.3 Identifiers: everything in its place

Having outlined the approaches that may be taken to designing an architecture at an abstract level, it is time to consider the application of a more concrete principle which is essential to the creation and maintenance of a fully integrated metadata (and data) environment. This is Principle 6, 'Impose a logical system of identifiers'.

A digital library, like its analogue counterpart, is a hugely complex affair. Both may host many thousands of items, each of which must have its allotted place on their virtual or physical shelves if it is to be found, retrieved and consulted. The digital library is even more complicated than its paper-based counterpart, as each item is often in itself a complex object, an aggregation of possibly hundreds or thousands of files, many of which may be duplicated in multiple forms, such as the archival, deliverable and thumbnail versions of the image of a page in a book. This complexity makes it all too easy for chaos to rule and for the valuable items in collections, and the files that make them up, to become lost in the morass. Needless to say, we should try to avoid this at all costs.

A key part of ensuring that nothing gets mislaid is to mark everything, data and metadata, with an unambiguous label which delineates its place in the entirety of the digital library's architecture. This is akin to a shelfmark label on a book in a physical library, but somewhat more pervasive: it needs to encompass the library as a whole, its collections, the items which populate these, the files from which they are constituted, every metadata record and every significant component or section in each of these. Ideally, the file system that holds the library should also be structured according to this system of identifiers. The aim is to create an integrated architecture for the library as a whole where the place of every component is clear and explicit within it.

One principle should be established at the outset. The identifiers that allow this to happen should not attempt to incorporate any descriptive information on the item or component that they label: this is the function of metadata, not of identifiers. The names of directories or files should similarly avoid any semantic labelling of this kind. If we had a digital edition of the first folio of Shakespeare's works, for instance, we should avoid directory names such as **hamlet** or **julius_caesar** and filenames such as **page1.tif** or **ophelia.jpg**; instead, it is the descriptive metadata attached to these that should spell out their content.

We should aim as a second principle to ensure that the structure of the identifiers mirrors the logical structure of our collections. This means that it should follow a pattern that establishes a hierarchy which begins at the top level (for the repository as a whole) and then moves through collections, sub-collections and items down as far as individual files. The further down the hierarchy we get, the longer the identifiers become; but this ensures that whenever we come across any component, for instance a stray image file, we can see exactly where it fits into the overall structure. For this reason we should not worry about the length or potential redundancy of any identifiers: it is much better to be verbose than to risk any ambiguity or potential duplication because of a concern for concision.

One final consideration is that for ease of processing it is helpful if all identifiers with the same function (for instance filenames) are of the same length and are ordered sequentially. If they are alphabetical they should begin at a (or aa, aaa, aaaa) and end at z (or zz, zzz, zzzz); if they are numeric they should be numbered in sequence and padded with zeros to ensure this (0001 ... 9999, for instance).

How might such a system of identifiers work in practice? The following discussion explains the one implemented in the Warburg Institute's Digital Library[C11.4], which forms the first case study in Chapter 11. At the start of every identifier is a three-letter code to indicate that it applies to this digital library and not to other collections housed within the Institute.

```
wdl
```

The library is divided into a number of discrete collections, each of which receives another three-letter code. One of these collections is a set of digitised Italian opera libretti which is assigned the code **opl**; it is identified by appending this code to the one for the digital library as a whole.

```
wdl-opl
```

Each item within this collection is assigned an additional code in the form of an alphabetical sequence of four letters beginning at **aaaa** for the first and then incrementing (**aaab**, **aaac**) for each subsequent one. Once again, these are appended to the string for the collection itself.

```
wdl-opl-aaaa
```

Using four letters in this way allows for a total of 456,976 items in a collection, which should be enough for most, but if more are needed an extra letter would bring the potential total to 11,881,376 and one more would advance it to 308,915,776.

For the sake of tidiness, and ensuring that identifiers with the same function are of the same length, it is best to decide in advance on a likely maximum size for a collection and hence the number of letters for this part of the identifier. Should this prove to be an underestimate, it is always possible to create a new collection with a different three-letter code; this need not necessarily be presented to the end-user as a separate one if it is undesirable to do so.

Below this level are the file or files that are brought together to make up what we see as the item. This may be a simple object consisting of one file only (for instance a film encoded as a single video file), or it may be a complex item made up of many, for instance a digitised book with an image for each page. What we call a 'file' here may itself consist of multiple files in different formats or fulfilling different functions. A video, for instance, may be made available in multiple encodings (AVI, WMV or MPEG). A page image from a book may also have several manifestations such as a high-quality TIFF for archival purposes, a compressed JPEG for delivery to the end-user and a smaller JPEG to act as a thumbnail for browsing. In addition to the data files that make up an object, each object will have at least one metadata file associated with it which should also be incorporated into the system of identifiers.

When we reach the level of the files that constitute a digital object, a simple numerical sequence, padded with zeros at the beginning, is used for each one that has the same format or function; in the Warburg Digital Library these numbers are four digits in length (0000 ... 9999), so allowing 10,000 files of the same type per item. To indicate the format or function of a file, a single digit or letter is appended at the end; the meaning of this suffix is determined by a local scheme devised at the Warburg Institute. For still images, **0** indicates an uncompressed, archival TIFF file, **1** a compressed JPEG derived from this for delivery purposes and **9** a small, thumbnail image in JPEG format. The archival TIFFs for the first three images from the digitised book with the item identifier **wdl-opl-aaaa** are labelled in the following way.

```
wdl-opl-aaaa-0001-0
wdl-opl-aaaa-0002-0
wdl-opl-aaaa-0003-0
```

Their corresponding JPEGS are identified as:

```
wdl-opl-aaaa-0001-1
wdl-opl-aaaa-0002-1
wdl-opl-aaaa-0003-1
```

and thumbnails for these as:

```
wdl-opl-aaaa-0001-9
wdl-opl-aaaa-0002-9
wdl-opl-aaaa-0003-9
```

Metadata files for each object follow the same convention; in this digital library they use letters rather than numbers to make their status as metadata clear. The suffix **a** indicates this file for the same book:

```
wdl-opl-aaaa-0001-a
```

The identifiers described here label every item within the digital library's collections, its place within them and the files (data and metadata) that either make up or describe the item. They have a vital function within the complex metadata that is needed for each object and so, as we shall see in Chapter 6, will feature everywhere in each item's canonical metadata file. They also have a role in the naming conventions for both the directory structure and filenames within the digital library.

Every file in the digital library is named using its identifier and the appropriate suffix for its type. The TIFF files, for instance, will be called:

```
wdl-opl-aaaa-0001-0.tif
wdl-opl-aaaa-0002-0.tif
wdl-opl-aaaa-0003-0.tif
```

the JPEGS derived from these will be called:

```
wdl-opl-aaaa-0001-1.jpg
wdl-opl-aaaa-0002-1.jpg
wdl-opl-aaaa-0003-1.jpg
```

and their respective thumbnails will be called:

```
wdl-opl-aaaa-0001-9.jpg
wdl-opl-aaaa-0002-9.jpg
wdl-opl-aaaa-0003-9.jpg
```

This item's metadata file, which is encoded in XML, will be named:

```
wdl-opl-aaaa-0001-a.xml
```

These filenames are somewhat verbose, but it is important to include all parts of their identifiers in them because they pin down precisely their place in the digital library architecture and make clear the functions that they perform. If a file goes astray somewhere in the often complicated operations that are involved in ingesting, managing, preserving and disseminating these objects they can be readily identified if they are labelled in this way. This can save much time and trouble, particularly in the future when the collection is no longer managed by those who created it and the place and function of ambiguously named files may be difficult to determine.

It is sensible to maintain a directory structure for the library as a whole which follows the hierarchy embedded within these identifiers. The Warburg Digital Library is arranged in this way (Figure 4.5).

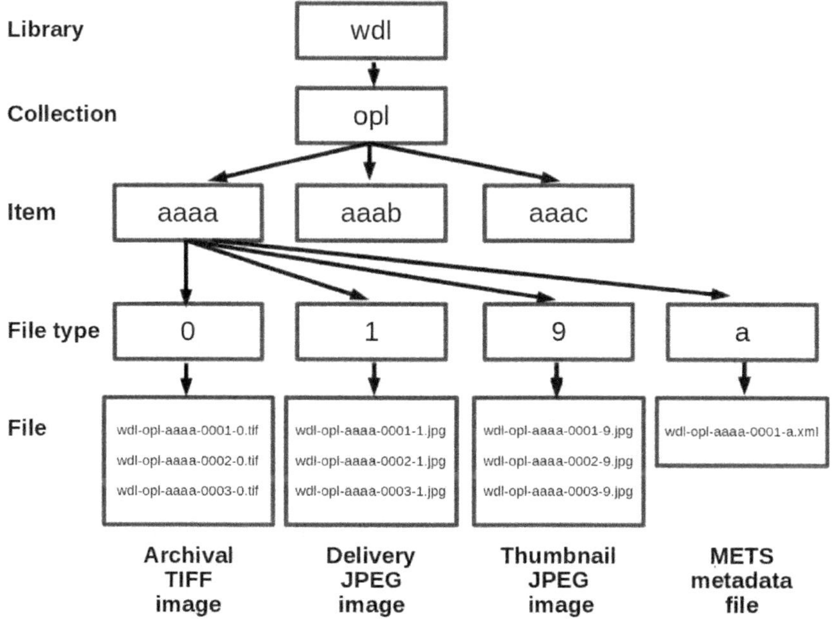

Figure 4.5 *Structure of Warburg Digital Library file system based on system of internal identifiers*

This follows the structure of the identifiers as far as the item level; the next layer below this subdivides into directories by file type, each of which then contains the files that conform to its respective type.

A system such as this, which is centred on labelling items and their constituent files on the basis of their place within an overall architecture, works effectively in structuring collections and minimising the chances of anything getting mislaid. It is, however, limited to acting as an internal set of identifiers only. The problem is that, while a string of characters such as **wdl-opl-aaaa** may be unique within a single library, there is no guarantee that this will be the case throughout the internet as a whole. We cannot, therefore, rely on them to act as unambiguous identifiers if we wish to share data and metadata outside our own institution.

To enable this, we need identifiers which are unique throughout the internet as a whole. A scheme for these does exist in the form of what are known as Uniform Resource Identifiers (URI). A URI for the first item in this collection of digitised opera libretti could take the following form.

```
http://wdl.warburg.sas.ac.uk/id/wdl/opl/aaaa
```

This should look familiar to anyone who has accessed the internet, as it resembles the sequence of letters that one types into the address window of a web browser to find and retrieve an online resource. Such a string is in fact a URI – although it is usually called by the more specific term Uniform Resource Locator (URL) – an identifier which references a document or other item on the internet and provides the address where it can be located. URIs are much broader than this, however, and can be applied to anything, tangible or intangible, to identify it wherever it is on the internet as a whole.

This could be something wholly abstract: **http://id.loc.gov/authorities/subjects/sh85046376**, for instance, is a URI defined by the Library of Congress for the philosophy of existentialism. It could be something rather more concrete, although perhaps more conceptual than physical, such as **http://vocab.getty.edu/page/tgn/7008546**, the URI for the Italian city of Genoa in the Getty Thesaurus of Geographic Names. It could also represent something more tangible, albeit digital, such as **www.theguardian.com/uk**, the address of the website of *The Guardian* newspaper, in which case it is more commonly called a URL as noted in the previous paragraph.

How can these cryptic URIs be deciphered? How can one tell that **http://id.loc.gov/authorities/subjects/sh8504637** refers to existentialism when its relationship to the philosophies of Jean-Paul Sartre and his associates is far from obvious from the URI as we encounter it? The most important part of the string that makes this deciphering possible is the first, in this example **http://id.loc.gov/**. This designates the authority which has defined the URI, in this case the Library of Congress. This will be unique whenever and wherever it is found on the internet, and so any URI that begins in this way will also be exclusive to the authority that has created it, however its subsidiary parts are constituted.

This gets us only so far: the URI is still opaque to us even when we know that it is assigned by the Library of Congress. This is where the prefix **http://** can come to our rescue, as it allows browsers to read this as a web address. Putting the URI into a web browser enables it to act as a URL and take us to a page on the Library of Congress website where it is explained that this URI denotes 'existentialism'. This is known as a *de-referenceable* URI, one which the authority that maintains it makes resolve to an online explanation of what it defines. This can be a very useful feature, although it is by no means obligatory to make a URI de-referenceable in this way.

Converting internal identifiers to URIs is a straightforward process as the foregoing example from the Warburg Digital Library shows. Each of the dashes (-) in the original is replaced with a forward slash (/), the preferred way of indicating divisions between hierarchical levels in URIs, and the prefix **http://wdl.warburg.sas.ac.uk/id/** is added at the beginning to show the authority which has defined it. The **/id/** at the end of this prefix is not obligatory but is a useful indicator that this is a URI and not a URL.

The internal identifiers outlined above will appear frequently in the examples that appear in the forthcoming chapters, where they will play key roles in linking components of metadata together. We cannot use URIs directly for this purpose, as XML has strict rules for formatting identifiers to which these external counterparts do not conform. Most of the schemes used in the metadata architecture recommended here have slots to record URIs for every significant component; these will be noted and examples given wherever this applies.

Much of this chapter has been devoted to detailing this system of identifiers in order to follow Principle 6, 'Impose a logical system of identifiers'. This attention to what may initially seem a relatively minor principle is merited, as it allows us to map out the overall shape of a digital library and also stakes out the internal anchor points needed to define the interrelationships between the components that make up its complex metadata architecture. It also provides the cornerstone to making our metadata (and data) interoperable, should we wish to share it with others.

Standards and identifiers are the foundations on which a coherent metadata strategy can be built. The next stage is to define the syntax, the encoding mechanism for the containers which will hold our metadata; this will be the focus of the following chapter.

5

XML: The Syntactical Foundation of Metadata

5.1 Introduction

Syntax as it is defined in information science describes the way in which metadata is encoded in order to assemble its semantic components into structures which mean more than the contents of these basic units alone. We must be able to read metadata and understand how it is structured if we are to use it and share it with others; this requires an understanding of its syntactical underpinnings. The choice of syntax is for this reason the first important decision that must be made in the design of an integrated metadata strategy.

There are a number of criteria that we should apply to our choice of encoding mechanism in order to follow the basic principles outlined earlier. We need metadata to be flexible and malleable enough to be able to support all stages of the digital curation lifecycle (Principle 1). This means that we should be able to manipulate and transform it into a form which allows it to perform its role at each of these stages. This feature is also needed if it is to act as the three types of information package within the OAIS model (Principle 2).

For long-term preservation (Principle 2 again) it should be in a format that is robust for archival purposes. This requires it to be independent of any single software application (Principle 5) for decoding, reading and processing. It should be interoperable as far as possible (Principle 3), and so capable of being transferred between systems with minimal manipulation. It should also be a widely recognised standard in its own right (Principle 7).

The recommendation for metadata syntax here is XML. This 'language' has a long history stretching back to the 1960s, when it began life as the Standard Generalised Markup Language (SGML), a mechanism for tagging electronic texts for linguistic analysis. XML is a slightly simplified variant of the now almost entirely superseded SGML which has found a key role as a vehicle for metadata. It is text based in the same way as SGML, is one of the simplest formats available and is decodable by almost any application. Although the way in which XML is encoded is simple, it can encompass metadata of great richness and complexity because it contains sophisticated mechanisms for storing it and building up elaborate structures of semantic interrelationships between its constituent parts.

5.2 What XML looks like

To get an idea of what an XML record (technically known as an *instance*) looks like, let us take a very simple example of metadata (and data) for a poem.

```
<?xml version="1.0"?>
<poem>
     <metadata>
      <title>odi et amo</title>
      <author>
             <name type="commonly known as">Catullus</name>
             <name type="full">Gaius Valerius Catullus</name>
      </author>
      <genre>poem</genre>
     </metadata>
     <text>
      <line number="1">odi et amo. quare id faciam, fortasse requiris</line>
      <line number="2">nescio. sed fieri sentio et xcrucior</line>
     </text>
</poem>
```

Example 5.1 *Poem by Catullus encoded in XML with metadata*

The first feature to note is that each component is enclosed in a set of tags, for example:

```
<genre>poem</genre>
```

These delineate what are known as *elements*, the semantic units that are recorded in XML. They usually consist of opening and closing tags, the latter of which is distinguished from the former by the addition of a forward slash (/) before its name.

One key feature of XML is that elements can nest or contain other elements. In this example all of those that make up this verse are nested within a **<poem>** element (marked by the opening and closing **<poem>...</poem>** tags). Within this further nesting occurs: the **<metadata>** element contains **<title>**, **<author>** and **<genre>** (the second of these in turn contains **<name>** which occurs twice) and **<text>** contains **<line>** elements (which again repeat). This allows a complex hierarchical structure to be built up in which semantic relationships between elements are concisely expressed: the multiple **<name>** elements, for instance, are shown to refer to the author of the poem by their place within their **<author>** 'parent'.

A further feature to note from this example is that elements can be qualified by the use of what are termed *attributes* to render their semantics more specific. The two **<name>** elements in this poem are treated in this way to indicate which form of the author's name is present within each:

```
<name type="commonly known as">Catullus</name>
<name type="full">Gaius Valerius Catullus</name>
```

Here the attribute **type** is used to perform the role of narrowing the semantic width of the **<name>** element to indicate the type of name recorded in each of its two occurrences. Attributes always take this form: the name of the attribute is followed by an equals sign and then by its content in inverted commas.

It is also possible for elements to consist of attributes alone: in this poem, for instance, **<genre>** could have taken an alternative form:

```
<genre type="poem"/>
```

Here its value is shown by the content of a **type** attribute instead of the text within its opening and closing tags. Elements of this type are known as empty elements and add the forward slash of a closing tag at the end to show that they contain no content beyond their attributes.

The markup that we see here is known as *semantic markup*, as it tells us something of the meaning of the content that it contains: each element and attribute makes a statement about this meaning. XML makes an excellent medium for holding metadata because of this. We could, for instance, extract some of the metadata for this poem (including Catullus's full name) and put it in an XML file whose elements conform to fields defined in a very simple form of DC:

```
<?xml version="1.0"?>
<dublin_core>
    <title>odi et amo</title>
    <creator>Gaius Valerius Catullus</creator>
    <type>poem</type>
</dublin_core>
```

Example 5.2 *Metadata from poem by Catullus in Dublin Core*

5.3 XML schemas

XML does not itself prescribe what elements or attributes we should use or how they relate to each other (for instance, which elements should nest within which); nor does it stipulate which are mandatory or optional, whether they can be repeated, what form their content should take and so on. It confines itself to defining the syntax and conventions within which all of these can be specified. A specification of this type is performed by a formal description, itself encoded in XML, which is known as an XML Schema.

Such a schema is written to perform a specific function and all of the metadata standards which will be discussed throughout this book are either published as XML schemas or available in that form among others. A schema prescribes both the content and structure of an XML instance, including any constraints on what it can include. Among the features that it spells out are:

- the elements that are allowed, which ones are mandatory, which are optional, which are repeatable and whether their content should conform to a particular type (for instance, text, numeric or date);
- the attributes which may qualify these elements, which are mandatory, which optional and what form their content can take (for instance, whether it can contain free text or whether it must be taken from a fixed list of values);
- the relationships between elements, most significantly which ones can nest within others to build up hierarchical semantic structures within an XML instance.

The potential features of an XML schema are much more extensive than those listed here. It may define a relatively simple application such as the DC record in Example 5.2 or it may form a very sophisticated and complex set of specifications which can take some time and effort to learn and employ effectively.

A schema file usually has the extension **.xsd**. We can declare that an XML instance adheres to its rules by adding a declaration in the form of two attributes to its opening element: if our poem complies with a (very simple) schema named poem.xsd, it would now appear as shown in Example 5.3.

```
<?xml version="1.0"?>
<poem xmlns:xsi="http://www.w3.org/2001/XMLSchema-instance"
    xsi:noNamespaceSchemaLocation="poem.xsd">
      <metadata>
            <title>odi et amo</title>
            <author>
                  <name type="commonly known as">Catullus</name>
                  <name type="full">Gaius Valerius Catullus</name>
```

```
            </author>
            <genre>poem</genre>
      </metadata>
      <text>
            <line number="1">odi et amo. quare id faciam, fortasse
                requiris</line>
            <line number="2">nescio. sed fieri sentio et excrucior</line>
      </text>
</poem>
```

Example 5.3 *The poem from Example 5.1 with a declaration of conformity to the schema 'poem.xsd'*

The meaning of these rather cryptic attribute names will be explained later in this chapter.

If an XML instance follows all of the rules of the schema to which it conforms, it is said to be *valid*. Almost all XML-based applications require valid records in order to function effectively, and so it is necessary to test an instance to ensure its conformance. This is done by software applications known as *parsers*, which check through it and report as an error any divergence from the requirements set out by the schema. These are usually incorporated into XML editors, which do this as one works on a file; they may, alternatively, be standalone applications which verify a completed instance. The metadata that conforms to the schemas recommended in this book should always be validated in this way.

It is possible, although not recommended, to produce an XML instance that does not conform to a schema, known technically as *well-formed XML*. A file is well-formed if it follows the syntactical requirements of XML (such as the rules for formatting elements and attributes) and ensures that all elements are nested neatly within each other, in the manner of the poem as originally presented in Example 5.1. The instance as a whole must also be nested within the opening and closing tags of a single element (in this case **<poem>...</poem>**), which is known as the *root* element. Such an instance will be understood by an XML application and can be edited and transformed in the same way as valid XML but is of little use for our purposes, as conformance to a schema is an essential feature of any viable metadata in the context of an overall strategy.

For the remainder of this book the word *schema* will be used only to refer to XML schemas of this type. The term *scheme* will continue to apply, as it has from the beginning, to metadata standards and applications in general.

5.4 Namespaces

One very useful feature of XML is the potential it offers to include elements and attributes from multiple schemas in the same instance. This is made possible through a mechanism known as *namespaces*, a way of labelling elements with a prefix that indicates the schema in which they are defined. This ensures that there can be no confusion as to the origin of any element and, hence, its semantics. As long as they are marked accordingly, there can be no possibility of confusing, for instance, a **<title>** element from DC with one of the same name from MODS, even if they appear in the same instance.

Namespaces are declared at the beginning of an XML file by including an attribute to the root element. If we wished to include elements from MODS in our instance, for example, we would include a declaration in this form:

```
xmlns:mods="http://www.loc.gov/mods/v3"
```

The string at the beginning (**xmlns:**) stands for 'XML namespace': two components are specified to define it. The first of these is a prefix (**mods**) which will be used throughout the instance to identify an element and its attributes as belonging to the schema in question, the second is a URI for the schema itself.

It should be noted that the latter of these is a URI, not a URL; it is an identifier for the schema, not an indication of where it can be found. To provide this an additional declaration must be added in the form of a further attribute to the root element:

```
xsi:schemaLocation="http://www.loc.gov/mods/v3/ mods-3-0.xsd"
```

Here we give the URI from the previous declaration, a space and then the location of the schema file itself. In this example the file is stored locally but it is possible (and preferable) to give its location as a URL on the server of the authority that maintains it:

```
xsi:schemaLocation="http://www.loc.gov/mods/v3/
http://www.loc.gov/standards/mods/v3/mods-3-7.xsd"
```

This will ensure that the schema is always available, even if the XML instance that we construct is moved around (providing, of course, that the authority maintains a persistent URL for it).

Once this declaration has been made we can prefix an element with **mods:** to indicate that it and its attributes are those defined in this schema. If we decided, for instance, to employ the **<title>** element from MODS in the poem instead of the element with the same name defined in the original schema *poem.xsd*, we would mark it in this way:

```
<mods:title>odi et amo</mods:title>
```

If we are using only a single schema or if we are employing multiple schemas but wish to designate one as a default, we may find it more convenient not to have to add a prefix to all of its elements. In this case we can simply declare a namespace without a prefix: for instance, if we gave our poem schema a (fictional) URI such as:

```
http://www.myinstitution.org/schemas/poem
```

we could have a namespace declaration of the form:

```
xmlns="http://www.myinstitution.org/schemas/poem"
```

and a location declaration such as this:

```
xsi:schemaLocation="http://www.myinstitution.org/schemas/
poem poem.xsd"
```

Any element or attribute without a prefix would then be assumed to belong to this schema.

If the poem were now altered to incorporate the **<title>** element from MODS in addition to those in *poem.xsd* it would now look as shown in Example 5.4.

```
<?xml version="1.0"?>
<poem xmlns="http://www.myinstitution.org/schemas/poem"
   xmlns:xsi="http://www.w3.org/2001/XMLSchema-instance"
   xmlns:mods="http://www.loc.gov/mods/v3"
   xsi:schemaLocation="http://www.myinstitution.org/schemas/poem poem.xsd
                       http://www.loc.gov/mods/v3
                           http://www.loc.gov/standards/mods/v3/mods-3-7.xsd">
       <metadata>
            <mods:title>odi et amo</mods:title>
            <author>
                  <name type="commonly known as">Catullus</name>
                  <name type="full">Gaius Valerius Catullus</name>
            </author>
            <genre>poem</genre>
       </metadata>
       <text>
              <line number="1">odi et amo. quare id faciam, fortasse
                   requiris</line>
              <line number="2">nescio. sed fieri sentio et excrucior</line>
       </text>
</poem>
```

Example 5.4 *Poem by Catullus marked up with elements from schema poem.xsd and MODS*

You may notice that there is one additional namespace prefix declared here (xsi:). This references a small set of elements and attributes which are designed to associate XML schemas with their instances; here it links the namespaces for each schema to the location of its schema file. A slightly different declaration was used in Example 5.3 to indicate where the schema file for the poem could be found:

```
xsi:noNamespaceSchemaLocation="poem.xsd"
```

This is a way of referencing schema files where no namespaces are declared, a viable option when a single schema is used, as in that example. The strategy in this book, however, relies on the integration of metadata from diverse schemas into a single structure, and so requires extensive use of namespaces. In the next chapter we will introduce METS, a 'packaging' schema which is designed to provide a framework of this kind by employing precisely this mechanism.

5.5 Creating and editing XML

The complexity of XML instances and the ample possibilities for errors that they present makes it impractical to create or edit them with a standard text editor. It is instead necessary to use a specialist editor which can read an XML schema, interpret its rules and ensure that only valid instances which fully conform to it can be created. There are several software packages available which are designed to do this. A powerful and widely used commercial option is Oxygen[C5.1]; a highly recommended free alternative is XML Copy Editor[C5.3].

A screenshot (Figure 5.1 opposite) of the editing screen in Oxygen demonstrates such a package in operation.

Here the poem from Example 5.3 is being edited to insert the second line of text: Oxygen has parsed the schema and shows that the only valid elements that can be used here are **`<line>`** and the closing tag for **`<text>`**. A small square at the top right of the editing window warns that we do not currently have a valid instance that fully conforms to the schema, although this is because we have yet to insert the new element and its mandatory attribute **`(number)`**. Once this is done the square will change colour to confirm that the instance is valid.

The same application can also be used to design XML schemas. This is done by a simple graphical interface which uses drag-and-drop to define elements, attributes and their relationships to each other (Figure 5.2).

Once the schema has been defined in this way Oxygen saves it with an .xsd extension; it can then be used with this or any other editor to create XML instances.

```
<?xml version="1.0" encoding="UTF-8"?>
<poem>

    <metadata>
        <title>odi et amo</title>
        <author>
            <name type="commonly known as">Catullus</name>
            <name type="full">Gaius Valerius Catullus</name>
        </author>
        <genre>poem</genre>
    </metadata>
    <text>
        <line number="1">odi et amo. quare id faciam, fortasse requiris</line>
        <
    </text>
</poem>
```

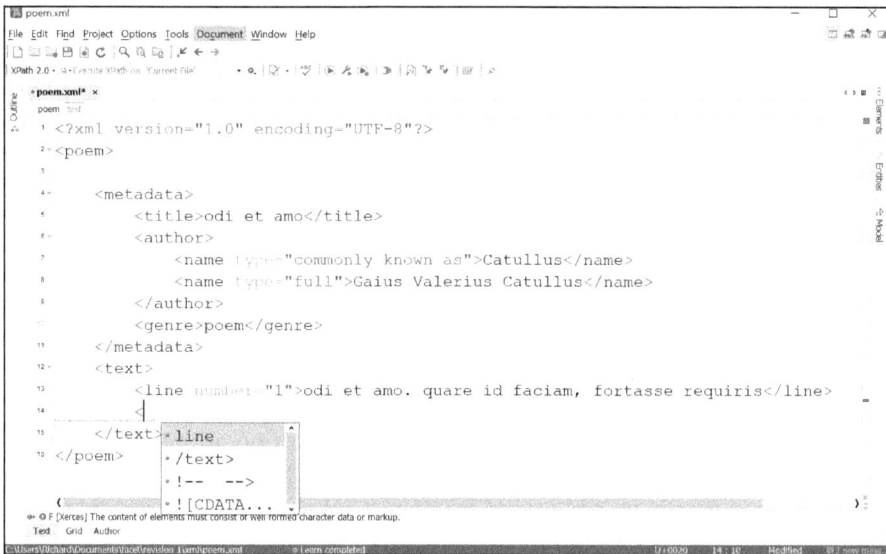

Figure 5.1 *Editing an XML file in Oxygen (inserting an element)* (Oxygen screenshots reprinted courtesy of Syncro Soft)

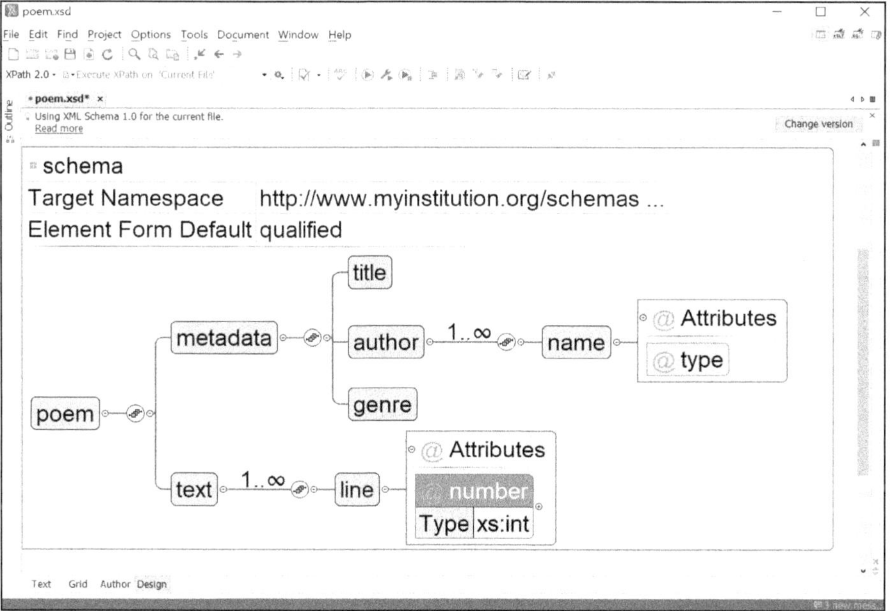

Figure 5.2 *Creating an XML schema in Oxygen* (Oxygen screenshots reprinted courtesy of Syncro Soft)

It should in practice be very rarely (or never) that one needs to construct a schema in this way; in almost all cases a published one outlined in the following chapters will meet our requirements. The only circumstances in which this might be necessary would be when our needs are so specialised that we are forced to create our own metadata scheme in the form of a data dictionary, the option of last resort detailed in the previous chapter. If we do go down that route, it is best to use the dictionary as the template for an XML schema, as this will allow integration with others that use this syntax and so ensure at least a limited degree of interoperability. The World Wide Web Consortium (W3C) provides an excellent introductory tutorial on constructing schemas[C5.4] for those who need to do so.

It can take some time to get to know an XML editor because they are complex applications capable of performing complex operations. In addition to editing files and creating schemas they can also carry out transformations, an important feature of XML and one of the prime reasons for employing this syntax. The implementation of the strategy outlined here requires very little, if any, direct XML editing, but it is still worthwhile investing in such an editor and getting to know how it works for when it is needed. The one area where this may be helpful is when using the standard outlined in the next chapter to design the packages that form the AIPs at the centre of this strategy.

5.6 Transforming XML

One of the most useful features of XML, and one which is central to its role in the integrated architecture outlined in this book, is that it is malleable. It is a straightforward matter to convert metadata encoded in one schema to another or to translate it into another format altogether. The processes that do this are not in the least complicated, although the transformations themselves can be highly complex; how complex will be dictated by the syntactic and semantic distance between the original schema and the destination of its converted metadata.

This malleability is essential if XML-encoded metadata is to function as an AIP in the OAIS model; it is this which makes possible its role as the canonical form into which ingested metadata (the SIP) can be translated and from which any metadata needed for dissemination (the DIP) can be generated. The integrated strategy proposed here would not be feasible without the ability to convert to and from this AIP while retaining its expressive power. This is particularly important as we look towards the long term. Without XML's transformative potential we could not feel confident about its viability for preservation, as there would be no guarantee that it would be able to generate metadata in a form compatible with future systems.

Although it is possible to convert XML using the pattern-matching features of programming languages such as Python, it is best instead to employ XSLT (eXtensible Stylesheet Language Transformations), a 'language' devised specifically for carrying out this function. XSLT instances, which are known as stylesheets, are themselves written in XML in a similar way to schemas (and so can be created in editors such as Oxygen). A conversion is done by running an XML file and XSLT stylesheet through a processor which generates a file in the destination format; this may be in XML conforming to another schema or in other formats such as text, PDF or PostScript. These processors may be standalone applications (a well known and widely used one is Saxon[C5.2]) or incorporated into editors such as Oxygen.

The advantage of using XSLT over a programming language is that it is capable of navigating the structures of an XML instance with a great degree of sophistication. This is because it incorporates XPath (XML Path Language), a query language which allows it to traverse these precisely and extract any content housed within them. In the poem by Catullus from Example 5.1, for instance, we could pull out his full name using a simple XPath statement:

```
/poem/metadata/author/name[@type='full']
```

This instructs XPath to begin at the top level of the instance's hierarchy (specified by the forward slash (/) at the beginning of the string) and then descend one level at a time through the elements **<poem>**, **<metadata>**, **<author>** and **<name>**. At this point it should then choose the **<name>** element, whose **type** attribute is set to 'full' (an instruction given by the expression **name[@type='full']**). The result of a query using this statement will then be:

```
Gaius Valerius Catullus
```

This is a very simple example of an XPath statement; much more complicated routes through the dense hierarchies of an XML instance can be mapped out as and when required.

XSLT works by executing XPath statements to retrieve content from an XML instance and then providing instructions on how this should be translated into the desired output format. This may be as simple as inserting it into new elements and attributes, or something much more complicated, such as reformatting strings or performing complex calculations on numerical content. Example 5.5 shows an XSLT stylesheet which can be used to extract the metadata from the poem in Example 5.1 and convert it into the DC record in Example 5.2.

```
<xsl:stylesheet xmlns:xsl="http://www.w3.org/1999/XSL/Transform" version="2.0">
  <xsl:template match="/">
        <dublin_core>
              <xsl:for-each select="/poem/metadata/title">
                     <title><xsl:value-of select="."/></title>
              </xsl:for-each>

              <xsl:for-each select="/poem/metadata/author/name[@type='full']">
                    <creator><xsl:value-of select="."/></creator>
              </xsl:for-each>

              <xsl:for-each select="/poem/metadata/genre">
                    <type><xsl:value-of select="."/></type>
              </xsl:for-each>
        </dublin_core>
  </xsl:template>
</xsl:stylesheet>
```

Example 5.5 *XSLT stylesheet to extract Dublin Core metadata from poem in Example 5.1*

The stylesheet works by extracting three elements from the poem using XPath statements:

[Original element in poem	XPath statement to extract element
<title>odi et amo</title>	/poem/metadata/title
<name type="full">Gaius Valerius Catullus</name>	/poem/metadata/author/name [@type='full']
<genre>poem</genre>	/poem/metadata/genre

The XSLT command **<xsl:for-each>...</xsl:for-each>** performs this function: it runs through the original XML file from beginning to end, searching for the content that satisfies the XPath statement contained within its **select** attribute. When it finds a match, it executes whatever is contained within its opening and closing tags. Here it extracts the content of the original element and inserts it into its DC equivalent, for instance:

```
<xsl:for-each select="/poem/metadata/genre">
            <type><xsl:value-of select="."/></type>
</xsl:for-each>
```

We use the command **<xsl:value-of select="."/>** to take the value of the element matched by its surrounding **<xsl:for-each>...<.xsl:for-each>** and surround it with the tags for the new element **<type>...</type>**.

One final detail must be attended to in order to generate the well-formed DC instance: the opening and closing tags for the root element

`<dublin_core>`. To do this we use a further XSLT command **`<template>...</template>`** within which the remainder of the stylesheet is nested. The **match** attribute of **`<template>`** is here set to '/', which instructs XSLT to match the whole XML instance beginning with its root element. We then locate the **`<dublin_core>...</dublin_core>`** tags immediately within **`<template>`** and the remaining XSLT commands within these in order to generate the DC instance with everything nested neatly in its appropriate place.

These three commands and their corresponding XPath statements are all that is needed to realise basic transformations of XML instances; they will probably be sufficient on their own to carry out most, if not all, of any conversions required to implement this metadata strategy. More can be done with a deeper knowledge of XSLT, but much can be achieved with as little as this. However, the time and effort involved in learning it in more depth is undoubtedly well spent and is highly recommended for the metadata librarian. There are many useful online tutorials available which can assist in this. A basic introduction from W3C, which is more than enough to get started writing useful stylesheets, is listed in the 'Useful Resources' section at the end of this volume[C5.5].

In many cases it is also possible to use XSLT produced by the authorities responsible for metadata standards. The Library of Congress, for instance, produces multiple stylesheets for the principal ones that it maintains which can be used to convert their instances to equivalents conforming to other schemas. However, it is still useful to have a least a basic knowledge of XSLT for occasions when these do not meet our exact requirements and so need to be edited or supplemented.

5.7 Why use XML?

On an initial encounter XML may appear a rather intimidating and complex way of holding metadata, but it is hoped that this chapter has shown that it has an internal logic based on straightforward principles which should make it relatively simple to learn and understand. It is the foundation on which a metadata strategy that aims to follow the principles laid out in Chapter 3 should be built, for several reasons.

XML is a well-established standard for data and metadata encoding and interchange and so supports Principle 7 ('Use standards whenever possible'). It is the primary standard specified by W3C for this purpose (World Wide Web Consortium 2008) and is itself derived from SGML, a format long approved by the International Organization for Standardization (ISO) for textual markup (International Organization for Standardization 1986). Its long pedigree and approval by these key bodies mean that we will not be leaving our metadata in a syntactical cul-de-sac if we employ XML.

XML is also a safe option for enhancing the interoperability of metadata (Principle 3). Its software independence (Principle 5), its realisation in one of the most readily interchangeable encoding mechanisms (text) and its ability to combine the human- and machine-readable in one file ensure that it presents few obstacles to the transfer and sharing of metadata at the level of syntax. To achieve full interoperability it must, of course, be complemented by a semantic congruence which will be supplied by the use of the standards specified in the following chapters.

For the long-term preservation of metadata, XML, like its predecessor SGML (Coleman and Willis 1997), is considered one of the most archivally robust formats available. Much of its strength in this area derives from the features that enhance its interoperability, particularly its text-based encoding and its independence from software packages which will inevitably become obsolete in the medium to long term. This archival role does not impede its capacity for the delivering of objects in the here and now, as its malleability, the way in which it can be transformed with such flexibility, ensures that it can deliver metadata in any required format. It is therefore a safe option for safeguarding the preservation of digital collections in the future (Principle 2) as well as supporting all stages of the digital curation lifecycle (Principle 1) in the present.

XML provides a syntactical foundation on which a metadata strategy can be built, but it is only the first stage in defining an architecture which can fulfil the essential principles that such a strategy needs to implement. The next stage is to define an overall framework for integrating the components which will populate this architecture, the package (in OAIS terms) which will bring these diverse elements together. The standard recommended to fulfil this role, METS, is introduced in the next chapter.

6

METS: The Metadata Package

6.1 Introduction

This chapter introduces the metadata standard that forms the centre of the architecture on which this strategy is built. METS[S.17], which stands for Metadata Encoding and Transmission Standard, is an XML schema designed to provide a framework for packaging all of the metadata (and potentially data) for a complex digital object. This includes its descriptive, administrative and structural components. METS allows all of this to be combined in a single XML instance, each type clearly delineated by an unambiguously defined place in its structure. As its name implies, packaging all of the metadata associated with a digital object in this way allows for its easy transmission and sharing with others.

METS was designed and is maintained by an international body of experts from the digital library community and is based at the MARC Standards Office at the Library of Congress. For the most part it does not supply semantics for the metadata that it houses; instead, it allows instances conforming to other XML standards, technically known as *extension schemas*, to be either embedded within its structures or held externally and referenced from within them. Any XML metadata can be incorporated into a METS instance in this way, although some schemas are specifically recommended for this purpose; using these enhances the interoperable potential of a record. The only exception to this, where METS itself provides a mechanism for recording metadata directly, is the type that records the internal structure of a digital object.

6.2 Why use METS?

METS has established itself as the predominant packaging schema within the digital library community, as might be expected from its provenance in the central bodies responsible for the definition of library metadata standards. For this reason it immediately fulfils Principle 7 ('Use standards whenever possible'). More pertinent than this, however, is its potential for meeting the requirements of Principle 2, 'Support the long-term preservation of the digital object', because of its congruence with the OAIS model.

As was shown in Chapter 3, the core of OAIS lies in its three information packages, the SIP, AIP and DIP. These are intended to bring together data objects and their associated metadata in discrete packages with clear boundaries which can then be used for their submission to an archive, its storage and preservation there and its dissemination to users. The metadata strategy that this book advocates follows this model by concentrating on the construction of a 'canonical' statement of metadata, equivalent to an AIP, which should also be in a discrete package that can be easily maintained, transferred and transformed as necessary.

METS fulfils this role very effectively, as it was designed specifically to act as an SIP, AIP or DIP within the OAIS framework. As an SIP or DIP, METS provides a standardised syntax for the transfer of metadata, and as an AIP it can function as its primary archival or 'canonical' form. Although it is generally used for the metadata of a digital object whose files are held externally, it is also possible for these to be converted to a format that allows them to be embedded directly within a METS instance, so rendering it a *bona fide* OAIS information package suitable for long-term preservation.

METS can act so effectively as an information package because it is designed to be generated easily from diverse metadata sources and to be capable of easy conversion to other formats as required. Part of this is due to its architecture, which separates different types into a clearly delineated structure connected by a system of internal identifiers. This approach ensures that a METS instance combines flexibility in how it interacts with other metadata sources, for both input and output, with a clear and logical internal arrangement which makes it easy to process its contents. This flexibility also extends to the ways in which it allows metadata to be either embedded within its architecture or referenced from within it, making its interaction with legacy data and metadata in particular much easier to achieve.

The drawback to this flexibility can be a reduction in its interoperable potential. Very little of a METS file is mandatory, and its implementer has multiple options to choose from when deciding on such issues as which types of metadata to include, which schemas to use and how the internal structure of an object is expressed. This makes it difficult to ingest a METS instance from another source without some clear documentation of the choices that have been made and how they have been applied. Such a mechanism, in the form of XML documents known as METS Profiles[C10.7], will be covered in Chapter 10.

One further problem that can arise when using extension schemas in a METS application is that they may not always find an obvious place in its structure. As we shall see particularly in respect of PREservation Metadata: Implementation Strategies (PREMIS)[S.23], a core standard for preservation metadata, some semantic components may not fall unambiguously into one of the categories that METS prescribes. They may also have components which duplicate functions that are already provided by the packaging standard, something which could prove problematic when processing a record. These issues are best resolved by implementing community-approved guidelines if they exist (as they do, for instance, for PREMIS) or ensuring the consistent documentation of local practices if they do not.

Other approaches to packaging standards are available, some of which have found a degree of acceptance in their respective communities. One of these, roughly contemporaneous in its initial appearance with METS, was designed by the Los Alamos National Laboratory to collate data and metadata for the complex digital objects in their digital library. MPEG-21, also known as the Digital Item Declaration Language (DIDL)[S.12], takes a different approach to METS in its overall design, collocating all types of metadata for an object's component together rather than separating each into a different part of its architecture and forming linkages between them by the use of identifiers (Bekaert, Hochstenbach and van de Sompel 2003). This is a viable approach, although rather less flexible than METS, and so less useful for converting legacy collections in particular, which may be one reason why it has failed to establish itself widely within the digital library community.

As is clear from this discussion, METS is not the only way to handle the packaging of digital library metadata and is not without a number of problems which arise principally from what is also its major strength: its innate flexibility. All of these can be alleviated, however, by adopting best practice guidelines or using features such as METS Profiles to enhance interoperability, and so can be rendered relatively minor. With these caveats in mind, we can begin to examine how METS works.

6.3 The METS architecture

METS aims to package all of the metadata (and possibly data) for a digital object within a single XML instance. To do this in a way which is easy to process and decode, it divides its contents into the seven sections shown in Figure 6.1 on the next page, each of which contains a different type of metadata.

The only one of these that is mandatory is the Structural Map, which records, as its name implies, the structural metadata for an object; all of the others are optional, although if none is present there would be little point in using METS at all.

The following discussion covers each of these sections with examples taken mainly from a METS record for a digitised book, the title page of which is shown in Figure 6.2. This is a libretto for an 18th-century oratorio which contains 30 pages, each of which has been scanned as a separate image.

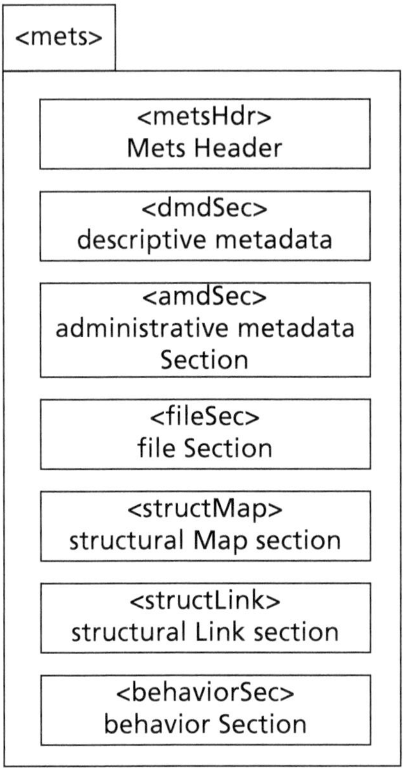

<mets>

<metsHdr>
Mets Header

<dmdSec>
descriptive metadata

<amdSec>
administrative metadata
Section

<fileSec>
file Section

<structMap>
structural Map section

<structLink>
structural Link section

<behaviorSec>
behavior Section

Figure 6.1 *The seven major sub-divisions of a METS file*

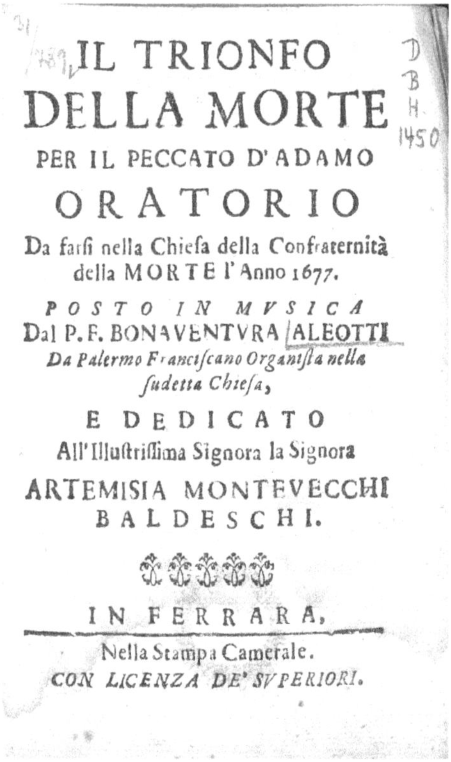

IL TRIONFO
DELLA MORTE
PER IL PECCATO D'ADAMO
ORATORIO
Da farſi nella Chieſa della Confraternità
della MORTE l'Anno 1677.
POSTO IN MVSICA
Dal P.F. BONAVENTVRA ALEOTTI
Da Palermo Franciſcano Organiſta nella
ſudetta Chieſa,
E DEDICATO
All'Illuſtriſſima Signora la Signora
ARTEMISIA MONTEVECCHI
BALDESCHI.
IN FERRARA,
Nella Stampa Camerale.
CON LICENZA DE' SVPERIORI.

Figure 6.2 *Title page of digitised book: the METS-encoded metadata for this is used as examples throughout this chapter*

Where appropriate, examples will also be given for other types of digital objects (for instance, video or audio files).

6.4 Identifiers within METS

The overall architecture of METS, which separates out the different metadata types shown in Figure 6.1, ensures its overall clarity, but to function effectively it is necessary for the sections into which it is divided to operate as a coherent whole. To enable this, METS employs an extensive system of identifiers to label every component of moment and a complementary system of pointers to reference these; together, these provide a comprehensive network of linkages which can express all of the relationships between the metadata constituents of even highly complex objects.

Every significant element in METS has an **ID** attribute which identifies it and allows it act as a reference point. Attributes of this type in XML must follow specific rules which are designed to ensure that they can be used in this way. First of all, they must be unique within the instance itself; should any be duplicated, an XML validator will produce an error message. Second, they are constrained in terms of how they may be formatted: they must begin with a letter and can contain only letters, numbers, hyphens, underscores, colons and full stops.

This is where the system of identifiers introduced in Chapter 4 comes in: they are designed to conform to the requirements of XML, and so can be used as valid IDs within a METS instance. All of the IDs for this digitised book are derived from its item identifier:

```
wdl-opl-aaaa
```

As each section of a METS instance is discussed, a recommended format for its IDs will be suggested. We will also demonstrate how the schema's linking mechanisms may be used to reference the IDs in other sections.

At this point we can begin our guided tour of the METS architecture itself.

6.5 The METS root element

A METS instance, like any XML file, must have a root element within which all of its content is nested. As well as fulfilling this basic role, this element, unsurprisingly named **<mets>**, performs the essential function of declaring all of the namespaces which will be used.

Namespaces, as we will remember from the preceding chapter, allow us to employ elements from multiple XML schemas in a single instance. METS itself prescribes very little in the way of semantics, preferring instead to allow the use of external extension schemas for most of this. If these are to be embedded within the METS architecture, it is necessary to define their namespaces, the abbreviated prefixes which will be used to identify their elements and the locations where their schemas can be found. This is done by attaching attributes to the **<mets>** element using the mechanisms introduced in the last chapter. If, for example, we intend to use MODS for descriptive and PREMIS and MIX (NISO Metadata for Images in XML Schema) for technical metadata (all of which are discussed in later chapters), we would define their namespaces in this way:

```
<mets xmlns="http://www.loc.gov/METS/"
     xmlns:xsi="http://www.w3.org/2001/XMLSchema-instance"
     xmlns:mods="http://www.loc.gov/mods/v3"
     xmlns:mix="http://www.loc.gov/standards/mix/v20"
     xmlns:premis="http://www.loc.gov/premis/v3"
```

```
    xsi:schemaLocation="http://www.loc.gov/METS/
        http://www.loc.gov/standards/mets/mets.xsd
    http://www.loc.gov/mods/v3 http://www.loc.gov/standards/mods/v3/mods-3-5.xsd
    http://www.loc.gov/standards/mix/v20
        http://www.loc.gov/standards/mix/mix.xsd
    http://www.loc.gov/premis/v3
        https://www.loc.gov/standards/premis/v3/premis-v3-0.xsd"
    OBJID="wdl-opl-aaaa">
```

Example 6.1 *Defining namespaces in the <mets> element*

Note that we also define here the 'default' namespace, the one which applies where no prefix is given to element names, which is, of course, that of METS itself.

One final component in this element is the **OBJID** (Object ID) attribute, in which we give the identifier for the digital object itself, in this case **wdl-opl-aaaa**; all subsequent IDs within the METS instance will be derived from this.

6.6 The METS Header

The first section within a METS instance, like all except the Structural Map, is optional, but its use is highly recommended. The METS Header **<metsHdr>** contains information on the METS file itself, including its provenance (its creator and maintainer) and the dates of its creation and last modification. Including this assists in following the last principle, Principle 8: 'Ensure the integrity of the metadata itself', by providing basic information which can be used to verify the authenticity of the metadata record.

Example 6.2 shows a simple METS Header which includes details of the record's creation, modification dates and the organisation which produced it. Note that the dates must be given in the ISO 8601[C6.1] format defined by the ISO; this includes a time of day, which is perhaps a little over-pedantic for recording the creation of a METS instance and so is often given as midnight:

```
<metsHdr ID="wdl-opl-aaaa-hdr"
        CREATEDATE="2017-03-17T00:00:00"
        LASTMODDATE="2020-07-07T00:00:00">
    <agent ROLE="CREATOR" TYPE="ORGANIZATION">
        <name>Warburg Digital Library</name>
    </agent>
</metsHdr>
```

Example 6.2 *Sample METS Header (metsHdr) element and subelements*

Note also that this section is given an ID derived from the identifier for the object. In this case it is simply formed by the addition of the suffix **-hdr** (standing for header).

6.7 Descriptive Metadata Section

One of the most important sections of a METS instance holds the descriptive metadata for a digital object. The Descriptive Metadata Section **<dmdSec>** does not specify any elements for this in itself; instead, it acts as a container within which it can be embedded if it is already encoded in XML or from which it can be referenced if it is held externally, usually because it is in another format.

This section is repeatable as many times as required. We may choose to do this if we wish, for instance, to include metadata that conforms to more than one schema, such as DC and MODS, or if we wish to include a highly detailed record and a more basic one to serve different purposes. Whether it is repeated or not, it is sensible to provide the **<dmdSec>** with an ID derived from the object identifier. In Example 6.3 it takes the form **wdl-opl-aaaa-dmd-0001**, where **dmd** stands for descriptive metadata and a sequential number is added as a suffix to account for any multiple instances of this section.

Of the two options for handling descriptive metadata, embedding or referencing, the former is much to be preferred for ease of processing and to better equip the METS instance as a vehicle for preservation. To allow embedding, METS makes use of the namespaces declared in the **<mets>** root element. In the very truncated Example 6.3 a MODS file is treated in this way, using the namespace prefix **mods:** to indicate that each element here conforms to that schema:

```
<dmdSec ID="wdl-opl-aaaa-dmd-0001">
 <mdWrap MDTYPE="MODS">
     <xmlData>
       <mods:mods>
          <mods:titleInfo>
            <mods:title>Il trionfo della morte per il peccato
                        d'Adamo</mods:title>
          </mods:titleInfo>
       </mods:mods>
     </xmlData>
  </mdWrap>
</dmdSec>
```

Example 6.3 *Embedding a MODS file within a METS Descriptive Metadata Section*

The METS element **<mdWrap>** is used to signify that an XML instance is embedded here. Its attribute **MDTYPE** indicates the metadata scheme to which the wrapped content conforms.

The alternative to embedding XML metadata is to maintain it externally and provide a reference or pointer to it, which is done by an alternative element to **<mdWrap>** called **<mdRef>**. In Example 6.4 on the next page an additional Descriptive Metadata Section uses this feature to provide a link to a record for the book in the online catalogue of the library that holds it:

```
<dmdSec ID="wdl-opl-aaaa-dmd-0002">
  <mdRef LOCTYPE="URL" MDTYPE="MARC"
      xlink:href="https://catalogue.libraries.london.ac.uk/record=b3012601~S12"/>
</dmdSec>
```

Example 6.4 *Using <mdRef> to point to an external descriptive metadata record*

<mdRef> is an empty element containing only attributes: **LOCTYPE** records the type of reference that it contains (here a URL), **MDTYPE** the type of scheme that the external descriptive metadata conforms to (here a MARC record) and **xlink:href** the address of the external metadata itself. Note the prefix **xlink:** which indicates that this attribute comes from a further set designed for recording linkages; its namespace must also be declared in the root **<mets>** element for its use to be valid here.

Using **<mdWrap>**, the preferred option, or **<mdRef>** is very straightforward, leaving the choice of descriptive metadata scheme as the main issue to be decided. The pros and cons of various options for this are discussed in the next chapter.

6.8 Administrative Metadata Section

The next section of a METS instance contains the extensive set of administrative metadata which is needed to ingest, manage, disseminate and preserve a digital object. It follows the approach of its predecessor in not supplying a set of elements itself but instead acting as a container within which this information can be embedded if encoded in XML or from which it can be referenced if held externally. It is partitioned into four subdivisions, each for a different subset of administrative metadata, as shown in Figure 6.3 opposite.

The first of these, **<techMD>**, covers technical metadata about the files that make up the digital object. For still images this may include such details as file formats, dimensions, colour depth and any compression algorithms that have been employed to reduce their sizes. For moving images we may wish to record frame rates, aspect ratios and the codecs used for compression and decompression. This type of metadata is particularly important for preservation purposes, as it provides information that will be needed by future systems as they attempt to understand and decode these files.

The second, **<rightsMD>**, covers the IPR attached to a digital object or to its parts. This includes any copyright declarations associated with it, a statement of who its copyright holders are and any information necessary to deliver it in accordance with the requirements of these property rights (for

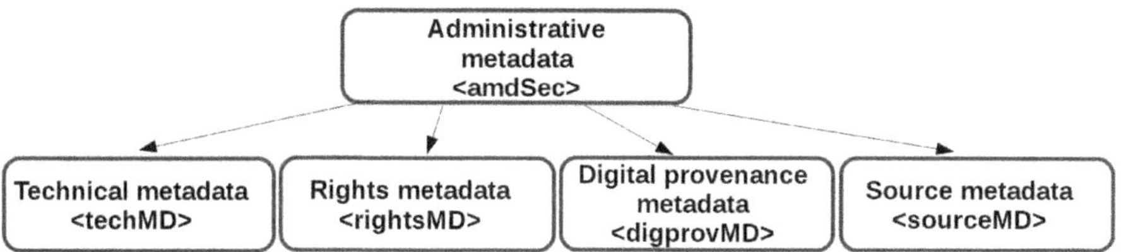

Figure 6.3 *The four subdivisions of the METS Administrative Metadata Section*

instance, restricting access to specific groups of users such as paying subscribers to a commercial service).

The third, **<digprovMD>**, covers information that records an audit trail of what has been done to a digital object since its creation. This type of information comes under the umbrella of preservation metadata, specifically the part which is designed to record the provenance of an object and so verify its authenticity, enabling future users to trust that it is what it claims to be. This type is handled by the preservation standard PREMIS, which is discussed in detail in Chapter 9.

The final subdivision, **<sourceMD>**, is designed for use in cases where digital objects have been digitised from physical resources (such as the online book shown in Figure 6.2). It is intended to contain descriptive and administrative metadata that relates to the analogue original rather than the digital surrogate made from it.

In theory, descriptive metadata that relates to the digital object itself should go into the Descriptive Metadata Section (**<dmdSec>**), while any related to the item that has been digitised should go here. In practice this is very rarely done. All such descriptive metadata is usually located in **<dmdSec>** for the sake of clarity and simplicity. The employment of **<sourceMD>** is generally limited to administrative information needed for the physical maintenance and preservation of the original (for instance, recording in the case of a manuscript whether it is on paper, parchment or vellum and whether it has been damaged). The recommendation here, therefore, is to use **<dmdSec>** for all descriptive metadata and **<sourceMD>** only for essential administrative information related to the original physical object.

The Administrative Metadata Section and all of its subdivisions are repeatable. Each should be labelled with an ID that is unique within the METS instance. It is recommended that they follow similar conventions to those suggested for **<dmdSec>**, adding in the case of technical metadata (**<techMD>**) only a suffix to indicate the type of the file in question, using the conventions outlined in Chapter 4 (here, for instance, a '0' designates an archival TIFF image):

```
<amdSec ID="wdl-opl-aaaa-amd-0001">
<techMD ID="wdl-opl-aaaa-amd-tmd-0001-0">
<rightsMD ID="wdl-opl-aaaa-amd-rgt-0001">
<digprovMD ID="wdl-opl-aaaa-amd-dpr-0001">
<sourceMD ID="wdl-opl-aaaa-amd-src-0001">
```

Each of these subdivisions can relate to the digital object as a whole or any component within it. The second option is particularly relevant to **<techMD>**, where the technical metadata for every file of which a complex object is composed can be recorded in a separate iteration of this element. These IDs make this level of granularity possible by providing the anchor points with which each subdivision can be referenced from anywhere in the METS instance. How this works will be illustrated in the following sections of this chapter.

Every subdivision of Administrative Metadata works in the same way as for Descriptive Metadata: embedding is done using an **<mdWrap>** element and referencing an external source by **<mdRef>**. A highly truncated technical metadata entry, in this case using MIX for a still image of the title page from the libretto, would look as shown in Example 6.5.

```
<amdSec ID="wdl-opl-aaaa-amd-0001>
    <techMD ID="wdl-opl-aaaa-tmd-0001-0">
       <mdWrap MDTYPE="OTHER" OTHERMDTYPE="MIX">
          <xmlData>
             <mix:mix>
                <mix:BasicDigitalObjectInformation>
                   <mix:FormatDesignation>
                      <mix:formatName>JPEG</mix:formatName>
                    </mix:FormatDesignation>
                </mix:BasicDigitalObjectInformation>
             </mix:mix>
          </xmlData>
       </mdWrap>
    </techMD>
</amdSec>
```

Example 6.5 *A MIX instance containing metadata for a still image file embedded within a <techMD> sub-division of <amdSec>*

As we saw for the MODS instance in Example 6.3, the prefix **mix:** indicates elements which conform to this extension schema rather than METS itself; its namespace will have been declared earlier in the **<mets>** root element. The attribute **MDTYPE** again indicates the schema to which this instance belongs; in this case it is set to 'OTHER', as MIX is not in the closed list specified for this attribute by the METS schema and the **OTHERTYPE** attribute used to record its name instead.

The MIX schema and others which can record technical metadata will be covered in more detail in Chapter 9, along with those for other types of administrative metadata.

6.9 The File Section

At this stage in our journey through the pathways of METS we leave metadata and come to data, specifically the files of which a digital object is composed. The File Section **<fileSec>** provides an inventory where they are listed and their locations noted. It is here that delivery and archival systems will look to find the files that they will provide to the end-user.

At the top level of the File Section are one or more elements called File Group (**<fileGrp>**). These are designed to group a digital object's files together in ways which make the organisation of the File Section as a whole logical and easy to maintain. Within each File Group are nested the elements named **<file>** which contain information on each file itself. The whole File Section may contain a single File Group if no internal arrangement is required, or File Groups may make multiple appearances to structure the section in any way needed. File Groups may also nest within each other to add further possibilities for the ordering of this section.

A very simple File Section containing a single File Group with three files would look as shown in Example 6.6.

```
<fileSec ID="wdl-opl-aaaa-fls-0001">
  <fileGrp ID="wdl-opl-aaaa-flg-0001">
     <file ID="wdl-opl-aaaa-fil-0001-0">
        <FLocat LOCTYPE="URL"
           xlink:href="https://warburgarchive.com/wdl/opl/aaaa/0/wdl-opl-aaaa-
                 0001-0.tif"/>
      </file>
      <file ID="wdl-opl-aaaa-fil-0002-0">
         <FLocat LOCTYPE="URL"
            xlink:href="https://warburgarchive.com/wdl/opl/aaaa/0/wdl-opl-aaaa-
                 0002-0.tif"/>
       </file>
       <file ID="wdl-opl-aaaa-fil-0003-0">
          <FLocat LOCTYPE="URL"
             xlink:href="https://warburgarchive.com/wdl/opl/aaaa/0/wdl-opl-aaaa-
                 0003-0.tif"/>
        </file>
    </fileGrp>
</fileSec>
```

Example 6.6 *Simple File Group with three* **<file>** *elements*

The File Section, the File Group and all of its **<file>** elements receive unique IDs derived from the identifier for the digital object as a whole. The section itself gets an ID of the form **wdl-opl-aaaa-fls-0001**, where **fls** stands for 'file section' and a sequential number comes afterwards. The File Group's ID takes the form **wdl-opl-aaaa-flg-000** – the digital object's ID supplemented by the three-letter code **flg** to indicate its status as a file group and a sequential number. For **<file>** the object's identifier is followed by the letters **fil**; after this is a running number and finally a suffix to indicate what type of file this is, following the convention mentioned earlier (in this case a '0' for an archival TIFF image once again).

In its simplest form the **<file>** element contains nothing more than information on the location of the file itself, as shown in Example 6.7.

```
<file ID="wdl-opl-aaaa-fil-0001-0">
   <FLocat LOCTYPE="URL"
       xlink:href=https://warburgarchive.com/wdl/opl/aaaa/0/wdl-opl-aaaa-
            0001-0.tif"/>
</file>
```

Example 6.7 *Sample (very simple)* **<file>** *element*

This is given in the File Location (**<FLocat>**) element nested within **<file>**. Several ways of pointing to the file's location are possible; the type used here is a simple URL as indicated in the **LOCTYPE** (Location Type) attribute.

The file shown in Example 6.7 is held externally to the METS instance and referenced from within it. This is the way that the **<fileSec>** is usually deployed, but if we wish or need to it is also possible to embed a data file directly within a **<file>** element. In this case the **<FLocat>** element is replaced by an alternative named **<FContent>** (File Content).

If the data file is itself encoded in XML, for instance an electronic text marked up in a schema designed for this purpose such as the Text Encoding Initiative (TEI)[S.25], it may be embedded directly within an **<xmlData>** element in the same way as we saw in Examples 6.3 and 6.5.

```
<file ID="wdl-opl-aaaa-fil-0001-4">
   <FContent>
     <xmlData>
        <tei:TEI>
                <tei:teiHeader>
                 [content omitted]
                <tei:/teiHeader>
                <tei:text>
                   <tei:body>
                      <tei:p>Il trionfo della morte</tei:p>
                         [content omitted]
                   </tei:body>
```

```
            </tei:text>
        </tei:TEI>
      </xmlData>
    </FContent>
</file>
```

Example 6.8 *Embedding a (very truncated) XML file within a* **<file>** *element*

In Example 6.8 we embed a (very truncated) XML file containing a transcription of the oratorio libretto marked up in the TEI. This could perhaps be used by a delivery system to display the textual content of the volume next to the images or to provide full-text searching of its content.

This works neatly for XML data files, but how can we handle the vast majority, such as image files, which are not encoded in this way? The answer is to convert them to a textual form using a simple utility known as **base64**. This is available in a number of applications which are readily downloadable for free on the internet and converts any binary file (image, audio, video, etc.) to text which can then be inserted directly into a METS instance. These files are larger than the originals but not inordinately so; for instance, a still image file grows by around 25% when converted. This data is embedded using the element **<binData>** (Example 6.9).

```
<file ID="wdl-opl-aaaa-fil-0001-5">
   <FContent>
     <binData>
        DI0ODdjam0gIDIyMDA1ODkgYSA0NU0wMDAxMDA...(etc.)
      </binData>
   </FContent>
</file>
```

Example 6.9 *Embedding a binary file directly within METS*

There is little reason to go through this process and embed binary data when creating the records which will be used to support a working digital library system but it has value when using METS for long-term preservation. Combining all of the data and metadata for a digital object in one file produces a self-sufficient, discrete AIP within the OAIS architecture which does not rely on any external files and linkages to be decoded and used at a future date. METS instances of this type may be too large and unwieldy to use in a working system, but it can be useful to generate them for long-term preservation purposes in tandem with their smaller counterparts which reference rather than embed their data files.

These examples of the **<file>** element in use show it with a single attribute, **ID**, only. It does, however, come with a range of other attributes that can provide useful additional information. Four of these are shown in

Example 6.10, which is an enhanced version of Example 6.7.

```
<file ID="wdl-opl-aaaa-fil-0001-0"
     CHECKSUM="31be5a2916cba255c5c7...(etc)"
     CHECKSUMTYPE="SHA256"
     ADMID="wdl-opl-aaaa-tmd-0001-0"
     GROUPID="0">
   <FLocat LOCTYPE="URL"
          xlink:href="https://warburgarchive.com/wdl/opl/aaaa/0/wdl-opl-aaaa-
              0001-0.tif"/>
</file>
```

Example 6.10 *Simple* **<file>** *element from Example 6.7 with additional attributes*

The first two, **CHECKSUM** and **CHECKSUMTYPE**, are used for providing information designed to verify the authenticity of the file, to confirm that it is the one referred to and that it has not been corrupted in any way. A checksum is a string, usually 64, 128 or 256 characters long, which is generated by a software utility from the bits and bytes of a file. It is almost certainly unique to the file from which it is derived; change a single byte, for instance one pixel in an image, and it will be completely different. Various utilities can generate these; the one used in this example is called SHA256 and its name is recorded in the **CHECKSUMTYPE** attribute. The checksum for this file, which is 64 characters in length, is given in the **CHECKSUM** attribute itself. The use of checksums is good practice in the administration of a digital library and is highly recommended.

The third attribute, **ADMID**, is an example of the rich set of internal linking mechanisms available in METS. This allows us to point to an element in the Administrative Metadata section containing the technical, rights, digital provenance or source metadata relating to the file. In this case we use it to point to technical metadata encoded in MIX by recording here the ID of the Technical Metadata (**<techMD>**) element from Example 6.5 that contains it. Every file can be linked to its respective technical or other administrative metadata in this way. A complementary attribute, **DMDID**, can also be included to point to descriptive metadata that relates only to this file, in this case by including the ID of the subdivision in the Descriptive Metadata (**<dmdSec>**) section that contains this information.

The final attribute here, **GROUPID**, is used to align a file to a secondary grouping in addition to its placement in the file group. These groupings can be defined in any way that we wish and the content of the attribute can follow any appropriate convention. In Example 6.10 it is used to specify the type of file that this is (TIFF, JPEG etc.), following the scheme outlined earlier where **GROUPID="0"** again indicates that it is an archival TIFF image.

The File Section shown in Example 6.6 demonstrates this section in its most basic form, with a single **<fileGrp>** containing a simple sequential listing of **<file>** elements. However, the File Group is capable of much more sophisticated arrangements than this. One way of using it which is highly recommended is to group multiple manifestations of the same component. For the digitised libretto, for instance, it could be used to bring together different image variants (archival TIFF, delivery JPEG, thumbnail JPEG) of the same page (Example 6.11).

```
<fileSec ID="wdl-opl-aaaa-fls-0001">
  <fileGrp ID="wdl-opl-aaaa-flg-0001">
     <file ID="wdl-opl-aaaa-fil-0001-0"
           CHECKSUM="31be5a2916cba255c5c7...(etc)"
           CHECKSUMTYPE="SHA-256"
           ADMID="wdl-opl-aaaa-tmd-0001-0"
           GROUPID="0">
        <FLocat LOCTYPE="URL"
           xlink:href="https://warburgarchive.com/wdl/opl/aaaa/0/wdl-opl-aaaa-
               0001-0.tif"/>
     </file>

     <file ID="wdl-opl-aaaa-fil-0001-1"
           CHECKSUM="10y569g3jrps30f5enfa...(etc)"
           CHECKSUMTYPE="SHA-256"
           ADMID="wdl-opl-aaaa-tmd-0001-1"
           GROUPID="1">
        <FLocat LOCTYPE="URL"
           xlink:href="https://warburgarchive.com/wdl/opl/aaaa/0/wdl-opl-aaaa-
               0001-1.jpg"/>
     </file>

     <file ID="wdl-opl-aaaa-fil-0001-9"
           CHECKSUM="p0pdmulh3xabnreqw7u5...(etc)"
           CHECKSUMTYPE="SHA-256"
            ADMID="wdl-opl-aaaa-tmd-0001-9"
            GROUPID="9">
        <FLocat LOCTYPE="URL"
           xlink:href="https://warburgarchive.com/wdl/opl/aaaa/0/wdl-opl-aaaa-
               0001-9.jpg"/>
      </file>
  </fileGrp>
</fileSec>
```

Example 6.11 *Sample <fileGrp>(File Group) for variants of a still image*

In this example, each page image is represented by a separate **<fileGrp>** which in turn contains three **<file>** elements, one for each variant. Their **GROUPID** attributes indicate which is which.

The use of multiple **<fileGrp>**s is a very straightforward way to organise a File Section neatly and logically, which will make it much easier to process when we come to deliver its content. It is well worth the time and effort required to design a well-structured File Section in this way.

6.10 The Structural Map

The kernel of a METS file and its only mandatory component is the Structural Map (**<structMap>**), which is the section that details the internal structure of a digital object and is the central point from which the web of linkages that make up a METS instance flow. The Structural Map is repeatable, should it be necessary to record multiple views of a complex object's structure; for instance, a medieval manuscript may need to use one such map for its textual content and another for a detailed representation of its physical make-up.

A digital object may have a very simple structure; for instance, it could consist of a single uninterrupted sequence if it is a video which plays from beginning to end with no segmentation into subdivisions. It may be more complex, perhaps a book with multiple chapters, sections and subsections or a DVD with multiple chapters, supplementary material and a maze-like structure for navigating all of its features. All of these are readily accommodated within the Structural Map, which defines the overall shape of a digital object as encountered by the user. For this reason, it is mandatory in any METS application.

The primary model underlying this section is hierarchical: it assumes that a digital object can be depicted as a series of components or sections which nest neatly within each other. In its simplest form this type of object is depicted by a series of Division (**<div>**) elements which are arranged in this way. Example 6.12 is an example of a Structural Map for a (very short) book consisting of nothing more than a title page, its reverse (verso) and a chapter of only two pages.

```
<structMap ID="wdl-opl-aaaa-stm-0001">

  <div  ID="wdl-opl-aaaa-div">

     <div LABEL="Front Matter" ID="wdl-opl-aaaa-div-0001">
        <div LABEL="Title page"   ID="wdl-opl-aaaa-div-0001-0001">
           <fptr FILEID="wdl-opl-aaaa-flg-0001"/>
        </div>
        <div LABEL="Blank page" ID="wdl-opl-aaaa-div-0001-0002">
           <fptr FILEID="wdl-opl-aaaa-flg-0002"/>
        </div>
      </div>

      <div LABEL="Chapter 1"  ID="wdl-opl-aaaa-div-0002">
```

```
        <div LABEL="Page 1"  ID="wdl-opl-aaaa-div-0002-0001">
           <fptr FILEID="wdl-opl-aaaa-flg-0003"/>
        </div>
        <div LABEL="Page 2"  ID="wdl-opl-aaaa-div-0002-0002">
           <fptr FILEID="wdl-opl-aaaa-flg-0004"/>
        </div>
     </div>

  </div>

</structMap>
```

Example 6.12 *Simple Structural Map for a book*

The Structural Map gets an ID of the form **wdl-opl-aaaa-stm-0001**, where **stm** stands for 'structural map' and a sequential number follows. All such maps contain a root **<div>** element within which all of the subsidiary **<div>**s are nested. The book is divided into two sections, the first "Front Matter" and the second "Chapter 1", each of which is represented by the highest-level **<div>**s nested immediately within the root. In this example their opening and closing tags are shown in bold. Within these are the next level of **<div>**s, each of which represents a single page of the book. Any number of levels of nested **<div>** elements are possible within the Structural Map, so allowing us to represent the structure of a digital object in any depth required.

The Structural Map itself and its subsidiary **<div>** elements all receive IDs in the usual manner for significant elements within METS. Those for the **<div>**s are designed to reflect their places in the overall hierarchy: **wdl-opl-aaaa-div** designates the 'root' element, each top-level **<div>** within this is numbered sequentially (**wdl-opl-aaaa-div-0001, wdl-opl-aaaa-div-0002** etc.) and every one nested within these has an additional numerical suffix of the same type (**wdl-opl-aaaa-div-0001-0001**, **wdl-opl-aaaa-div-0001-0002** etc.).

The other attribute for each **<div>** is **LABEL**, which contains the text that will be presented to the user when they browse through the internal structure of the object. Here we record the headings for each section ("Front Matter" and "Chapter 1") and the designation for each page within these ("Title page", "Blank page", "Page 1" and "Page 2"). With this attribute a delivery system can build tools such as virtual tables of contents for users to find their way around a resource.

One further element appears within the lowest-level **<div>**s: this is **<fptr>**, which stands for File Pointer. This is where we point to the part of the File Section within which details of the file or files that correspond to this **<div>**, including of course their location, can be found. The **FILEID** attribute establishes this link by supplying the **ID** of the relevant element in the File Section. In this example it is used to reference the File Group (**<fileGrp>**) that contains the **<file>** elements (archival TIFF, delivery JPEG and thumbnail JPEG) for each image: for the title page, for instance, the **ID** attribute of the **<fileGrp>** in Example 6.11 is given to make this connection.

The metadata in this Structural Map and the linkages that it supplies to the location of the files for each image provide a delivery system with all the information that it needs to let the user browse through this virtual book and view any page that they wish. Figure 6.4 on page 86 shows how the chain of linkages from the Structural Map to the File Section allows this to happen.

We begin at the Structural Map in the lower left-hand corner. From the **<div>** elements here we generate a table of contents: the **LABEL** attributes of the top level of these produce the section or chapter headings and those of the next level the designation of each page. Once the user clicks on a page (here the 'Title page') the system notes the **FILEID** attribute of the **<fptr>** within the page's **<div>** and then locates the **<fileGrp>** whose **ID** attribute matches it. As we wish to display the delivery JPEG image, which has the code **1** to identify it, it looks for the **<file>** element with the **GROUPID** attribute set to '1'; it then moves down to this element's **<FLocat>** and uses its **xlink:href** attribute to find the URL of the image and display it.

This may seem to be a fiendishly circuitous way of displaying an image but it is easy to design a delivery system that follows this route because each step along the way is logical and everything has a clear and unambiguous place in the METS architecture. This is why a coherent system of identifiers is so important for METS to function effectively: they mark out each metadata component with its unique location within this potentially complex structure, and so make navigation possible.

Much more complex structures than this basic hierarchy can be laid out using additional features of the Structural Map architecture. A very useful one allows us to divide a file into sub-units. In an image of a painting, for instance, we may wish to highlight figures represented within its frame with hot links which, when clicked, bring up their respective descriptions from the Descriptive Metadata section. It is most useful, perhaps, for audio-visual materials, where we may wish to segment an audio or video file to make it possible to skip to a particular sequence within it. A very simple map for a video of a five-minute film that is treated in this way may take the form shown in Example 6.13.

```
<structMap ID="wdl-zaa-aaaa-stm-0001">
 <div ID="wdl-zaa-aaaa-div">
    <div ID="wdl-zaa-aaaa-div-0001">
      <fptr FILEID="wdl-zaa-aaaa-fgrp-0001-0">
```

```
        <area BEGIN="00:00:00" END="00:01:30" BETYPE="TIME" LABEL="Opening
          titles"/>
        <area BEGIN="00:01:31" END="00:03:45" BETYPE="TIME" LABEL="Shots of
          London landmarks"/>
        <area BEGIN="00:03:46" END="00:05:10" BETYPE="TIME" LABEL="Interview
          with man on street"/>
      </fptr>
     </div>
  </div>
</structMap>
```

Example 6.13 *Structural map for a video of a short film*

The whole film is presented in a single file which is referenced as usual by the **FILEID** attribute of the File Pointer **<fptr>**. Each of its three segments is represented by a new element **<area>** nested within this **<fptr>**. We use its **BEGIN** and **END** attributes to mark the beginning and end of each of these, setting the **BETYPE** (Beginning Type) attribute to 'TIME' to show that it is timecodes which mark these boundaries. As usual, we use the **LABEL** attribute to provide the short description that will appear in the navigation menu when our users view the film.

There is no space here to go into details of the other sophisticated features of the Structural Map. It is capable of recording structural metadata as simple as in these examples or of great complexity if that is required. It is also, as stated earlier, capable of being repeated, should multiple representations of an object's structure be needed.

6.11 Structural Links and Behavior Section

Two subdivisions of the METS architecture remain, both of which are relatively little used in practice. The first, Structural Links (**<structLink>**), is an adjunct to the Structural Map which allows us to record linkages between the latter's parts that cut across its hierarchical structure. The second, the Behavior Section (**<behaviorSec>**), provides a way to associate the Structural Map or parts of it with the software programs or code needed to render or display a digital object.

The Structural Links section has mainly been employed when using METS to record and archive websites. One pilot project at the Library of Congress attempted to do this by recording the structure of web pages in the Structural Map and then invoking the Structural Links section to encode the hyperlinks within these (Guenther and Myrick 2007). Although this worked effectively within the context of that project, it proved rather cumbersome and METS has not been adopted widely for this purpose. The Structural Map and its mechanisms for recording complex structures have proved more

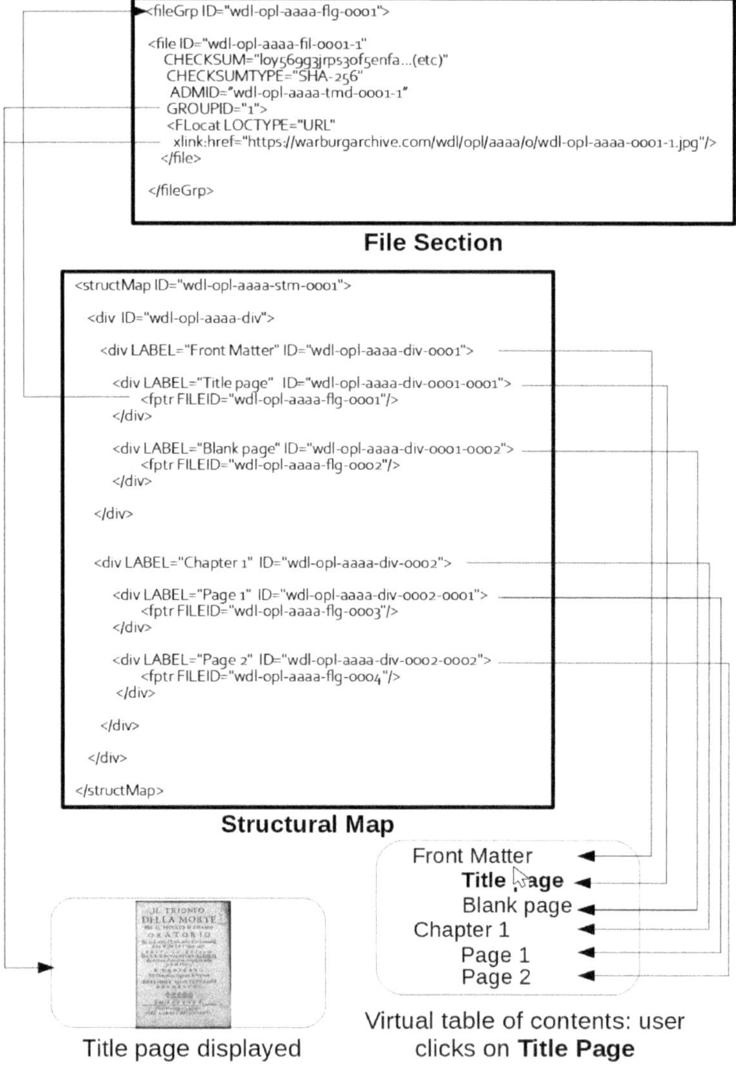
<fileGrp ID="wdl-opl-aaaa-flg-0001">
<file ID="wdl-opl-aaaa-fil-0001-1"
CHECKSUM="loy569g3jrps3of5enfa...(etc)"
CHECKSUMTYPE="SHA-256"
ADMID="wdl-opl-aaaa-tmd-0001-1"
GROUPID="1">
<FLocat LOCTYPE="URL"
xlink:href="https://warburgarchive.com/wdl/opl/aaaa/o/wdl-opl-aaaa-0001-1.jpg"/>
</file>
</fileGrp>
File Section
<structMap ID="wdl-opl-aaaa-stm-0001">
<div ID="wdl-opl-aaaa-div">
<div LABEL="Front Matter" ID="wdl-opl-aaaa-div-0001">
<div LABEL="Title page" ID="wdl-opl-aaaa-div-0001-0001">
<fptr FILEID="wdl-opl-aaaa-flg-0001"/>
</div>
<div LABEL="Blank page" ID="wdl-opl-aaaa-div-0001-0002">
<fptr FILEID="wdl-opl-aaaa-flg-0002"/>
</div>
</div>
<div LABEL="Chapter 1" ID="wdl-opl-aaaa-div-0002">
<div LABEL="Page 1" ID="wdl-opl-aaaa-div-0002-0001">
<fptr FILEID="wdl-opl-aaaa-flg-0003"/>
</div>
<div LABEL="Page 2" ID="wdl-opl-aaaa-div-0002-0002">
<fptr FILEID="wdl-opl-aaaa-flg-0004"/>
</div>
</div>
</div>
</structMap>
Structural Map
Front Matter
Title Page
Blank page
Chapter 1
Page 1
Page 2
IL TRIONFO
DELLA MORTE
ORATORIO
Title page displayed
Virtual table of contents: user clicks on Title Page

Figure 6.4 *Using the METS Structural Map and File Section to display the image of a page*

than adequate for the needs of most digital collections.

The Behavior Section has had even less uptake. This allows us to record information on the interface or code necessary to render a digital object. It may have some use if we are archiving objects which can be viewed only with specific software, for instance a document in a now obsolete word processing format such as Wordstar. However, a contemporary digital library would purposely avoid formats which are tied to specific packages, particularly proprietary ones, and so would have little need to document rendering mechanisms in this way. For this reason it is very rare to find this section implemented within a digital library, archive or repository.

6.12 Creating and using METS in practice

This completes our tour of the METS schema, albeit a concise one that has covered only its main features. Although there is more to METS than this, what has been touched on here should be more than enough to implement it in a working digital library. For a taste of all of its capabilities in their full glory, the reference work to consult is the METS Primer and Reference Manual[C6.2] produced by its editorial board at the Library of Congress. This 142-page volume can be rather intimidating, but more concise and easier-to-digest guides and introductions are available from the standard's website at the Library of Congress[S.17].

It is important to note at this point that in a working environment we do not create METS instances manually using an XML or any other editor. We may wish to map out a template for METS files in this way during the initial design of a metadata strategy, a skeletal version which would assist us in deciding on such basics as the extension schemas for descriptive and administrative metadata, the system of identifiers that will be applied and the shape of the Structural Map. After that it will be up to the developers, either ourselves or our technical team, to devise the mechanisms that will generate METS files conforming to this template from the disparate sources of metadata which need to be brought together.

The tools to do this can be various, but the recommended one to use is XSLT, a very powerful mechanism designed specifically for generating and transforming XML files. XSLT is very effective in integrating XML metadata from various sources, and so is ideal for this purpose. In most digital library operations it can be used in conjunction with simple scripting languages, such as bash in Unix/Linux, or more sophisticated programming languages such as Python. The skills needed to do this should lie well within the comfort zone of any technically adept library staff member and almost certainly any digital or systems librarian. The first case study in Chapter 11 demonstrates how METS files are generated in this way using simple XSLT and bash scripts.

At this point we can begin to examine the external sources of metadata that may be slotted into a METS instance, the extension schemas that supply its descriptive and administrative ingredients. We begin with the descriptive variety, the most visible, and so the most familiar to librarians and their users.

7

Descriptive Metadata: Semantics

7.1 Introduction

Descriptive metadata forms the core of any library, archive or repository, analogue or digital, where it plays the indispensable role of ensuring that the contents of its collections can be discovered and unlocked. It is the type that is most visible to end-users, for whom it provides signposts through the physical or virtual shelves, making it possible for them to locate what they need and to avoid what they do not. Without adequate descriptive metadata a digital library is almost unusable, the time and effort expended in creating and maintaining its collections going to waste.

Its central position in a library's work necessitates a place of commensurate importance in its overall metadata strategy. For this reason alone it should certainly adopt the principles outlined in Chapter 2. In particular, it should adhere to Principle 7 ('Use standards whenever possible') and so follow established practices which have developed within professional communities and been proven robust and viable. Descriptive metadata should also take particular note of Principle 4 ('Ensure interoperability') so that it can readily be shared with others and so widen its potential audience well beyond the boundaries of the collections within which it is created.

This chapter concentrates on the semantics of descriptive metadata, the containers that hold it and how they are labelled and described. It introduces three metadata schemes, DC, MARCXML and MODS, all of which are compatible with METS and all of which have established themselves firmly within the digital library community. These are generic schemes which can accommodate descriptive metadata for a wide range of digital objects; more specialised ones which can either replace or supplement them for specific collections will be discussed briefly at the end of the chapter.

7.2 Dublin Core

Dublin Core[S.13], or DC as it is often called, owes its name to the city of Dublin, Ohio, where in 1995 a group of experts from computer science, libraries, archives, museums and online information services met to put together a standard for describing resources on the internet. They were attempting to emulate the way in which the MARC cataloguing standard had opened up new avenues for discovery in libraries by enabling the sharing and exchange of metadata in a logical machine-readable format. Those who formulated MARC had it easier in some ways, as it was based on established bibliographic principles for a relatively narrow range of materials; the challenge for DC was to find something that could cope with the diversity of objects that can be found in digital form on the internet.

Rather than create a large and daunting array of elements to accommodate this heterogeneity, the DC team chose instead to aim for simplicity. They devised a small set of only 15 fields, none of them mandatory and all repeatable, which could handle in at least a basic way the requirements for documenting and describing almost anything; these constitute what is usually known as Simple Dublin Core[C7.2] (Figure 7.1).

These fields have relatively broad definitions which are quite easy to understand and employ by the specialist and non-specialist alike. The libretto which served as the primary example in the preceding chapter could be catalogued with Simple DC in this way (Table 7.1 opposite).

Fitting the metadata for this object into DC is relatively straightforward, but already some issues emerge. We have had to use the **Identifier** field twice, once for the internal object ID and again for the URL of the resource in the digital library. How will our delivery system know which is which?

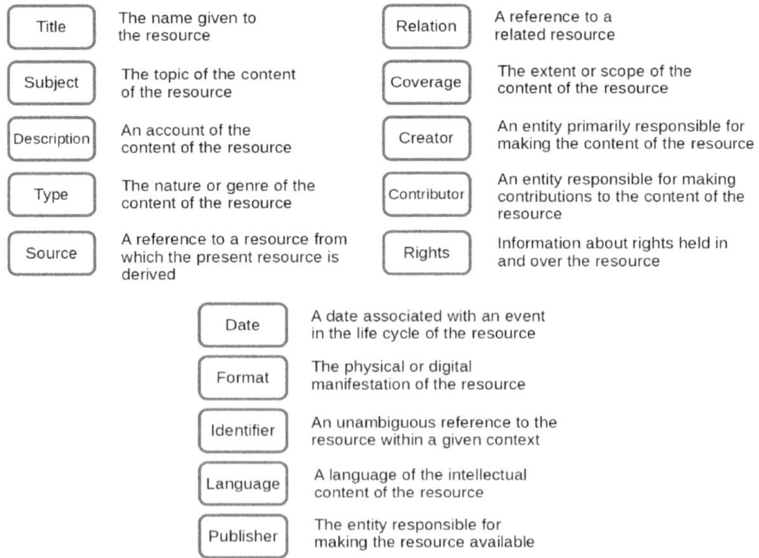

Title
The name given to the resource
Subject
The topic of the content of the resource
Description
An account of the content of the resource
Type
The nature or genre of the content of the resource
Source
A reference to a resource from which the present resource is derived
Relation
A reference to a related resource
Coverage
The extent or scope of the content of the resource
Creator
An entity primarily responsible for making the content of the resource
Contributor
An entity responsible for making contributions to the content of the resource
Rights
Information about rights held in and over the resource
Date
A date associated with an event in the life cycle of the resource
Format
The physical or digital manifestation of the resource
Identifier
An unambiguous reference to the resource within a given context
Language
A language of the intellectual content of the resource
Publisher
The entity responsible for making the resource available

Figure 7.1 *The 15 fields of Simple Dublin Core*

Table 7.1 *Simple Dublin Core record for oratorio libretto*

Title	Il trionfo della morte per il peccato d'Adamo: oratorio da farsi nella chiesa della Confraternità della Morte l'anno 1677
Subject	Oratorios
Description	Posto in musica dal p.f. Bonaventura Aleotti da Palermo franciscano organista nella sudetta Chiesa, e dedicato all'illustrissima signora la signora Artemisia Montevecchi Baldeschi
Type	Libretti
Creator	Aliotti, Bonaventura, approximately 1640-approximately 1690
Rights	This copy is licensed under a Creative Commons Attribution-NonCommercial 3.0 Unported License
Date	1677
Identifier	wdl-opl-aaaa
Identifier	https://wdl.warburg.sas.ac.uk/islandora/object/islandora%3A3790
Language	Italian
Publisher	Nella stampa camerale

We are fortunate that this is the only major ambiguity here. For something more complicated, such as a video of a feature film, things can get a good deal more convoluted. How, for example, should we apportion people involved in its production into the **Creator** and **Contributor** fields, the former of which is meant to record the primary intellectual input into a work and the latter any secondary contributions? Should we include the director alone as the Creator, or should we add the producer, screenwriter, cinematographer and composer of the music? Should actors be regarded as creators or contributors? Once we have made these difficult decisions, how will we know when we come across a field labelled simply 'Creator' or 'Contributor' the exact role of the people listed there? What about dates? Should we record the date of filming, the date it was edited and released, the dates of reissues or the date when it was made available for home viewing? If the field just says 'Date', how do we know which one we are dealing with?

It is clear that the simplicity of DC is at the expense of semantic precision: the fields are broad in meaning, which ensures that they are capable of accommodating metadata for a wide range of objects, but are too vague if we want to be clear about what exactly is recorded. This problem was recognised from the beginning and several approaches have been adopted which attempt to alleviate it.

The first of these is known as Qualified Dublin Core[C7.1], which was defined at the same time as the standard was first conceived. This allows suffixes to be attached to Simple DC field names to qualify them and constrain their semantic scope. The **Creator** field for the record in Table 7.1, for instance, may be treated in this way to clarify that it refers to the composer of the oratorio:

```
Creator.Composer
```

Any qualifiers may be used for this purpose, although the Dublin Core Metadata Initiative (DCMI), who maintain the standard, suggest using controlled lists for these and recommend a number of their own.

Adding qualifiers in this way ensures greater precision, but it comes at the cost of reduced interoperability, particularly if locally defined terms are used instead of those recommended by DC. This circle can be squared to some extent by the fact that Qualified DC follows what is rather unflatteringly called the Dumbing Down Principle: if a system does not understand a qualified field name (such as **creator.composer**), it can remove the qualifier and comprehend it as a Simple DC element instead (in this case **creator**). At the cost of less precise semantics it is possible to exchange metadata in this way with other DC-based systems which will have at least a basic understanding of the contents of each field.

This approach is something of a fudge and never proved popular with DC implementers. The DCMI themselves have deprecated (advised against implementing) it since 2008 and replaced it with a new set of fields which supplements the initial Simple DC collection with a further 40 derived from the qualifiers that it recommended for use in Qualified DC. This new scheme is known as DCMI Metadata Terms[S.9]. Its major additions include fields to specify the relationships between resources (such as `<HasPart>` or `<HasVersion>`), more precise rights information (such as `<license>` and `<AccessRights>`) and more specific details of dates (`<created>`, `<DateCopyrighted>` and so on).

DCMI Metadata Terms is what is technically known as an application profile, a scheme which uses the 15 Simple DC fields as its kernel and supplements them with an additional set appropriate to the application for which it is designed. Many application profiles of this type have been devised since DC was first drawn up; some notable ones include PBCore[S.22] for audiovisual content, Darwin Core for sharing information on biodiversity[S.6] and DC-Libraries[S.8] for bibliographic metadata in libraries. DC also forms the basis of the Open Archives Initiative Protocol for Metadata Harvesting[S.21], a standard for harvesting and sharing metadata which will be discussed in Chapter 10.

DC is a scheme which limits itself to specifying semantics, the fields in which metadata content is to be held. It does not mandate any given syntax – the way in which DC records are to be encoded for storage. It is certainly possible to use XML for this, and so to embed DC directly into METS files; the DCMI themselves have created schemas for Simple and Qualified DC and DCMI Metadata Terms for this purpose[C7.3]. The metadata record from Table 7.1 for the oratorio libretto could be encoded using the Simple DC schema as shown in Example 7.1.

```
<?xml version="1.0" encoding="UTF-8"?>
<simpledc>
    <title>Il trionfo della morte per il peccato d'Adamo: oratorio da farsi
      nella chiesa della Confraternità  della Morte l'anno 1677 </title>
    <subject>Oratorios</subject>
    <description>Posto in musica dal p.f. Bonaventura Aleotti da Palermo
      franciscano organista nella sudetta Chiesa, e dedicato all'illustrissima
      signora la signora Artemisia Montevecchi Baldeschi</description>
    <type>Libretti</type>
    <creator>Aliotti, Bonaventura, approximately 1640-approximately
      1690</creator>
    <rights>This copy is licensed under a Creative Commons Attribution-
      NonCommercial 3.0 Unported License</rights>
    <date>1677</date>
    <identifier>wdl-opl-aaaa</identifier>
    <identifier>https://wdl.warburg.sas.ac.uk/islandora/object/islandora
      %3A3790</identifier>
    <language>Italian</language>
    <publisher>Nella stampa camerale</publisher>
</simpledc>
```

Example 7.1 *Simple Dublin Core record for oratorio libretto encoded in XML*

The ubiquity of DC and the fact that it has formed the basis of other metadata schemes undoubtedly attest that is has succeeded in its primary objective of creating a universally applicable standard for describing internet resources. Its relatively broad semantics do, however, represent a problem for many digital library applications where more precise metadata is usually to be preferred. It may be a useful option to consider if an appropriate application profile is found for the specific requirements of a collection, but in general we may wish to employ a more extensive and precise set of metadata elements than DC can offer. If we do adopt a more extensive schema of this kind we can, if necessary, always supplement it with a DC record in a separate Descriptive Metadata Section within METS (for instance, to share it with other systems that apply this simpler standard).

7.3 MODS: the Metadata Object Description Schema

The descriptive metadata scheme which is the primary recommendation in this book is one which largely succeeds in offering the same flexibility as DC, and hence a similarly wide applicability to a diverse range of digital objects, while providing a greater degree of semantic precision and potential for interoperability. It does this by defining a more extensive element set than DC, an internal structure which allows the detailing of more sophisticated relationships between its components and, should the need arise, the potential to extend its semantics to meet the needs of a particular application.

MODS[S.18] was created by and is maintained by the MARC Standards Office at the Library of Congress, the custodians of the MARC standard for bibliographic metadata. Most of its semantics are derived from this latter standard, which makes it readily compatible with pre-existing records in library catalogues, but its emphasis is on providing a generic scheme capable of recording descriptive metadata for any object, digital or analogue, not only those which have their origin in library collections. In this it has broadly realised its ambitions. It has not quite achieved the reach of DC, partly because it has a slightly steeper learning curve, but it has established itself as a preferred standard for many significant digital library projects, particularly those that deal with historical materials or have an academic focus.

MODS's core element set numbers 83 in total. Of these, 19 are top-level elements, roughly similar to the 15 of Simple DC, while 64 are nested within these at lower levels in a hierarchical structure. Example 7.2 demonstrates how the DC record from Example 7.1 may be encoded in MODS.

```
<mods ID="wdl-opl-aaaa-dmd-0001-0001">
  <titleInfo>
      <nonSort>Il </nonSort>
      <title>trionfo della morte per il peccato d'Adamo</title>
      <subTitle>oratorio da farsi nella chiesa della Confraternità della
           Mortel'anno 1677</subTitle>
   </titleInfo>
  <name type="personal" authority="lcnaf"
       authorityURI="http://id.loc.gov/authorities/names"
       valueURI="http://id.loc.gov/authorities/names/no2002111866">
       <namePart>Aliotti, Bonaventura</namePart>
       <namePart type="date">approximately 1640-approximately 1690</namePart>
       <role>
         <roleTerm type="text">composer</roleTerm>
         <roleTerm type="code" authority="marcrelator">cmp</roleTerm>
       </role>
   </name>
  <typeOfResource>text</typeOfResource>
  <originInfo>
       <place>
           <placeTerm type="code" authority="marccountry">it</placeTerm>
       </place>
       <place>
           <placeTerm type="text">In Ferrara</placeTerm>
       </place>
```

```
        <publisher>Nella stampa camerale</publisher>
        <dateIssued encoding="iso8601">1677</dateIssued>
        <issuance>monographic</issuance>
    </originInfo>
    <note type="statement of responsibility">posto in musica dal p.f.
         Bonaventura Aleotti da Palermo franciscano organista nella sudetta
         Chiesa, e dedicato all'illustrissima signora la signora Artemisia
         Montevecchi Baldeschi.</note>
    <subject authority="lcsh"
        authorityURI="http://id.loc.gov/authorities/subjects"
        valueURI="http://id.loc.gov/authorities/subjects/sh85095291">
        <topic>Oratorios</topic>
    </subject>
    <subject authority="lcsh"
        authorityURI="http://id.loc.gov/authorities/subjects"
        valueURI="http://id.loc.gov/authorities/subjects/sh85076744">
        <genre>Librettos</genre>
     </subject>
     <location>
        <url>http://warburg.sas.ac.uk/pdf/DBH1450b3012601.pdf</url>
     </location>
     <classification authority="warburg"
         authorityURI="http://warburg.sas.ac.uk/id/class">DBH 1450
     </classification>
     <recordInfo>
        <descriptionStandard>aacr</descriptionStandard>
        <recordCreationDate encoding="marc">070411</recordCreationDate>
          <recordOrigin>Converted from MARCXML to MODS version 3.5 using
                MARC21slim2MODS3-5_XSL2-0.xsl (Revision 2.23 2014/12/19)
                  </recordOrigin>
     </recordInfo>
</mods>
```

Example 7.2 *Sample record for oratorio libretto encoded in MODS*

In this simple record, which uses 9 of the available 19 top-level elements (marked in bold), it should be immediately apparent that we can describe an object with much greater precision than is possible in Simple DC. The internal structure of the subsidiary elements which are available within most of the top-level ones, as well as the array of attributes available for many, clarify explicitly much of the detail that must be left implicit in a DC record. This should become clearer as we look at this record in more detail.

The only mandatory element in MODS is **<titleInfo>** which is equivalent to DC's **Title**. It can contain five subelements, three of which are shown here: these are used to distinguish the main title (**<title>**) from its sub-title (**<subTitle>**) and to designate any words, in this case the definite article in Italian, which should be ignored if we use it to create an alphabetical title index (**<nonSort>**). Although they are not shown in this example, we could add attributes to the **<titleInfo>** element to indicate such facets as its type (if it is a uniform title, for instance, for a work which appears under several variants), its language and how it has been transliterated if it was originally written in another script.

Names are also treated with much more sophistication than is possible in the **Creator** and **Contributor** fields of DC. The name itself (**<name>**) can be subdivided into separate parts using repeatable **<namePart>** elements. In Example 7.2 they record the composer's name proper and his dates of birth and death. Even more useful is the ability to designate precisely the role of the person who is named here: the **<roleTerm>** element allows us to indicate this with a textual description (here 'composer') or a code from an authority list (in this case 'cmp' from the MARC Relator Codes[C8.11] maintained by the Library of Congress). This resolves the issues of imprecision associated with the DC **Creator** and **Contributor** fields and also renders it unnecessary to determine the relative importance of a person's contribution to a work in order to determine to which of these they should be allocated.

As one might expect from a standard rooted in the practices of the library sector, MODS offers an array of detailed information on the origin of an object. Its **<originInfo>** element, which broadly covers the same semantic area as DC's **Publisher** and **Date**, contains an extensive array of subelements which allow us to record its place of publication (or more broadly, origin), its publisher and a range of options for any relevant dates within its lifecycle. These include its date of issue (as shown in the example), creation, capture (for digitised versions of physical objects), modification and copyright.

The MODS counterpart to the single **Subject** element of DC is also much more sophisticated in its semantic precision. Multiple subelements allow us to differentiate the type of subject clearly. In Example 7.2 **<topic>**, the most generic of these, is shown in conjunction with **<genre>**, but others that could be used include **<geographic>**, **<temporal>** and **<name>**. In DC the **Subject** field also contains non-textual subject indicators such as Dewey Decimal Classification numbers, but MODS provides a separate **<classification>** element for this: in Example 7.2 it contains a subject code from a local classification scheme.

Many MODS elements, in this example **<name>**, **<subject>** and **<classification>**, allow for two attributes to record the authority file, thesaurus or scheme from which their content is taken. The first, **authority**, contains a free-text code for this, while the second, **authorityURI** (the preferred option), houses a URI to identify it precisely. Both are shown in Example 7.2 for demonstration purposes, although in most cases one is sufficient on its own. These are invaluable for ensuring the integrity of metadata, as it allows us to pin down the semantics of an element precisely.

The use of either **authority** or **authorityURI** is therefore highly recommended when applicable.

One final element to note from this example is **<recordInfo>**, which provides information on the MODS record itself. Here we can note such information as the cataloguing standard followed, the date on which the record was created and how this was done – in this case by conversion from a pre-existing record in MARCXML, the next format to be discussed. This is particularly significant for the application of Principle 8 ('Ensure the integrity of the metadata itself') because it allows us to maintain an audit trail for a descriptive metadata record, including important details of its provenance, and so provides a way of verifying its authenticity. It is therefore highly recommended and will be much appreciated by those who have to handle this metadata in the future.

Example 7.2 is an example of a record for a digitised book, but MODS is designed to be applicable to any object, analogue or (particularly) digital, in a similar way to DC. Its extensive element set should satisfy almost all of a digital collection's needs, but if a highly specific requirement arises it is possible to supplement it with the top-level element **<extension>**, which allows us to embed metadata from an external schema. If, for example, we were describing an image of a piece of Bronze Age jewellery we could augment a record with metadata from VRA Core, a standard for the description of visual culture, as shown in Example 7.3.

```
<extension>
 <vra:vra>
    <vra:work>
      <vra:culturalContextSet>
         <vra:culturalContext>British</vra:culturalContext>
      </vra:culturalContextSet>
      <vra:stylePeriodSet>
         <vra:stylePeriod>Late Broze Age</vra:stylePeriod>
         <vra:stylePeriod>Neolithic</vra:stylePeriod>
      </vra:stylePeriodSet>
    </vra:work>
  </vra:vra>
</extension>
```

Example 7.3 *VRA Core record embedded within the MODS* ***<extension>*** *element*

Embedding metadata here operates in a similar way to METS: a namespace declaration for the schema is made in the **<mets>** root element which defines the prefix (**vra:**) that identifies its elements when deployed in the **<extension>**.

One other useful feature of MODS is that it is highly granular: it can describe the digital object as a whole or any of its sub-components in equal detail, all within a single instance. This can be done by employing a further top-level element, **<relatedItem>**, with its **type** attribute set to 'constituent'. This is a container which allows us to nest any MODS elements, effectively creating a full record in its own right. If we are describing a feature film, for instance, we may wish to provide information on the movie itself and a synopsis for each segment. In Example 7.4 we use **<relatedItem>** to provide simple metadata for the video file from Example 6.13 in the previous chapter.

```
<relatedItem type="constituent" ID="wdl-zaa-aaaa-dmd-0001-0001-0001">
       <titleInfo>
              <title>Opening titles</title>
       </titleInfo>
       <abstract>Opening credits for the film</abstract>
</relatedItem>

<relatedItem type="constituent" ID="wdl-zaa-aaaa-dmd-0001-0001-0002">
       <titleInfo>
              <title>Shots of London landmarks</title>
       </titleInfo>
       <abstract>Montage of London landmarks including Buckingham Palace and
              Houses of Parliament</abstract>
</relatedItem>

<relatedItem type="constituent" ID="wdl-zaa-aaaa-dmd-0001-0001-0003">
       <titleInfo>
              <title>Interview with man on street</title>
       </titleInfo>
       <abstract>Vox pop interview with man who explains the attraction for him
                 of living in London</abstract>
</relatedItem>
```

Example 7.4 *Use of <relatedItem> element to describe segments of a video*

A separate **<relatedItem type="constituent">** element is deployed for each segment: this contains the very basic metadata of a title and description (using the top-level **<abstract>** element).

Note that each **<relatedItem type="constituent">** element is given an ID; in a similar way to METS, every significant component within a MODS file can be identified in this way. This proves very useful when we use MODS in the context of the wider METS architecture, as it allows us to reference a component of an object's descriptive metadata from anywhere in the METS Structural Map: every **<div>** element there has an attribute (**DMDID**) which can point to IDs within MODS and so reference precisely the descriptive metadata that relates to the part of the digital object that it covers. It is therefore recommended that IDs are provided at least for the root **<mods>** and subsidiary **<relatedItem>** elements within a MODS instance (as in Examples 7.2 and 7.4).

MODS manages to reconcile the conflicting requirements of precision and interoperability by offering a rich but not excessive element set in combination with a facility to extend this if the requirements of a given application so demand. For this reason it is recommended in preference to DC as the central descriptive metadata schema for use in an integrated, METS-based architecture. It is supported by extensive documentation maintained by the Library of Congress, who also produce a very useful set of XSLT stylesheets to convert metadata to MODS from other standards (including DC and MARCXML) and vice versa. All of this makes it a sound recommendation for descriptive metadata either on its own or in conjunction with more specialised schemas, some of which are considered below.

7.4 MARCXML

One potentially useful schema for digital collections whose contents are derived from those in physical libraries is MARCXML[S.15]. As its name implies, this translates records in MARC, the long-established standard for library catalogues, into the XML syntax. It is unlikely that we would embed MARCXML records directly within a METS instance in preference to MODS, but it is possible that we could use them as a stepping stone from a library's pre-existing online catalogue to a digital library's descriptive metadata.

MARCXML is a direct representation of the fields and subfields of a MARC record in XML: each is mapped directly to an element or attribute in this schema. A (slightly truncated) MARC record for the libretto in an online catalogue would look as shown in Example 7.5.

```
LEADER 00000nam 2200109 a 4500

008 070411s1677 it r 000 ita
040 UK-LoURL
100 1 Aliotti, Bonaventura,|dca. 1640-ca. 1690.
245 13 Il trionfo della morte per il peccato d'Adamo :$boratorio
da farsi nella chiesa della Confraternità della Morte
 l'anno 1677 /$cposto in musica dal p.f. Bonaventura
 Aleotti da Palermo franciscano organista nella sudetta
 Chiesa, e dedicato all'illustrissima signora la signora
 Artemisia Montevecchi Baldeschi.
260 In Ferrara :$bNella stampa camerale,$c[1677]
300 24 p. ;$c15 cm.
530 Also available online.
650 0 Oratorios|vLibrettos.
951 25 Warburg Digital Collection DBH
991 crr
```

Example 7.5 *MARC record for oratorio libretto*

And its manifestation in MARCXML would take the form shown in Example 7.6.

```
<?xml version="1.0" encoding="UTF-8"?>
<record>
  <leader>00000nam 2200109 a 4500</leader>
  <controlfield tag="008">070411s1677 it r 000 ita</controlfield>
  <datafield tag="040" ind1=" " ind2=" ">
      <subfield code="a">UK-LoURL</subfield>
  </datafield>
  <datafield tag="100" ind1="1" ind2=" ">
       <subfield code="a">Aliotti, Bonaventura,</subfield>
       <subfield code="d">ca. 1640-ca. 1690.</subfield>
   </datafield>
   <datafield tag="245" ind1="1" ind2="3">
        <subfield code="a">Il trionfo della morte per il peccato
           d'Adamo :</subfield>
        <subfield code="b">oratorio da farsi nella chiesa della ConfraternitaÌ€
           della Morte l'anno 1677 /</subfield>
        <subfield code="c">posto in musica dal p.f. Bonaventura Aleotti da
            Palermo franciscano organista nella sudetta Chiesa, e dedicato
            all'illustrissima signora la signora Artemisia Montevecchi
            Baldeschi.</subfield>
    </datafield>
    <datafield tag="260" ind1=" " ind2=" ">
        <subfield code="a">In Ferrara :</subfield>
        <subfield code="b">Nella stampa camerale,</subfield>
        <subfield code="c">[1677]</subfield>
    </datafield>
    <datafield tag="300" ind1=" " ind2=" ">
        <subfield code="a">24 p. ;</subfield>
        <subfield code="c">15 cm.</subfield>
    </datafield>
    <datafield tag="530" ind1=" " ind2=" ">
         <subfield code="a">Also available online.</subfield>
    </datafield>
    <datafield tag="650" ind1=" " ind2="0">
         <subfield code="a">Oratorios</subfield>
         <subfield code="v">Librettos.</subfield>
    </datafield>
</record>
```

Example 7.6 *The same record in MARCXML*

The mapping to MARCXML is very straightforward. Most MARC fields are represented by a **<datafield>** element: its **tag** attribute contains their three-digital identifiers and their indicators can be found in its **ind1** and **ind2** attributes. In this way the 245 field, which records an item's main title and in this case has the indicator digits **13**, becomes

```
<datafield tag="245" ind1="1" ind2="3">.
```

An element's subfields, for instance the $a, $b and $c in the 260 field, which detail an item's place of publication, publisher and date respectively, are represented by **<subfield>** elements nested within their parent **<datafield>**:

```
<marc:datafield tag="260" ind1=" " ind2=" ">
  <marc:subfield code="a">In Ferrara :</marc:subfield>
  <marc:subfield code="b">Nella stampa camerale,
    </marc:subfield>
  <marc:subfield code="c">[1677]</marc:subfield>
</marc:datafield>
```

This direct translation of the structure of a MARC record to XML produces something that is comprehensible to cataloguers who have been trained in this standard but rather less so for those who have not. For this reason it is not recommended in preference to MODS, which is more readily understandable by a wider community of practitioners. Where MARCXML can be useful, however, is as an intermediary from an existing online catalogue to a digital library.

Almost all library management systems make it possible to download records in MARCXML. In many cases there may be an option to do this directly. If not, it should certainly be possible to pull them down in native MARC format and then convert them to MARCXML using simple utilities (for instance, the freely available package MarcEdit[C7.4]). They can then be converted to MODS using one of the XSLT stylesheets provided by the Library of Congress. The MODS record in Example 7.2 was created from a MARCXML file retrieved from a library catalogue in exactly this way.

This method allows us to create descriptive metadata for a digital library which is based on pre-existing records produced to professional standards. For digital collections which co-exist with or derive from their traditional counterparts MARCXML can be a useful go-between.

7.5 Other descriptive metadata standards

MODS is the primary recommendation for descriptive metadata, as its extensive element set should accommodate the demands of most collections. However, there are a number of standards which have become established within their respective professional communities and can be deployed instead of MODS, or preferably in conjunction with it, for more specialised classes of materials. All of the following are available as XML schemas and can be readily embedded within the METS Descriptive Metadata section or the MODS **<extension>** element.

7.5.1 VRA Core

VRA Core[S.29] was briefly introduced as an extension to MODS in Example 7.3. It was originally created by the Visual Resources Association, a professional body for those working with images in such areas as libraries, archives, galleries and the commercial sector. Its stated aim, according to its website, is to act as 'a data standard for the description of works of visual culture as well as the images that document them'; works of visual culture in this context include 'paintings, drawings, sculpture, architecture, photographs, as well as book, decorative, and performance art'. As its name implies, it was loosely inspired by DC in its aspiration to produce a relatively simple element set which would be easy to learn and implement. It is now maintained by the Library of Congress and is approved by METS as an extension schema.

Its schema provides 19 top-level elements and a limited number of subelements that can be used to describe collections, the works within them and images of these works. These cover such areas as their cultural context, the people or bodies involved in their design, creation or production, their material make-up, the styles or historical periods that they embody, the techniques used in their creation and their iconographic subjects. The schema is available in two versions: an unrestricted variant which allows any values to go into its elements, subelements and attributes (and so is useful for converting legacy metadata), and a restricted alternative which imposes a closed list of types for every element to ensure greater potential for the interoperable exchange and aggregation of VRA Core records.

This schema is undoubtedly an appropriate option as a complement to MODS for collections which are centred on images of works of art or visual culture in general.

7.5.2 Text Encoding Initiative P5 Manuscript Description

The Text Encoding Initiative (TEI) is an XML application for the detailed encoding of texts aimed primarily, but not exclusively, at the creation of scholarly digital editions. It also includes an extensive set of elements for descriptive metadata which are more detailed than those provided by MODS or other more generic schemas. For manuscripts and other textual objects (such as early printed books) which require highly detailed and specialised metadata it provides a set of elements designed expressly for this purpose.

The TEI P5 Manuscript Description[S.26] includes in its compass such features as the information needed to identify a work (including its repository and shelfmark), its intellectual content, physical description and history. These can go into great detail and can describe the work as a whole or any of its constituent parts. For those working in the field of historical bibliography it has established itself as the primary standard, and so may be worth consideration for a digital library of scholarly editions, digitised manuscripts or incunabula.

7.5.3 Schemas from the sciences and social sciences

Descriptive metadata schemas are not limited to the humanities. A number have been designed within the sciences and social sciences to meet the specific requirements of their disciplines. Some of the more widely used include:

Darwin Core[S.6]: an extension to DC which covers the field of biological diversity, specifically for detailing the occurrence of biological specimens;

Ecological Metadata Language (EML)[S.14]: a schema for documenting data sets in the ecological sciences;

Data Documentation Initiative (DDI)[S.7]: a schema for describing the data produced by surveys and other observational techniques in the social, behavioural, economic and health sciences;

Common European Research Information Format (CERIF)[S.5]: a schema for documenting information relating to research projects, including details of the research undertaken, funding bodies and outputs: this can be useful for providing context to a digital object that results from such a project.

7.5.4 Using these schemas

All of these schemas can be readily integrated into the METS framework by embedding their instances directly within the Descriptive Metadata Section. This may be repeated as many times as required, and so it is entirely feasible to have multiple occurrences, each containing metadata conforming to a different, complementary schema. If we take this approach it is recommended to implement it in addition to MODS rather than replacing it entirely. In this way we will maintain the interoperable potential of the metadata record that the generic standard allows while retaining the precision of the more specific one as and when it is required.

An alternative strategy is to employ the MODS `<extension>` element to incorporate this metadata in the way that was shown for VRA Core in Example 7.3. This is a valid way to include the additional semantics of a specialised schema if one wishes to avoid the use of multiple Descriptive

Metadata Sections. It may even be preferable if we intend to share the descriptive metadata for an object with others in, for example, a union catalogue. In such a case, having all of the descriptive metadata in a single, discrete MODS file would be more convenient than having it spread out among different Descriptive Metadata Sections in its parent METS instance.

7.6 Descriptive metadata: from semantics to content rules

This concludes our tour of key descriptive metadata standards and how they may be implemented within METS. This discussion is only part of our journey through this type of metadata; it has covered its semantics, the fields that contain it and their interrelationships. The next, and equally important, component is the way in which we control what goes into these fields, the metadata content itself. How this is done by the use of content rules, authority lists and thesauri is the subject of the next chapter.

8

Descriptive Metadata: Content Rules

8.1 Introduction

The previous chapter covered the semantics of descriptive metadata, the meaning of the fields or elements that contain it. Agreeing on a standard for these, such as MODS, is an important step towards creating a coherent metadata strategy for discovery, preservation and interoperability but it fulfils only part of the requirements for achieving these. We must also exercise some control over the content that populates these fields, specifically, what goes into each and the way in which it is formatted. Only by imposing some degree of consistency in both of these can we begin to realise the potential of a collection's descriptive metadata.

Enforcing content rules is one of the basic principles for a metadata strategy outlined in Chapter 3 (Principle 4: 'Control metadata content wherever possible'). To do so effectively requires us to apply Principle 7 ('Use standards whenever possible') in order to root our work in the best practices of a professional community. This will enhance our ability to apply Principle 3 ('Ensure interoperability') by making our metadata readily accessible to others in form and content. Controlling content will also 'Support all stages of the digital curation lifecycle' (Principle 1) and 'Support the long-term preservation of the digital object' (Principle 2) by providing metadata that is consistent and intelligible now and in the future.

8.2 Why content rules are needed

The aim of content rules is to ensure a degree of consistency in metadata beyond that provided by the semantics of the standards discussed in the previous chapter. A field in a scheme and its definition as documented can go only so far in clarifying what its content should be. This is particularly true of Simple DC, the semantic scope of whose fields is deliberately broad and, inevitably, imprecise; for instance, knowing that the Title field contains a 'name given to a resource' tells us little about what to expect to find there.

Even the stricter semantics of MODS leave plenty of room for inconsistency. The `<titleInfo>` element from Example 7.2 in the previous chapter provides more details than DC Title but does not tell us exactly what its content is.

```
<titleInfo>
   <nonSort>Il </nonSort>
   <title>trionfo della morte per il peccato
          d'Adamo</title>
   <subTitle>oratorio da farsi nella chiesa della
          Confraternita della Mortel'anno 1677</subTitle>
</titleInfo>
```

Should we expect to find here the libretto's title in its original language (Italian) or, if we are looking at a rendering of its text into English, the translated version? Perhaps both should be provided? If the book is instead a work of literature in Arabic, should we record it in the original script or a transliteration? What form of the title should we use if it is commonly called by more than one? Should we list the theatrical work by Peter Weiss known in its full English title as 'The Persecution and Assassination of Jean-Paul Marat as Performed by the Inmates of the Asylum of Charenton Under the Direction of the Marquis de Sade' in this form? Should we perhaps use the abbreviated form 'Marat/Sade', by which it is more usually known or its German original 'Die Verfolgung und Ermordung Jean Paul Marats dargestellt durch die Schauspielgruppe des Hospizes zu Charenton unter Anleitung des Herrn de Sade'?

Similar questions regarding the choice of content may arise in any part of a metadata record.

- If a work has more than one author, how many should we include? A scientific article may have 300 of these – should we list them all or, if not, how many and which ones?
- What about pseudonyms? Should the author of Middlemarch be listed as George Eliot or under her real name, Mary Ann Evans?
- If we are an audiovisual archive hosting a feature film, who, among the potentially hundreds of those credited in its production, should be included?
- Which are the dates associated with an object's history that should be documented? For a published book we might settle for its date of publication, but what about second editions and revisions? For items such as films, sound recordings or images of works of art the problems multiply.
- How should we describe an object's subject matter, and in what depth?

Metadata rules covering these and many other issues are essential to ensure consistency across a collection; this is as true for a digital library as for its analogue counterpart. Rationalising the *choice* of content in this way is only part of what is needed: it must be complemented by a harmonisation of the *form* that this content takes.

Personal names are a prime example of this.

- Should a compound name like George Bernard Shaw be listed as 'Shaw, George Bernard' or 'Bernard Shaw, George'?
- How can we differentiate people with the same name? The union catalogue WorldCat lists 4,564 authors named John Smith – how can we tell them apart from each other?
- How should we handle geographic names? If we came across 'Helset' or 'Stadi' as a place of publication how would we know that this referred to Helsinki, the capital of Finland? Would we recognise that 'Handoverpia' or 'Antwerpis' is the Belgian city of Antwerp? All of these are variants of the 7 or 26 names by which these cities are or have previously been known.

To achieve consistency over the form that metadata content takes we have to impose some form of *authority control*. This is best done by employing lists of terms which have been compiled specifically for this purpose. For personal and geographic names we can employ *authority files*, extensive compilations of consistently formatted versions of these names. For subjects we may prefer to use a hierarchical listing known as a *thesaurus* which allows us to move between broader and narrower terms to pinpoint the one that should be used.

We therefore have two components to employing content rules as part of a metadata strategy: the first, which we call *cataloguing rules*, mandates what should go into records and the second, usually termed *authority control*, dictates the form or format that this content should take.

8.3 Cataloguing rules

An initial decision that must be made when planning a metadata strategy is whether to apply an established set of cataloguing rules or to devise one's own. If we take the latter course it is preferable not to start with a completely blank sheet and sensible to base locally compiled rules on a pre-existing standard as far as possible; we will then have to decide which one this should be and how to tailor it to meet our requirements. The choice of approach will be influenced by the type of resources in a collection, their intended audience and the professional environment within which it is located.

8.3.1 Established standards for cataloguing rules

A digital library may in some cases populate its metadata with records that have been already been compiled by others. If, for example, we implement MODS by converting MARCXML records exported from a library's online catalogue these will conform to the cataloguing rules that are established as standard practice within that library's professional community. In that case we do not need to concern ourselves with deciding on a set of rules, as the choice will already have been made for us. Our concern will then be to apply the same rules to any new records which have not come via this route, in order to ensure an overall degree of consistency across all our metadata.

Even if we do not import records from an existing catalogue, the application of pre-existing cataloguing rules may be the obvious choice if we work within sectors that have adopted these as standards for professional practice. The drawback to this is that they can be extensive in scope and complex in application, and so require extensive instruction to learn and implement. Training in their use is often incorporated into professional education or development programmes such as courses in library science. Others may have shallower learning curves, particularly if they have been devised specifically for use in digital collections whose curators may not have gone through the same educational routes as librarians.

Some of the key standards to consider are the following.

8.3.1.1 Anglo-American Cataloging Rules, Second Edition (AACR2)[S.1]

The most commonly employed standard for cataloguing rules in libraries dates back to 1967 and was last updated in 2005. The vast majority of library catalogues have employed, and in many cases still employ, these rules which govern bibliographic information for materials of all types including electronic resources. AACR2 is highly detailed and based on standards which have evolved over many years, most notably the International Standard Bibliographic Description. Records conforming to it are generally created by cataloguers who have undergone formal training in its use. For those who have not, a concise edition is available which may be more approachable than the full version.

Digital collections which are created from physical library materials will probably base their descriptive metadata on AACR2, as it is likely to be the standard to which their existing catalogue records conform.

8.3.1.2 Resource Description and Access (RDA)[S.24]

RDA was initially released in 2010 as an intended replacement for AACR2 which would be more appropriate for resources in a digital environment. One of its features is that it conforms to the Functional Requirements for Bibliographic Records (FRBR)[C8.3], a set of principles defined by the International Federation of Library Associations which are designed to enhance bibliographic description to encompass all types of materials, including the electronic. A key component of RDA is the definition of multiple levels of description, each of which may need to be treated in its own way. An object, for instance a recording of Beethoven's Ninth Symphony, may be described as a *work* in the abstract (the symphony as a concept), an *expression* of the work (its musical content), a *manifestation* (a performance) or an *item* (a digital file or compact disc containing a recording of the performance). Each of these may require different metadata to handle its intellectual content and technical characteristics: RDA is designed to supply this in ways which can be difficult with AACR2, owing to its origins in the pre-digital bibliographic world.

These are sound principles on which to base digital-era cataloguing rules, but the take-up of RDA has been patchy as it is as complex as AACR2 and so requires as much investment in training and professional development as its predecessor. Some major libraries, including the Library of Congress and the British Library, have implemented it for new records since 2013, but many persist with AACR2 to this day.

Most of the comments relating to AACR2 in the digital library also apply to RDA. If we employ records exported from library catalogues which conform to this new standard we will by default implement RDA as the bedrock of our descriptive metadata. Outside the context of a pre-existing library and its catalogue, it will be a judgement call as to whether this complex standard, with its steep learning curve in at least its complete and unedited form, is the most appropriate for a digital library.

8.3.1.3 Cataloging Cultural Objects (CCO)[S.3]

CCO is a set of cataloguing rules devised by the American Library Association to address the needs of curators in the cultural heritage sector for 'describing and documenting works of art, architecture, cultural artifacts, and images of these things' (Baca et al. 2006) in areas where AACR2 and RDA fall short. It recognises a distinction between a work of art and an image that documents it and provides rules and guidance appropriate to each. These include suggestions for what to include in a metadata field, rules for formatting this content and guidance on appropriate authorities and controlled vocabularies. Although it is far from a minimal or skeletal set of guidelines, running as it does to almost 400 pages, it is more approachable than AACR2 and RDA and undoubtedly a viable course of action for cataloguing rules in the cultural heritage sector.

8.3.1.4 Describing Archives: A Content Standard (DACS)[S.10]

Another standard that merits consideration is DACS, a set of content rules produced by the Society of American Archivists. As its name implies, DACS is primarily intended to standardise the description of archival materials, including personal papers and manuscripts, but it is readily applicable to all types of content; for instance, it has been employed successfully in moving image collections (Rush et al. 2008). It is a more concise standard than the three discussed above, and so easier to learn and apply, but is nonetheless designed to be compatible with AACR2, RDA and ISAD(G), their counterpart in the archival sector. It is not tied to a given set of descriptive metadata semantics but can be readily applied to MARC (and hence MODS), among others. For all of these reasons it may be a judicious option to implement either directly or as the basis of a local set of rules.

8.3.1.5 Descriptive Cataloging of Rare Materials[S.11]

A final set of standards which should be considered for digital libraries hosting collections derived from rare or historical materials is a series of manuals produced by the Rare Books Section of the US Association of College and Research Libraries. These cover the cataloguing of manuscripts (ancient, medieval, renaissance and early modern), early printed books, maps, graphics, music and serials. They are designed to be compatible with MARC, and so are also a good fit with MODS. For specialised collections of this type they offer a solid basis for ensuring consistent and interoperable metadata.

8.4 Devising local guidelines

Although the standards discussed above have their significant merits and should definitely be employed if resources and circumstances allow, there may be reasons why this is not always feasible. We may not have access to AACR2- or RDA-compliant records from a pre-existing catalogue or the capacity to train staff to a sufficient level of expertise in these complex standards. The learning curves of the others may also be too steep to allow us to implement them in their entirety, or we may decide that they do not fully meet the specific requirements of our collections. In such circumstances we may have to devise a local set of rules or guidelines for the content of our descriptive metadata.

If we choose to do this we should nevertheless aim to base these on an established set of cataloguing rules if at all possible. This will ensure that we do not detach ourselves fully from the professional practices applied in our community, and so nullify our metadata's potential for interoperability; it will also prevent us from making fundamental mistakes that have been encountered before and corrected as these standards have been refined over time. We should work, therefore, to ensure that the rules we compile are compatible with a core standard, in effect producing a cut-down, digestible version with local additions if required.

One further design principle that should be looked at is whether or not to allow multiple levels of detail in our metadata records. Given the heterogeneous nature of many digital collections, it may be a viable approach to prescribe a series of levels from minimal to fully comprehensive. Each would then build on those below by adding extra fields and perhaps incorporating more complex content, akin to the way in which Qualified DC relates to its simpler counterpart. The most important principle to follow here is that the minimum-level fields can always act as a viable metadata record in their own right, with or without their higher-level complements: the latter should always add to the former rather than seek to replace them.

The exact form that these guidelines take will be dictated by local circumstances, but some general principles should be followed in all cases:

- they should document each field into which the cataloguer will be inputting metadata;
- they should make clear which fields are mandatory for all records, which are mandatory when relevant or applicable, which are recommended and which are entirely optional;
- they should indicate which are repeatable and in what circumstances;
- they should provide clear and unambiguous guidance as to the content of each, including:

  — what should be included, for example which forms of a title or author's name to use;
  — how it should be formatted (for instance, which convention to use for dates);
  — which controlled vocabularies, authority lists or subject thesauri should be applied to enforce this;

- they should aim to be as concise as possible while providing all relevant details.

To illustrate these principles the following examples show extracts from guidelines produced for Oxford University's Oxford Digital Library (ODL), one of the University's first attempts at a unified digital library. Metadata for the objects in the library's collections was inputted into online forms using

Simple DC fields enhanced by qualifiers; these were then converted to MODS for integration into the METS files which formed its canonical records. As might be expected for collections based on materials held in the University's libraries, the guidelines are based on AACR2 in their choice of content and its formatting.

They begin by introducing the fields and designating their status as **Mandatory for all records, Mandatory where applicable** and **Recommended where applicable** (Figure 8.1).

Help for the Descriptive Metadata entry form: DC categories

General Introduction

This document lists the Dublin Core fields which can be used in ODL records, and gives guidance and instructions on their use. You will see that they are divided into three categories:-

Mandatory for all records:

Title Subject Type Description	Every record must contain at least a minimal entry in each of these fields

Mandatory where applicable:

Creator Date Identifier Rights Format Source	Where an item has an identifiable creator, is datable, is digitized from a surrogate, or has a corresponding record on OLIS or has restrictions on access over and above those which apply to the entire collection, the relevant field in this category must be filled in. The **Format** field may also be used to indicate the physical extent of the original item.

Recommended where applicable:

Contributor Publisher Language Coverage Relation	You are strongly recommended to fill in these fields if they are applicable to this item.

Figure 8.1 *Oxford Digital Library cataloguing guidelines: introduction*

This tripartite division allows for a minimal-level record comprised of only four fields, supplemented by a further six if they are applicable to an object; the remaining five, which are recommended but not mandatory, allow for more detailed records when these are preferable.

Each is then covered in more detail, beginning with the Title (Figure 8.2 opposite).

Title

Definition	The name given to the digital object. Typically, a Title will be a name by which the resource is formally known.	
Procedure	- Use the title in the MARC field 245 of the record on OLIS, if there is a one for the resource already - If there is a Uniform Title for the resource, record this using the <uniform> qualifier in addition to the main title - If the item is a journal article, record the title of the article (the analytic title) using the <main> qualifier, and the title of the journal it comes from using the <serial> qualifier. If it a chapter etc from a monograph, use the <monograph> qualifier. - Record series titles with the <series> qualifier - If there is not a title on OLIS, apply AACR2 rules for titles to format your entry - Every record must have at least a **<main>** or a **<supplied>** title provided	
Qualifiers	**<main>**	The main title as defined above - this qualifier is **compulsory** unless a <supplied> title is provided
	<alternative>	Any alternative titles by which the item is known
	<subtitle>	A subsidiary title (often preceded by "or" on the title page)
	<supplied>	A title or subtitle supplied by the cataloguer (where no title page or equivalent is available) - this qualifier is **compulsory** unless a <main> title is provided
	<parallel>	An alternative rendering of a title in a language other than the primary one
	<uniform>	Uniform title
	<series>	The title of a series of which the item is a part
	<serial>	The title of the serial from which the item is taken
	<monograph>	The title of the monograph from which the item is taken
	<firstline>	The first line of the text if this is a relevant means of identification
Example	<main>Gentleman's Magazine, or Monthly Intelligencer#<alternative>Gentleman's Magazine <main>Candide or#<subtitle> Optimism <main>Democratization of forest management in Eastern and Southern Africa#<monograph>International Forestry Review	

Figure 8.2 *Oxford Digital Library cataloguing guidelines: Title*

The guidance for this field gives its (rather broad) definition as provided by DC but then offers more detailed instructions which enable the cataloguer to input a more focused entry than the unadorned DC explanation allows. It prescribes the source from which it should be taken as a MARC record on the Library's catalogue OLIS (Oxford Libraries Information System); if there is nothing there (for instance, for the many non-print items in the collections) the cataloguer is told to construct a title formatted to AACR2 rules. To make this easier for those who are not trained in this standard, the guidelines provide an appendix containing a concise summary of the relevant rules and how they should be applied (Figure 8.3).

Titles (AACR2 1.1B1)

Transcribe the title proper exactly as to wording, order, and spelling, but not necessarily as to punctuation and capitalization. Give accentuation and other diacritical marks that are present in the chief source of information (see also 1.0G). Capitalize according to appendix A.

Speedball technique charts
Les mis rables
(Diacritic supplied)
The materials of architecture
Supplement to The conquest of Peru and Mexico
The 1919/20 Breasted Expedition to the Near East
l-calculus and computer theory
Fourteen hours
IV informe de gobierno

Do not transcribe words that serve as an introduction and are not intended to be part of the title. Give the title including these words in a note (under <description>).

Sleeping Beauty
<description.note>Title appears on item as: Disney presents Sleeping Beauty
NASA quest
<description.note>Note: Title appears on item as: Welcome to NASA quest

If the title proper as given in the chief source of information includes the punctuation marks . or [ ], replace them by . and ( ), respectively.

If elected.

(Source of information reads: If elected .)

If the title proper as given in the chief source of information includes symbols that cannot be reproduced by the facilities available, replace them with a cataloguer.s description in square brackets. Make an explanatory note if necessary.

Figure 8.3 *Oxford Digital Library: summary of AACR2 rules for Title field*

The entry then concludes with a list of qualifiers (mandatory and optional) which can narrow the field's semantic scope to a particular type of title and a number of examples to illustrate its required content.

Controlled vocabularies, name authorities and subject thesauri are mandated for the Subject, Creator, Contributor, Publisher, Language and Coverage fields. It is recognised that occasional problems may arise in applying these because of the heterogeneity of these diverse collections: a generic thesaurus of subjects, for instance the Library of Congress Subject Headings (LCSH), may not be precise enough to describe their more idiosyncratic content, or a name authority list may not contain entries for some of the more obscure persons associated with them.

To address the first of these issues, a lack of precision in generic standards for subject headings, the Subject field requires that entries conform to a preferred thesaurus (in this case LCSH) but also allows the inclusion of extra subject terms from additional vocabularies, including ones created locally for some of its constituent collections. The source of any given term is indicated by a qualifier; for instance, `<bpcsh>` indicates an entry from British Political Cartoons Subject Headings, a list of subject headings devised by the Bodleian Library for subjects depicted in its collection of historical political cartoons.

For the second issue, missing entries for people, corporate entities or places in published name authorities, an additional procedure is prescribed, as shown in Figure 8.4.

ODL Name Authority Procedures

Go to: Personal Names Corporate Names Geographic Names

Personal Names

Primary resource: Library of Congress Name Authority File

- Choose Author search to search for author's name, or Subject search to search for personal names apart from authors.
- Carry out your search
- Click on the button marked **Authorized Heading** next to the correct entry
- Click on the name itself to display the MARC record for the entry
- The entry in the 100 field is the authoritative form of the name which you should use - copy and paste the entry starting at the **|a** marker. It will be converted automatically to the correct format when you save the record.

Alternatively, if you have access to Cataloguer's Desktop, use the name authority resource on this for your entry

If there is no entry, check on OLIS OLIS which contains many additional (mainly British) names: use the 100 field entry from the MARC display for your entry

If this fails, then look at the ODL authority list for personal names

If there is no entry here, create your own

- Look at AACR suggestions for formatting personal names
- Create your entry using the suggested format, and then add it to the ODL authority list

Figure 8.4 *Oxford Digital Library Name Authority Procedures*

The cataloguer is directed first of all to the primary resource for names, the Library of Congress Name Authority File (LCNAF). If no entry is found there, they are referred to the University's own catalogue, OLIS, which contains additional names, mainly British, that are missing from the US-based resource. Should they have no luck there, they then consult a list maintained by the ODL itself (Figure 8.5).

Oxford Digital Library: Personal names authority list

Add new entry

	Entry	Creator	Notes
Edit	$aBennigsen, Levin August Theophil,$cgraf von,$d1745-1826	A. Fran	Subject of caricature. Military. Source: Literature on the age of Napoleon project
Edit	$aBoyne, John, $d1750-1810	A. Fran	Caricaturist. Source: British Museum Catalogue of Political Satires
Edit	$aBuckingham, Mary Elizabeth Nugent,$cMarchioness of, $d1761-1812	A. Fran	Subject of caricature. Source: National Portrait Gallery
Edit	$aBuckinghamshire, Albinia Bertie,$cCountess of,$dd. 1816	A. Fran	Subject of caricature. Source: Genealogy web
Edit	$aBurdett, Jones,$dfl. 1808	A. Fran	Subject of caricature
Edit	$aByrne, Nicholas,$dfl. 1814	A. Fran	Subject of caricature
Edit	$aCawse, J. (John),$d1779-1862	A. Fran	Caricaturist. Source: OLIS
Edit	$aClarke, Henri Jacques Guillaume,$d1765-1818	A. Fran	Subject of caricature. Source: OLIS
Edit	$aCoates, Robert,$d1772-1848	A. Fran	Subject of caricature. Source: DNB
Edit	$aDabos	A. Fran	Artist

Figure 8.5 *Oxford Digital Library: Personal names authority list*

This is an index of personal names not found in LCNAF or OLIS which has been compiled by those cataloguing the ODL's collections. If one is listed here it should be input into the metadata field as formatted; if not, the cataloguer is directed to create a new entry following AACR2 conventions. This ensures a consistent application of authority control across the entire digital library from either published sources or locally maintained supplements to these.

Guidelines such as these demonstrate that it is possible to create a relatively concise set of content rules which meet the local requirements of a digital library while ensuring conformity with community-based standards for metadata content. Some degree of training in their application will still be needed but this will be much less demanding than that involved in achieving full competence in a standard such as RDA. The time and effort spent in creating a set of guidelines of this type will soon pay for itself in terms of metadata quality and future productivity. This expenditure need not be particularly onerous, as there are many examples of these on the internet that can act as models on which it can be based; some that can be recommended are listed in the 'Useful Resources' section at the end of this volume[C8.2, C8.12, C8.16].

8.5 Controlled vocabularies

The importance of controlled vocabularies has been emphasised repeatedly in this book: they are essential for ensuring consistency in the content of a record, and so for the overall viability and interoperability of metadata. It is important to apply them to names of any sort, personal, corporate and geographic, and also to subjects. They should also be used anywhere else where ambiguity is best avoided. We have already seen, for instance, the use of MARC Relator Codes in the MODS record of the previous chapter's Example 7.2 to define precisely the role of an individual in relation to a work. In addition to controlled vocabularies, it is also useful for the formatting of components such as dates to follow conventions which are defined in published standards.

This section will cover some of the major vocabularies that can be employed for this purpose. It is important to choose one of these to act as the primary source of content for any applicable field. If necessary further ones can be added as supplements to this as was demonstrated in the examples from the ODL. It is especially important when adopting this approach to indicate the vocabulary from which a term is derived; in MODS this is done by the **authority** and **authorityURI** attributes to elements such as `<name>` and `<subject>` as was shown in Example 7.2. Most of the vocabularies detailed here provide URIs for every entry to ensure that they can be identified exactly. It is highly recommended to include these in a descriptive metadata record; the **valueURI** attribute in MODS, which is available for most elements, is where they should be recorded.

Although these vocabularies are extensive and should cover most contingencies, it is possible that they will have omissions with respect to some of the materials in a large digital library. It may be necessary in these cases to supplement them with entries that are maintained locally in the manner described for the ODL in the preceding section. It is very important to maintain consistency with existing vocabularies if this is done. An order of precedence should be established to achieve this: first consult the external published list, then the local supplement and, as a last resort, add an entry to the latter, which should be formatted, if possible, in a way that follows the conventions of the external resource. In this way an overall consistency can be achieved without neglecting the requirements of a specialised collection.

It is worth keeping in mind as we build a local vocabulary that we may wish to share it with others and it should therefore be constructed with interoperability in mind. This requires the use of an interoperable encoding syntax (XML), a metadata standard for semantics and URIs to provide unique identifiers. How this may be done will be discussed in the section on 'Creating local name authorities and thesauri' later in this chapter.

8.5.1 Name authorities

One of the most extensive and wide-ranging resources for name authorities is the already-mentioned LCNAF[C8.7]. This includes over 8 million entries, including 6 million personal, 1.4 million corporate and 120,000 geographic names. Its breadth of coverage makes it a strong contender as a primary resource for a wide range of digital collections, particularly those whose provenance lies in materials that populate traditional libraries.

Accessing the LCNAF is done through a simple search facility at the Library of Congress website. If we look for Bonaventura Aliotti, the composer of the oratorio whose libretto featured throughout the last chapter, we encounter a screen such as the one in Figure 8.6.

The Library of Congress > Linked Data Service > **LC Name Authority File (LCNAF)**

Aliotti, Bonaventura, approximately 1640-approximately 1690

URI(s)
- http://id.loc.gov/authorities/names/no2002111866

Instance Of
- MADS/RDF PersonalName
- MADS/RDF Authority
- SKOS Concept

Scheme Membership(s)
- Library of Congress Name Authority File

Collection Membership(s)
- Names Collection - Authorized Headings
- LC Names Collection - General Collection

Variants
- Aleotti, Bonaventura, approximately 1640-approximately 1690
- Aliocti, Bonaventura, approximately 1640-approximately 1690
- Alioti, Bonaventura, approximately 1640-approximately 1690
- Aliotta, Bonaventura, approximately 1640-approximately 1690

Figure 8.6 *LCNAF entry for a personal name*

The preferred form of his name is shown in bold at the top and this is the version that we should input into a metadata record. Just below is the URI for this entry as assigned by the Library of Congress: we should also record this to identify him precisely. The record also shows variant names by which this person is known to make his identification easier in case of any ambiguity or confusion.

This entry would go into a MODS record in the manner shown in Example 7.2 from the previous chapter (Example 8.1).

```
<name type="personal" authority="lcnaf"
        authorityURI="http://id.loc.gov/authorities/names"
        valueURI="http://id.loc.gov/authorities/names/no2002111866">
        <namePart>Aliotti, Bonaventura</namePart>
        <namePart type="date">approximately 1640-approximately 1690</namePart>
         <role>
           <roleTerm type="text">composer</roleTerm>
           <roleTerm type="code" authority="marcrelator">cmp</roleTerm>
        </role>
</name>
```

Example 8.1 *Name entry in MODS using entry from LCNAF (from Example 7.2)*

Here the authoritative form of the name is recorded in two **<namePart>** elements for their respective components (the composer's name itself and his dates) and its URI in the **valueURI** attribute of **<name>**: the **authority** and **authorityURI** attributes identify its source as LCNAF.

This Library of Congress file is extensive but by no means comprehensive. Other authority lists exist which are either larger and broader in scope or more specialised in their remit. Among the former a notable initiative is the International Standard Name Identifier (ISNI)[C8.4], a collection of over 16 million names of contributors to a wide variety of media; according to its website, it includes 'researchers, inventors, writers, artists, visual creators, performers, producers, publishers' and many others, assigning a unique URI to each. Among the more specialist lists available a noteworthy one for the cultural heritage sector is the Getty Research Institute's Union List of Artist Names (ULAN)[C8.13], an inventory of over 720,000 names of artists, painters, sculptors, printmakers and photographers who, again, as its website says, 'have been involved in the design or production of architecture or visual arts that are of the type collected by art museums'.

If a collection requires coverage from more than one vocabulary a possible approach is to use a service which aggregates a number of these into a single resource. The most comprehensive and authoritative of these is the Virtual International Authority File (VIAF)[C8.14], which integrates names from (at the time of publication) 68 lists including LCNAF, ULAN and ISNI. A search for our composer on VIAF produces the following record (Figure 8.7).

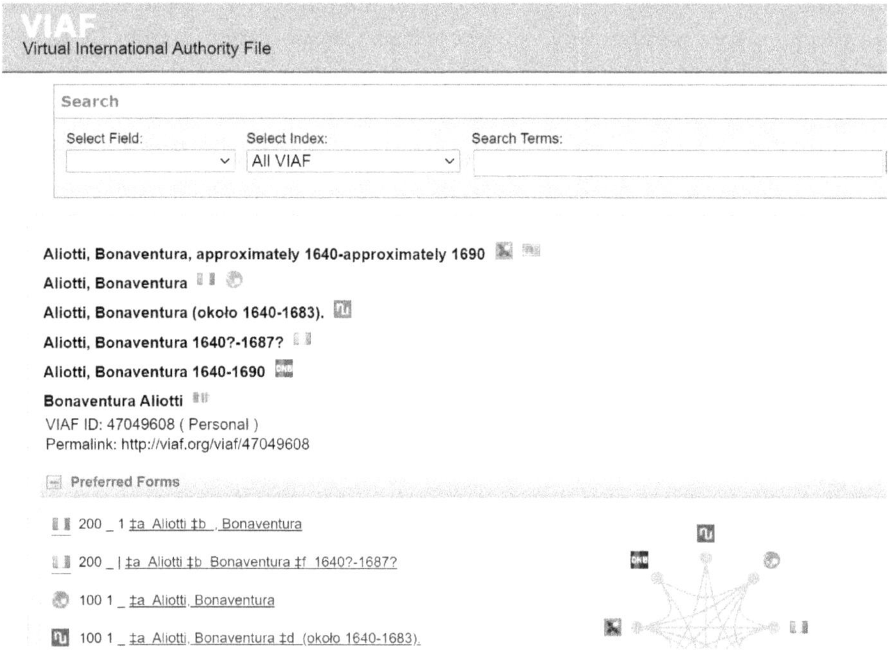

VIAF
Virtual International Authority File

Search
Select Field: Select Index: All VIAF Search Terms:

Aliotti, Bonaventura, approximately 1640-approximately 1690
Aliotti, Bonaventura
Aliotti, Bonaventura (około 1640-1683).
Aliotti, Bonaventura 1640?-1687?
Aliotti, Bonaventura 1640-1690
Bonaventura Aliotti
VIAF ID: 47049608 (Personal)
Permalink: http://viaf.org/viaf/47049608

Preferred Forms

200 _ 1 ‡a Aliotti ‡b , Bonaventura
200 _ | ‡a Aliotti ‡b Bonaventura ‡f 1640?-1687?
100 1 _ ‡a Aliotti, Bonaventura
100 1 _ ‡a Aliotti, Bonaventura ‡d (około 1640-1683).

Figure 8.7 *Entry for composer Bonaventura Aliotti on VIAF* (Image © 2013 OCLC, Inc.; used with permission of OCLC; VIAF is a trademark/service mark of OCLC, Inc.)

This entry shows the preferred form of this person's name in each of the sources where it can be found: the LCNAF entry from Figure 8.6 is indicated by the US flag next to the first entry. VIAF provides its own URI for each aggregated entry, labelled a **Permalink** on this screen.

As many of the lists which are brought together here differ in the ways in which they format their entries, it is necessary to establish an order of priorities when using VIAF; for instance, we could prioritise LCNAF, followed by ULAN and ISNI in that order. We could then use the unstructured MODS **authority** attribute to indicate the authority within VIAF from which the term derives. In Example 8.2 we set it to 'viaf/lcnaf' to identify an entry from LCNAF. We would then put the VIAF URI for the term in the **valueURI** attribute and identify VIAF as the source of this entry using **authorityURI**.

```
<name type="personal"     authority="viaf/lcnaf"
      authorityURI="http://viaf.org/viaf/data"
      valueURI="http://viaf.org/viaf/47049608">
      <namePart>Aliotti, Bonaventura</namePart>
```

```
    <namePart type="date">approximately 1640-approximately 1690</namePart>
    <role>
      <roleTerm type="text">composer</roleTerm>
        <roleTerm type="code" authority="marcrelator">cmp</roleTerm>
    </role>
</name>
```

Example 8.2 *Name entry in MODS using entry from VIAF/LCNAF*

For the tidy-minded digital librarian it is perhaps not ideal to incorporate entries which are formatted according to different cataloguing conventions, but it is a viable compromise if our collections require it. Any lack of consistency in this respect will be compensated for by the precise identification offered by the VIAF URI.

8.5.2 Subjects

Subjects are another part of a metadata record where some degree of authority control is essential. As is the case with names, multiple sources for subjects are available, some generic, some more specialised. Most of these are published as *thesauri*, hierarchical listings which allow the cataloguer to move between broader and narrower terms to locate one at their required degree of precision.

Where a digital collection is based on its counterpart in a physical library, the choice may be made for us if we incorporate its catalogue records into our descriptive metadata. If not, the choice of which to employ is an important one which requires careful consideration. A generic standard is probably the wisest course if a collection is relatively eclectic in scope. More specialised collections, for instance in the sciences, will probably require subject schemes which have been devised to meet the requirements of their respective disciplines. A compromise approach, such as that implemented by the ODL, may also be appropriate. It is feasible to use a generic scheme to provide subject access across the digital library as a whole and to supplement this with more specialised alternatives which provide better-focused entry points to its sub-collections.

One of the most widely used generic schemes is the LCSH[C8.9], a complement to the same library's name authority file. Accessing these headings is done in a way that is very similar to LCNAF. A search for 'oratorios' produces the entry shown in Figure 8.8 on the next page.

The preferred term is once again highlighted in bold at the top; this is followed by a scope note, a short description of when it is appropriate to use it. A URI is also provided which uniquely identifies this subject within the scheme. Below this we see two sub-headings for entries which are

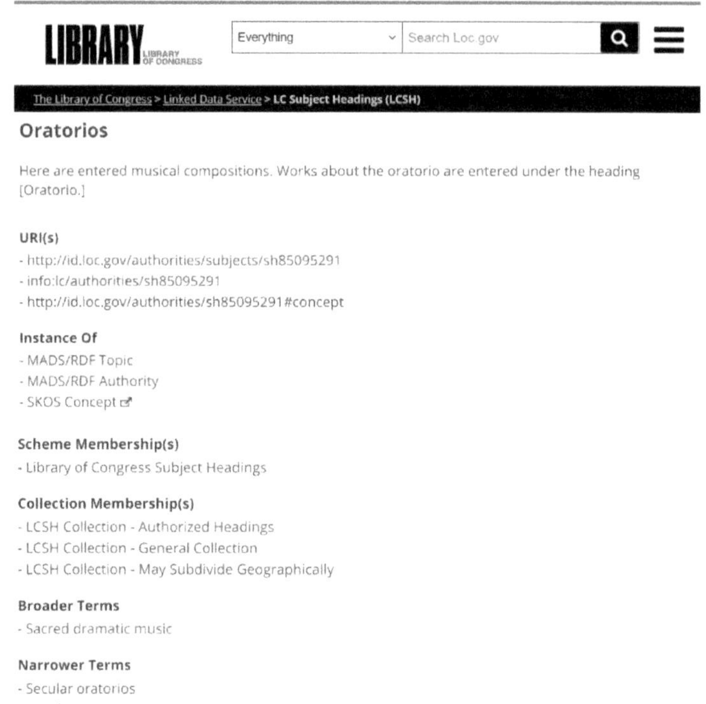

Figure 8.8 *LCSH entry for Oratorios* (beginning)

respectively broader and narrower than the current one; these allow us to navigate up and down the hierarchies of the subject thesaurus to find a wider or more specific term if required.

Using this entry we can enter a subject heading in MODS as in Example 7.2 of the previous chapter (Example 8.3).

```
<subject authority="lcsh"
        authorityURI="http://id.loc.gov/authorities/subjects"
        valueURI="http://id.loc.gov/authorities/subjects/sh85095291">
        <topic>Oratorios</topic>
</subject>
```

Example 8.3: *Subject entry in MODS using term from LCSH* (from Example 7.2)

As for the name authority entries in Examples 8.1 and 8.2, we use the **authority**, **authorityURI** and **valueURI** attributes to record the source and URI for this term, respectively.

If a more specialised scheme is required there are hundreds to choose from; the Library of Congress maintains a list of over 400 (Subject Heading and Term Source Codes[C8.8]). Each is assigned a short code which can be used to identify it in the MODS **authority** attribute. Most will also have a URI which may be included in **authorityURI**, and which should be noted in their documentation.

8.5.3 Codes and dates

In addition to these name and subject authorities, a number of other fields can benefit from controlled lists of codes to pin down their meaning precisely. The Library of Congress also maintains many of these. Some of the most useful are the following.

- **MARC Relator Codes**[C8.11]: three-letter codes which indicate the relationship of an 'agent' to a resource, for instance an author to a book. In Example 7.2, the code **cmp** is used in the **<role>** element to indicate the relationship of the 'composer' to the oratorio.
- **ISO 639.2 Language Codes**[C8.6]: three-letter codes to specify languages. Many elements in MODS (for instance **<titleInfo>**) include **lang** attributes which may be populated with these to indicate the language of the metadata element being referred to.
- **MARC Code List for Countries**[C8.10]: two-letter codes for countries. In Example 7.2 the **<placeTerm>** element in **<originInfo>** uses the code for Italy to indicate the country of publication.

One final feature that should be controlled in a metadata record is the format of dates. A standard for this, ISO 8601, is widely adopted and it is recommended that all dates, and times if relevant, follow its (very simple) format. For a year, an entry consists simply of its expression as four digits, as in this example from Example 7.2:

```
<dateIssued encoding="iso8601">1677</dateIssued>
```

An entry for a single day takes the form YYYY-MM-DD; for instance, the date of the first Moon landing would be recorded as:

```
1969-07-20
```

If we wished to be really precise we could also include its exact time, expressed here in Coordinated Universal Time (indicated by the suffix **Z**):

```
1969-07-20T20:17:40Z
```

This is a very simple and logical scheme; a concise guide to it is provided by W3C (W3C Date and Time Formats)[C8.15].

8.6 Creating local name authorities and thesauri: the MADS schema

As was highlighted earlier, it may be necessary to create local name authority lists or subject thesauri either as supplements to published standards or very occasionally as standalone works designed for a specific purpose. The approach taken by the ODL to ensure consistency in the application of name authorities is an example of the former. An example of the latter, the creation of a thesaurus designed to meet the particular requirements of a specific collection, will be presented in the case study of the Warburg Iconographic Database in Chapter 11.

If we do create such a list or thesaurus, it is important to remember that we may wish to share it with others now or in the future. This requires us to incorporate two features into it: we need to implement a consistent local system of URIs for all entries and to employ an interoperable syntax and semantics to hold them. To enable both of these, it is recommended to use another XML-based schema from the same family as METS and MODS, the Metadata Authority Description Schema (MADS)[S.16].

MADS is a relatively simple schema which can accommodate both flat name authority lists and hierarchical subject thesauri. For a simple name authority entry let us devise one for the dedicatee of the oratorio who, unsurprisingly, has no entry in LCNAF (Example 8.4).

```
<mads>
    <authority ID="wdl-id-name-00001">
        <name type="personal" authority="wdl"
              valueURI="http://wdl.warburg.sas.ac.uk/id/name/00001">
              <namePart type="family">Montevecchi Baldeschi</namePart>
              <namePart type="given">Artemesia</namePart>
        </name>
    </authority>
</mads>
```

Example 8.4 *Name authority entry in MADS*

This is all very straightforward: the root element **<mads>** contains an **<authority>** element for the record which in turn nests **<name>** for the personal name itself. The **<authority>** element has a unique **ID** attribute assigned to it for internal referencing and a **valueURI** to hold an external URI for this entry. The person's name is recorded in two **<namePart>** elements, one for her family and one for her given name.

Encoding entries in a hierarchical subject thesaurus is a little more complicated, as they must include pointers to their broader or narrower terms (Example 8.5).

```
<?xml version="1.0" encoding="UTF-8"?>
<madsCollection>
        <mads ID="wdl-id-subject-00001">
            <authority>
              <topic valueURI="http://wdl.warburg.sas.ac.uk/id/subject/00001"
                     authority="wdl">oratorios</topic>
            </authority>
        </mads>
        <mads ID="wdl-id-subject-00001-00001">
            <authority>
            <topic valueURI="http://wdl.warburg.sas.ac.uk/id/subject/00001/00001"
                   authority="wdl">oratorio volgaro</topic>
            </authority>
            <related type="broader" xlink:href="#wdl-id-subject-00001">oratorio
                   </related>
        </mads>
</madsCollection>
```

Example 8.5 *Broader and narrower subject authority entries in MADS*

Here we have two entries which are in this case both nested within an alternative root, **<madsCollection>**, a container for multiple **<mads>** elements. The first records the top-level subject 'oratorios' and the second a narrower term 'oratorio volgaro'. The broader/narrower relationship between the two is expressed by adding a further element **<related type="broader">** to the second entry; this is a pointer to its broader counterpart ('oratorio'), the link being made by the **xlink:href** attribute which contains its ID (preceded by a **#** symbol, a convention which indicates a reference to an ID in the same instance). This is somewhat verbose but allows us to build up logical hierarchies of terms which are easy for a delivery system to process.

Referencing entries in local authority lists from within a MODS record is done in exactly the same way as for published authorities. We could add a reference to the oratorio's dedicatee in this way, using the MARC Relator Code for her role (**dte**) (Example 8.6).

```
<name type="personal" authority="wdl"
      valueURI="http://wdl.warburg.sas.ac.uk/id/name/00001>
    <namePart type="family">Montevecchi Baldeschi</namePart>
    <namePart type="given">Artemesia</namePart>
    <role>
      <roleTerm type="text">dedicatee</roleTerm>
      <roleTerm type="code" authority="marcrelator">dte</roleTerm>
```

```
    </role>
</name>
```

Example 8.6 *Name entry in MODS using term from local authority file*

We could add a subject entry for 'oratorio volgaro' as shown in Example 8.7.

```
<subject authority="wdl" valueURI="http://wdl.warburg.sas.ac.uk/id/
        subject/00001/00001">
      <topic>oratorio volgaro</topic>
</subject>
```

Example 8.7 *Subject entry in MODS using term from local thesaurus*

This has been a long and complex chapter, but the importance of applying consistent and well-designed content rules to ensure high-quality, interoperable metadata merits the weight that they have been given. The time and effort spent in learning an established set of practices or devising local procedures which can be integrated with these will certainly not be wasted when it comes to employing and sharing metadata, and hence data, now and in the future.

9

Administrative and Preservation Metadata

9.1 Introduction

All libraries employ metadata to support the administration and delivery of their collections. In a traditional library much of this relates to the acquisition of materials and their processing before they reach the shelves. In a digital library its scope is likely to be more extensive and certainly more complex. There has to be a central place for this type of metadata in any integrated strategy. Although most of it will be invisible to the end-user, it has an essential role that cannot be neglected.

Much of the rationale for administrative metadata in a digital library stems from the imperatives of the long-term preservation of its collections. Two core features of the digital medium, the opacity of binary encoding and the subsequent need to decipher the files that make up an object before they can be read, necessitate at least basic technical metadata if a collection is to be viable in the future. This opacity also brings up issues of trust and authenticity: future users will need to know something of the provenance of an object, how and by whom it was created and what changes have been made to it since if they are to be fully confident that it is what it claims to be. For this we need what is known as digital provenance metadata, an audit trail of what has happened to a digital object from its creation to its present form.

Although it has an important role in ensuring the future viability of collections, administrative metadata also features significantly in the here and now. One significant area that it covers is IPR. These include the assertion of ownership in a digital asset, the statement of any copyright provisions that apply to it, the granting of permissions for access and the control of its delivery to users within the boundaries set by these rights and permissions. Rights metadata, which fulfils these functions, is therefore a key component here.

Administrative metadata clearly plays an important part in realising many of the strategic principles outlined in Chapter 3. It is a core feature of all stages of the digital curation lifecycle (Principle 1) and, of course, has a central role in preservation for the future (Principle 2). It also enhances the interoperability of metadata and data (Principle 3), particularly by recording technical information that assists others in reading a digital object and digital provenance information that ensures that its integrity can be trusted.

We should, if possible, use established standards (Principle 7) for this important part of an overall strategy. As is true of all metadata, there is no shortage of these to choose from. For technical metadata in particular we can find schemes for every digital format, including still images, video, audio and text. Others exist for digital provenance and rights metadata for all types of object. Some cover all of these within a single framework.

This chapter will recommend the use of a scheme which is designed primarily as a standard for preservation metadata, the information that is needed to ensure that digital objects are viable and usable in the long term. PREservation Metadata: Implementation Strategies (PREMIS)[S.23] is an umbrella for several schemes which record technical, digital provenance and rights metadata. Although devised as a medium for preservation metadata, much of the information recorded in PREMIS, particularly that covering the technical facets of digital objects and the IPR invested in them, functions effectively in supporting the day-to-day operation of a digital library.

PREMIS was initially devised as a data model and corresponding data dictionary, an extensive listing of elements and their interrelationships without any mandatory specification of how they should be encoded. It has also been published as an XML schema, which is the syntax recommended for the architecture prescribed in this volume. PREMIS metadata in XML can be integrated into the METS framework without difficulty, although some issues can arise from ambiguities as to where its components fit most neatly and some possible duplication of semantic components between the two. These concerns can readily be resolved by implementing guidelines which have been devised to address them; some of these will be covered later in this chapter.

PREMIS is not, of course, the only schema to encompass administrative metadata. Its generic remit and emphasis on preservation can result in its coverage being limited in range and depth, particularly in the case of technical metadata. It may be all that is required in some cases, but it may often be necessary to supplement it with other schemas which address more specifically and in greater detail the requirements of particular data types. This may be done either by adding multiple Technical Metadata sections within METS or by using an option within PREMIS which allows, in a manner similar to MODS, the embedding within extension elements of XML-encoded metadata conforming to other schemas. A number of the most important of these will be introduced later in the chapter.

9.2 PREMIS: an overview

PREMIS consists of four top-level components which it calls *entities*. Each of these provides a subset of the metadata needed for digital preservation. They are shown in Figure 9.1, a diagram from the PREMIS Data Dictionary.

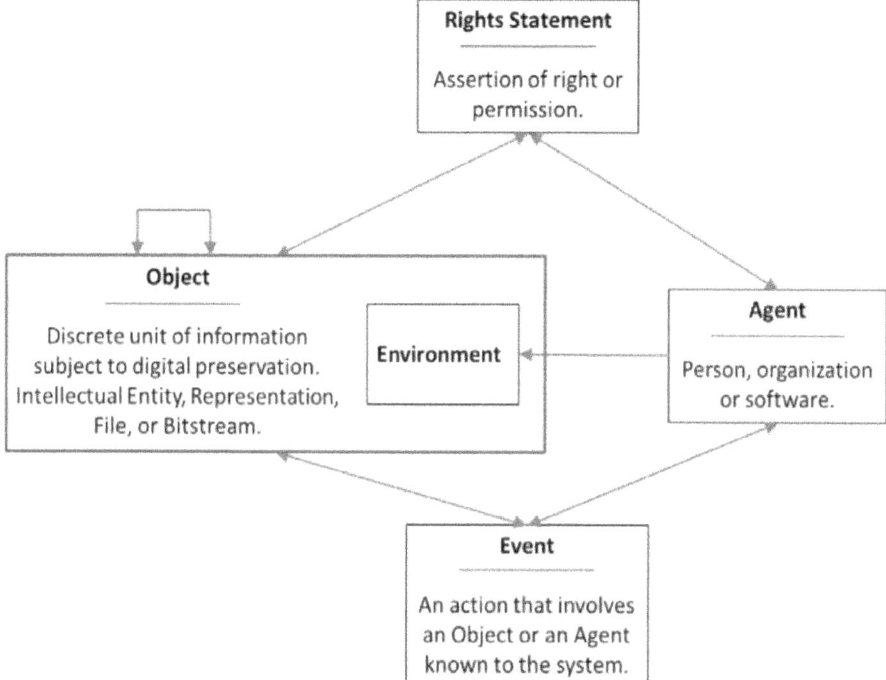

Figure 9.1 *The four top-level entities of the PREMIS data model*

The first of these, **Object**, concerns itself with information on the 'discrete unit of information subject to digital preservation', the digital object itself. This entity mainly contains the technical metadata necessary to enable it to be decoded and understood. It also includes as a subset **Environment**, information on any software and hardware that may be needed to render it usable. **Object** metadata in PREMIS generally finds its natural place within the METS architecture in the Technical Metadata (`<techMD>`) division of the Administrative Metadata Section (`<admSec>`) and its **Environment** subset in the rarely used Behavior Section (`<behaviorSec>`).

The second entity, **Event**, documents actions performed upon an object at any stage in its lifecycle. These may include its creation, editing, conversion to new formats and the production of any derivatives. It is closely related to the third entity, **Agent**, which records the people, organisations or things which perform these actions and may include, for instance, the camera operator who scans an image, the institution which employs them and the software and hardware that they use. These two entities provide the information necessary to record the audit trail that populates the METS Digital Provenance Section (**<digiprovMD>**) of its Administrative Metadata.

The final entity, **Rights,** supplies statements of IPR and permissions which are granted by the object's owners. It is intended primarily to detail rights associated with the processes required for digital preservation but may also be used to cover those needed to deliver objects in a working digital library. This entity provides the information that is found in the Rights Section (**<rightsMD>**) of Administrative Metadata within METS.

At this point, we should look at these entities in more detail. The examples given in the following subsections are shown in the context of their relevant sections within the METS architecture. They present minimal records and so provide only a subset of the extensive range of elements available. The extensive documentation on the Library of Congress home page for this standard provides comprehensive details of the full set.

9.2.1 Technical metadata: the PREMIS Object entity

PREMIS allows us to assign metadata to an object at four levels of granularity. The first of these, the Intellectual Entity, is the most abstract, corresponding roughly to the Work in FRBR. More concrete is the Representation, an object, such as a digitised book, as it is presented in the digital library itself. Next are the files of which it is comprised (File) and finally the binary digits (Bitstream) that make up these files. In Example 9.1, we will confine ourselves to the File level, which is where technical metadata is mainly concentrated.

A basic Object description for an image file of the oratorio's title page would look as shown in Example 9.1.

```
<amdSec ID="wdl-opl-aaaa-amd-0001">
  <techMD ID="wdl-opl-aaaa-tmd-0001">
    <mdWrap MDTYPE="PREMIS:OBJECT">
      <xmlData>
        <premis:object>
          <premis:objectIdentifier>
            <premis:objectIdentifierType>local (METS ID) </premis:objectIdentifierType>
            <premis:objectIdentifierValue>wdl-opl-aaaa-fil-0001-0</premis:objectIdentifierValue>
          </premis:objectIdentifier>

          <premis:objectCategory>file</premis:objectCategory>

          <premis:objectCharacteristics>
            <premis:fixity>
              <premis:messageDigestAlgorithm>SHA-256</premis:messageDigestAlgorithm>
              <premis:messageDigest>10y569g3jrps30f5enfa...(etc)</premis:messageDigest>
              <premis:messageDigestOriginator>WDL</premis:messageDigestOriginator>
            </premis:fixity>
```

```
          <premis:format>
            <premis:formatDesignation>
              <premis:formatName>image/tiff</premis:formatName>
            </premis:formatDesignation>

            <premis:formatRegistry>
              <premis:formatRegistryName>PRONOM</premis:formatRegistryName>
              <premis:formatRegistryKey>fmt/353</premis:formatRegistryKey>
            </premis:formatRegistry>
          </premis:format>
        </premis:objectCharacteristics>
      </premis:object>
    </xmlData>
  </mdWrap>
 </techMD>
</amdSec>
```

Example 9.1 *Simple technical metadata in PREMIS Object entity*

The first two sections in this example, **<premis:objectIdentifier>** and **<premis:objectCategory>**, are both mandatory: they provide respectively an identifier for the file and the PREMIS Object category (intellectual entity, representation, file or bitstream) that it fits into. Any relevant identifier may be used in the first of these; in the example we use its ID from the METS File Section.

The **<premis:objectCharacteristics>** section, also mandatory for all records, contains the key technical metadata itself. The first, **<premis:fixity>**, registers a checksum of the type we met in Chapter 6 (Example 6.10). This is a string generated from a binary file which will change if even a single byte is altered: it is used to check its authenticity, that it has not been corrupted or manipulated in any way, and so to establish its integrity. We may remember that METS itself has a slot for recording checksums in the form of attributes to the **<file>** element. This is an example of one of several possible redundancies between PREMIS and METS which must be resolved by the implementation of guidelines.

The **<premis:format>** section is optional but highly recommended and records details of the format in which the file has been encoded. There are two options for this, at least one of which must be included: both are shown here. In the first, **<premis:formatDesignation>**, we may enter the format using any widely understood convention. Here we use 'image/tiff', a two-part designation for naming formats on the internet known as a MIME type[C9.4].

The second option employs what is known as a format registry, a listing of file formats compiled and maintained by an approved authority. In this case we use PRONOM[C9.5], a service provided by the UK National Archives which was the first of its kind and remains the most widely accepted in operation today. PRONOM assigns each format a persistent unique identifier, in this case 'fmt/353', which allows a more precise identification than a MIME type alone.

For this reason the use of an identifier from a registry is highly recommended.

This is only a minimal technical metadata record within the PREMIS Object entity. Other features that may be recorded here include the file's size, the application that created it, whether it is encrypted and how it may be decrypted to be read. This is the limited information required by ourselves, anyone with whom we share an object and its future users in order to decode and understand it. In many cases, however, we may wish to add further technical information that goes beyond the bare essentials of making the file readable and decodable.

If, for example, we have a text file we may wish to record details of its character set, the fonts used, details of any markup, the direction of text flow and details of the ordering of its pages. For audio we may wish to know the sampling frequency of a digital recording and the encoding that it employs. For video such details as its frame rate, broadcasting standard and chrominance and luminance information are important. For still images we may wish to know such details as the extent to which a JPEG image has been compressed and the exact JPEG algorithm used to do this.

For this type of information, which goes beyond the basic metadata that PREMIS provides, we need additional technical metadata schemas that are designed for each type of format. A number of these are introduced in the section on 'Other useful schemas for administrative metadata' in this chapter. As mentioned earlier, they may be incorporated into an overall METS-based architecture in two ways. The first, which we saw in Chapter 6 (Example 6.5), is to insert a further **<techMD>** element and anchor this supplementary information directly within it. The second is to make use of PREMIS's own extension facility.

Several elements within PREMIS allow metadata from external schemas to be embedded in an instance directly. One of these is **<premis:objectCharacteristicsExtension>**, which can appear as the final subelement within **<premis:objectCharacteristics>**. XML-encoded metadata from any schema may be included here; the schema's namespace and location should be recorded in the **<mets>** root element to enable this, as shown in Example 6.1. We may choose, for example, to include an instance of metadata for a JPEG image in MIX, a standard for still image metadata (Example 9.2).

```
<premis:objectCharacteristicsExtension>
  <mix:mix>
     <mix:BasicDigitalObjectInformation>
        <mix:Compression>
           <mix:compressionScheme>JPEG 2000 Lossy</mix:compressionScheme>
           <mix:compressionRatio>10</mix:compressionRatio>
```

```
        </mix:Compression>
      </mix:BasicDigitalObjectInformation>
   </mix:mix>
</premis:objectCharacteristicsExtension>
```

Example 9.2 *Supplementary MIX metadata in PREMIS <objectCharacteristicsExtension> element*

Ten PREMIS elements allow extensions of this type. Incorporating metadata from a supplementary schema in this way produces a tidy technical metadata section and so is probably to be preferred to the more fragmented approach of duplicating METS **<techMD>** elements.

9.2.2 Digital provenance metadata: the PREMIS Event and Agent entities

Digital provenance metadata is important for ensuring the integrity and authenticity of digital objects and the collections of which they form a part. Within the METS architecture, it slots into the Digital Provenance (**<digiprovMD>**) portion of the Administrative Metadata Section. Two PREMIS entities, Event and Agent, are used in conjunction to hold this type.

An entry which documents the initial scan of this page's TIFF image might take the (rather verbose) form shown in Example 9.3.

```
<admSec ID="wdl-opl-aaaa-adm-0001">
 <digiprovMD ID="wdl-opl-aaaa-dpr-0001">
   <mdWrap MDTYPE="PREMIS:EVENT">
      <xmlData>
         <premis:event>

           <premis:eventIdentifier>
               <premis:eventIdentifierType>local (METS ID)
                    </premis:eventIdentifierType>
               <premis:eventIdentifierValue>wdl-opl-aaaa-dpr-0001-evt-0001
                    </premis:eventIdentifierValue>
           </premis:eventIdentifier>

           <premis:eventType>creation</premis:eventType>
           <premis:eventDateTime>2014-08-04T15:53:07</premis:eventDateTime>

            <premis:eventDetailInformation>
               <premis:eventDetail>Initial scan in library photographic studio
                    </premis:eventDetail>
            </premis:eventDetailInformation>

            <premis:linkingObjectIdentifier>
               <premis:linkingObjectIdentifierType>local (METS ID)
                    </premis:linkingObjectIdentifierType>
               <premis:linkingObjectIdentifierValue>wdl-opl-aaaa-fil-0001-0
                    </premis:linkingObjectIdentifierValue>
```

```
            </premis:linkingObjectIdentifier>

            <premis:linkingAgentIdentifier>
               <premis:linkingAgentIdentifierType>local (METS ID)
                    </premis:linkingAgentIdentifierType>
               <premis:linkingAgentIdentifierValue>wdl-opl-aaaa-dpr-0002
                    </premis:linkingAgentIdentifierValue>
            </premis:linkingAgentIdentifier>

         </premis:event>
      </xmlData>
   </mdWrap>
 </digiprovMD>

 <digiprovMD ID="wdl-opl-aaaa-dpr-0002">
   <mdWrap MDTYPE="PREMIS:AGENT">
      <xmlData>
         <premis:agent>

            <premis:agentIdentifier>
                <premis:agentIdentifierType>local (METS ID)
                     </premis:agentIdentifierType>
                <premis:agentIdentifierValue>wdl-opl-aaaa-dpr-0002-agent-0001
                     </premis:agentIdentifierValue>
            </premis:agentIdentifier>

            <premis:agentName>Bookeye 4 V2 Professional</premis:agentName>
            <premis:agentType>hardware</premis:agentType>

         </premis:agent>
      </xmlData>
    </mdWrap>
 </digiprovMD>
</admSec>
```

Example 9.3 *Recording details of initial scan of image using PREMIS Event and Agent entities*

Here we record the date and time that the image was initially scanned in the Event entity and the hardware used to capture it in its Agent counterpart; each goes into a separate **<digiprovMD>** element in the Administrative Metadata Section. PREMIS is not noted for its concision, but its structure is clear and logical. The **<premis:event>** element contains details of the event itself, the **<premis:agent>** contains details of the hardware. Both of these are required to have identifiers in the same manner as their counterparts in the Object entity. Here, **<premis:eventIdentifier>** and **<premis:agentIdentifier>** each have one derived from the **ID** attribute of its respective METS **<digiprovMD>**.

The Event entity contains two mandatory elements to record the type of event (**<premis:eventType>**) and the date and time on which it occurred

(**<premis:eventDate>**). For the former it is recommended to use a controlled list of types. The one suggested by PREMIS is maintained, as are so many, by the Library of Congress[C9.3], where we find 'creation', the term used here. The date is recorded in the ISO 8601 format which we met in the previous chapter. We follow this with a simple note in the optional element **<premis:eventDetailInformation>** which expands on that rather pithy term for the event type.

The next two nesting elements, **<premis:linkingObjectIdentifier>** and **<premis:linkingAgentIdentifier>**, perform the function of linking this event to the object it refers to and to the agent (in this case the hardware platform) that carries it out. In each case this is done by recording their respective METS **ID** attributes in the subelements **<premis:linkingObjectIdentifierValue>** and **<premis:linkingAgentIdentifierValue>**. In the former, this is the **ID** attribute of its **<file>** element in the File Section, in the latter, the same attribute of its **<digiprovMD>** element.

The Agent entity here contains two subelements, both optional, which hold the agent's name (**<premis:agentName>**) and the type of the agent that he, she, they or it is (**<premis:agentType>**). In this case the first records the name of the scanner used and the second registers its type as 'hardware'. The latter is best identified by an entry from a very short list, also maintained by the Library of Congress,[C9.2] which consists of only four terms: 'hardware', 'software', 'person' and 'organization'.

Recording events and the agents that enact them in this way is logical and straightforward, despite its verbosity. Additional PREMIS elements are available for each if more detail is required and they may also be supplemented in extension elements by metadata conforming to external schemas.

9.2.3 Rights metadata: the PREMIS Rights entity

Rights are the other core component of administrative metadata: this is the information necessary to assert ownership of the intellectual property in digital objects, including the legal basis on which it is claimed, and to control access to them in ways which respect and enforce it. PREMIS includes a further entity for this purpose, unsurprisingly titled Rights. This is specifically designed to administer IPR as they relate to digital preservation. One example of this could be permissions to reformat a digital object in order to ensure its longevity. It is nonetheless useful for handling rights in an operational digital library as well, and for this reason is recommended as the primary scheme for this type.

This is a very simple Rights statement which grants permissions to users under the terms of a licence defined by the non-profit organisation Creative

Commons[C2.1]. These licences allow copyright holders to declare the rights that they are willing to grant others to use, share and build on their work. Seven are in common use, ranging from the most liberal which assigns a work wholly to the public domain, to another which requires only an acknowledgement of the owner, to more restrictive ones which prohibit the production of derivatives or commercial use. Each is assigned a simple code by which it may be identified. In this case we are licensing works under the Creative Commons CC BY-NC 4.0 licence, which requires attribution of ownership and no commercial use but allows the creation of new works derived from our own.

The rights metadata section of a METS instance with this information documented in PREMIS looks as shown in Example 9.4.

```
<rightsMD ID="wdl-opl-aaaa-rgt-0001">
   <mdWrap MDTYPE="PREMIS:RIGHTS">
      <xmlData>
          <premis:rights>
             <premis:rightsStatement>
               <premis:rightsStatementIdentifier>
                  <premis:rightsStatementIdentifierType>local
                          (METS ID)</premis:rightsStatementIdentifierType>
                  <premis:rightsStatementIdentifierValue>wdl-opl-aaaa-rgt-0001
                           </premis:rightsStatementIdentifierValue>
               </premis:rightsStatementIdentifier>

               <premis:rightsBasis>license</premis:rightsBasis>

               <premis:licenseInformation>
                  <premis:licenseDocumentationIdentifier>
                  <premis:licenseDocumentationIdentifierType>
                          https://creativecommons.org/licenses
                          </premis:licenseDocumentationIdentifierType>
                  <premis:licenseDocumentationIdentifierValue>CC BY-NC 4.0
                              </premis:licenseDocumentationIdentifierValue>
                  </premis:licenseDocumentationIdentifier>
                  <premis:licenseNote>This digitized book is licensed under the
                          Creative Commons Attribution-NonCommercial 4.0
                          International license</premis:licenseNote>
               </premis:licenseInformation>

               <premis:rightsGranted>
                      <premis:act>Display</premis:act>
                      <premis:restriction>General public</premis:restriction>
               </premis:rightsGranted>

               <premis:rightsGranted>
                      <premis:act>Modify</premis:act>
                      <premis:restriction>Non-commercial</premis:restriction>
               </premis:rightsGranted>
```

```
            </premis:rightsStatement>
        </premis:rights>
    </xmlData>
  </mdWrap>
</rightsMD>
```

Example 9.4 *Creative Commons licence recorded in PREMIS Rights entity*

The Rights entity begins like its counterparts with an identifier (**<premis:rightsStatementIdentifier>**). In Example 9.4 the value given is the **ID** attribute of the METS **<rightsID>** element in which it is nested. This is followed by another compulsory element, **<premis:rightsBasis>**, which indicates the type of rights recorded and is usually set to 'copyright', 'license', 'statute' or 'other', terms taken from another list[C9.4] at the Library of Congress (hence the US spelling of 'license'). The value here determines what set of elements follows: for 'license' this is **<premis:licenseInformation>** and its subelements, for the others one of **<premis:copyrightInformation>**, **<premis:statuteInformation>** or **<premis:otherRightsInformation>**.

It is within the **<premis:licenseInformation>** element that we provide information on the licence itself. We identify it as a Creative Commons licence by providing the URI for these within **<premis:licenseDocumentationIdentifierType>** and the code for the specific licence (CC BY-NC 4.0) within **<premis:licenseDocumentationIdentifierValue>**. We supplement this with a human-readable note about the rights being granted within **<premis:licenseNote>**. Further subelements are available here to provide more extensive information, including detailed descriptions of the terms of the licence and the range of dates to which it applies.

A similar range of elements is available for the other types of rights ('copyright', 'statute' and 'other'), all of which are tailored to their specific requirements. The set relating to copyright includes such details as the jurisdiction whose laws are applicable to a work, its status ('in copyright' or 'public domain') and when it expires. The 'statute' set includes a citation for the applicable statute itself, its jurisdiction, references to the documentation supporting the rights which are claimed and the dates when it is in force. A similar, if more generic, set are also available for 'other' rights if **<premis:rightsBasis>** is set to this value.

Should we wish to grant more specific rights than those covered by copyright, licence or statute, or to state them more explicitly, an optional repeatable element within **<premis:rightsStatement>** allows us to do this. We may, for instance, wish to allow all users of a digital library to view or display a book but only non-commercial ones to download and modify it. This can be done with the `<premis:rightsGranted>` element, whose subelements allow us to define the act that we are granting the right to perform (`<premis:act>`) and any restrictions that apply. Here we stipulate those who are permitted to perform the actions of 'Display' or 'Modify', respectively (`<premis:restriction>`). In this way we can specify a range of permitted actions, who can undertake them and the circumstances in which they are allowed.

9.2.4 Using PREMIS with METS

PREMIS fits relatively neatly into the METS architecture: the Object entity finds a natural place in its Technical Metadata section, its Event and Agent counterparts in Digital Provenance and Rights within Rights. However, there are some potential issues that arise when the two do not wholly mesh together: the application of local guidelines is necessary to resolve frictions of this kind.

The most significant of these is redundancies between the two schemas where the same function is performed in each; this requires us to decide whether to duplicate information or, if not, which schema should be given priority. A prime example noted earlier is checksums, the strings generated from a binary file which are recorded as a check on its authenticity. In METS they may be found in the **CHECKSUM** attribute of the `<file>` element and in PREMIS in the `<premis:fixity>` element of the Object entity. A potential clash may also occur between METS's **ID** attributes and the system of identifiers which PREMIS prescribes for many of its components. PREMIS also has elements (not shown in the example) for expressing structural metadata which could compete with the role performed by the METS Structural Map.

These concerns are readily resolved if a consistent set of guidelines are followed when using PREMIS with METS. In general, it is probably better to give priority to the mechanisms in METS over those of PREMIS, as the packaging standard fulfils a wider variety of functions within the context of the digital library as a whole. For this reason the previous examples give primacy to the system of METS identifiers rather than those of PREMIS, using METS **ID** attributes or their derivatives to populate any mandatory PREMIS equivalents. Fixity information should similarly make use of the METS **CHECKSUM** attribute as its primary home, but there is no harm in duplicating this information in PREMIS.

One very useful guide to using these standards in conjunction is the Library of Congress's own 'Guidelines for using PREMIS with METS for Exchange'[C9.1], which address many of these issues in a clear and concise way.

They stress the need to document clearly whatever decisions are made. One mechanism for doing this, METS Profiles, is discussed in the next chapter.

9.3 Other useful schemas for administrative metadata

PREMIS can readily satisfy most requirements for basic administrative metadata, but other schemas are available which can act as useful supplements to it. These mainly apply to technical metadata, for which several format-specific schemas have established themselves as key standards. Rights metadata is also covered in a number of these, some of which are focused on the IPR requirements of particular sectors. Some also cover digital provenance metadata in more detail than is offered by PREMIS. All may be incorporated into any of the ten extension elements available within PREMIS or their appropriate METS sections.

9.3.1 Technical metadata

The choice of a technical metadata schema to extend the relatively basic element set offered by the PREMIS Object entity will depend primarily on the format of an object's constituent files. All of those listed here are maintained by the Library of Congress and recommended by the METS Editorial Board as extension schemas.

9.3.1.1 Still images

For still images the primary schema is MIX[S.20], which we have already encountered earlier in this volume. MIX allows us to record a very extensive set of technical metadata should we so wish, but most of its elements are optional, enabling us to choose the level of detail that is appropriate to our needs. In addition to the basic details already covered by PREMIS (for instance file sizes, formats and checksums) it also includes such specifics as an image's colour space, compression, encoding options, spatial metrics and so on. It offers the possibility of documenting meticulous information on an image's capture, such as the settings of the camera used, and any changes made to it since then. This digital provenance information is much more exhaustive than that offered by PREMIS.

For a specialist archive, such as a collection of photographs, the depth of detail offered by MIX may be appropriate. For a library of digitised books, each of which may consist of several hundred images, the basic information offered by the PREMIS Object entity, either on its own or perhaps supplemented by a small number of MIX elements, may be all that is needed.

9.3.1.2 Text

Text may appear to be one of the most transparent of digital formats, and so one of the easiest to decode. This is one of the reasons why XML is such a robust mechanism for the preservation of metadata. It is nonetheless good practice to record technical metadata when there is a textual component to an object in a digital library. There are many features that could usefully be documented to ensure that it will be understood and readable in the short and long term. These include the character set employed, the language(s) it is written in, any fonts used, the ordering of pages and characters (left-to-right for English or Italian, right-to-left for languages such as Hebrew or Arabic) and any schemas used if it is marked up in XML.

A relatively simple schema, TextMD[S.27], maintained, like so many others, by the Library of Congress, meets all of these requirements very adequately. Example 9.5 shows a basic TextMD record in a METS Administrative Metadata section.

```
<amdSec ID="wdl-opl-aaaa-amd-0002">
   <techMD ID="wdl-opl-aaaa-tmd-0003">
      <mdWrap MDTYPE="TEXTMD">
         <xmlData>
            <textmd:textMD>
                <textmd:character_info>
                     <textmd:charset>UTF-8</textmd:charset>
                     <textmd:byte_order>little</textmd:byte_order>
                     <textmd:byte_size>8</textmd:byte_size>
                     <textmd:linebreak>LF</textmd:linebreak>
                </textmd:character_info>

                <textmd:language>ita</textmd:language>

                <textmd:markup_language>TEI Lite</textmd:markup_language>

                 <textmd:pageOrder>left-to-right</textmd:pageOrder>

                <textmd:characterFlow>left-to-right</textmd:characterFlow>
            </textmd:textMD>
          </xmlData>
      </mdWrap>
   </techMD>
</amdSec>
```

Example 9.5 *Technical metadata for text marked up in TEI Lite*

In this example we assume that we have transcribed the text of the libretto and marked it up in the encoding schema TEI Lite[C9.6] to allow full-text searching as a supplement to the viewing of page images. In this TextMD instance we record information on the character set used (**<textmd:character_info>**), the language of the libretto (**<textmd:language>**), the schema used to mark it up (**<textmd:markup_language>**), the order in which the pages should be presented (**<textmd:pageOrder>**) and the direction in which the characters on each page should be read (**<textmd:characterFlow>**). This is all very straightforward information but invaluable for enabling present and future users to read the text as we have encoded it.

9.3.1.3 Audio

Another format, another schema. Audio recordings have their own specific technical metadata requirements to ensure that they can be decoded and played without problems. Details of their encoding format (Ogg, MP3, WAV etc.) are an obvious requirement for this. It may also be useful to include information on the frequency with which an audio recording has been sampled, the number of bits per sample and any compression employed to reduce file sizes. It is also good practice to record details of analogue originals, such as vinyl records or tapes, when a digital file has been created from them. For an LP these may include the type of groove that the stylus traverses and its rotation speed (33, 45 or 78 revolutions per minute), for a tape its physical format (for instance open-reel or cassette) and number of tracks.

A further schema from the Library of Congress, AudioMD[S.2], is designed to meet these requirements. A simple instance of this for a digital audio file might look as shown in Example 9.6.

```
<amdSec ID="wdl-opl-aaaa-amd-0003">
   <techMD ID="wdl-opl-aaaa-tmd-0003">
      <mdWrap MDTYPE="LC-AV">
         <xmlData>
            <audiomd:AUDIOMD ANALOGDIGITALFLAG="FileDigital">
              <audiomd:fileData>
                 <audiomd:bitsPerSample>24</audiomd:bitsPerSample>
                 <audiomd:formatName>OGG</audiomd:formatName>
                 <audiomd:formatVersion>1.3.3</audiomd:formatVersion>
                 <audiomd:samplingFrequency>44.1</audiomd:samplingFrequency>
              </audiomd:fileData>
              <audiomd:audioInfo>
                 <audiomd:duration>00:30:00</audiomd:duration>
              </audiomd:audioInfo>
            </audiomd:AUDIOMD>
         </xmlData>
      </mdWrap>
   </techMD>
</amdSec>
```

Example 9.6 *Sample AudioMD instance*

One component that should be noted is **ANALOGDIGITALFLAG**, a mandatory attribute to the **<audiomd:AUDIOMD>** root element. This must have one of three settings to indicate whether the object is a digital file ('FileDigital') or a recording on a physical medium, either digital ('PhysDigital') or analogue ('Analog'). Within the root are nested top-level elements which contain technical information on the file (**<audiomd:fileData>**) and the recording itself (**<audiomd:audioInfo>**), where we record such basic information as its file format (OGG version 1.3.3.), its sampling frequency in kHz, the number of bits per sample and the duration of the recording. Other elements are available to document details of any calibration used and the physical make-up of an analogue original if it has been digitised from a source of this type. Although it is possible to go into considerable detail in an AudioMD instance, every higher-level element is optional, and so we can readily adjust the scope of the technical metadata registered here to suit our requirements.

9.3.1.4 Video

Video objects in a digital library present a comparable, if somewhat more complex, set of technical metadata requirements to their audio counterparts. In addition to recording details of file formats, compression, encoding algorithms (codecs) and sampling frequencies, we may also note such features as pixel and line counts, aspect ratios, frame rates and chrominance and luminance information. If our digital objects are derived from an analogue original we may also include such details as the latter's physical format (VHS or Betamax tape, for instance) and its generation (how many times it has been copied, and so has deteriorated in quality).

A companion to the previous schema, in this case called VideoMD[S.28], allows us to record all of this clearly and concisely. Once again a very basic example demonstrates how it does this (Example 9.7).

```
<amdSec ID="wdl-opl-aaaa-amd-0004">
   <techMD ID="wdl-opl-aaaa-tmd-0004">
      <mdWrap MDTYPE="LC-AV">
         <xmlData>
            <videomd:VIDEOMD ANALOGDIGITALFLAG="FileDigital">
             <videomd:fileData>
                 <videomd:sampling>4:2:2</videomd:sampling>
                 <videomd:bitsPerSample>24</videomd:bitsPerSample>
                 <videomd:compression>
                     <videomd:codecName>MPEG-4</videomd:codecName>
                 </videomd:compression>
                 <videomd:frameRate>30</videomd:frameRate>
             </videomd:fileData>
                  <videomd:videoInfo>
```

```
                <videomd:aspectRatio>4:3</videomd:aspectRatio>
                <videomd:duration>00:05:10</videomd:duration>
            </videomd:videoInfo>
          </videomd:VIDEOMD>
        </xmlData>
      </mdWrap>
    </techMD>
</amdSec>
```

Example 9.7 *Sample VideoMD instance*

VideoMD follows a similar pattern to AudioMD in its overall structure. It also includes a mandatory **ANALOGDIGITALFLAG** attribute to indicate the type of video object being described and a corresponding set of top-level elements providing technical information on the file (**<videomd:fileData>**) and details of the video recording itself (**<videoInfo>**). Others (not shown here) include calibration details and information on any analogue source. Here we use a small selection from its extensive element set to record details of the video's sampling, compression, frame rate, aspect ratio and duration. As is the case with AudioMD, we can choose the level of detail to record, as every higher-level element is optional.

9.3.2 Rights metadata

A final component of administrative metadata for which we may wish to consider an additional schema to supplement PREMIS is that of rights. As we saw in Example 9.4, PREMIS offers an extensive set of elements to record the legal framework within which IPR are asserted and the permissions given to those who interact with the contents of a collection. When it comes to granting rights, however, it can be a tad imprecise. A typical PREMIS rights granted statement takes this form:

```
<premis:rightsGranted>
    <premis:act>Display</premis:act>
    <premis:restriction>General public</premis:restriction>
</premis:rightsGranted>
```

The subelements of **<premis:rightsGranted>** use free text to specify which acts are allowed and what restrictions are imposed on them. This is fine within the context for which PREMIS Rights is primarily designed, the recording of permissions for actions needed to ensure the future preservation of digital objects. Human-readable text of this sort fulfils this purpose well enough. In a working system, however, where we wish to use this metadata to control access to the materials in a digital collection, something more precise and easier for machines to process may be required.

One schema which does this is METSRights[S.19]. As its name implies, this was devised in conjunction with METS to administer the IPR of digital objects and is, of course, an approved extension schema to it. A simple instance including and extending the rights granted under Creative Commons in Example 9.4 would look as shown in Example 9.8.

```
<amdSec ID="wdl-opl-aaaa-amd-0005">
   <rightsMD ID="wdl-opl-aaaa-rmd-0001">
      <mdWrap MDTYPE="METSRIGHTS">
         <xmlData>
            <rightsmd:RightsDeclarationMD RIGHTSCATEGORY="LICENSED">

               <rightsmd:Context CONTEXTCLASS="GENERAL PUBLIC">
                        <rightsmd:Permissions DISCOVER="true" DISPLAY="true"
                                              COPY="true" MODIFY="true"
                                              DUPLICATE="true" PRINT="true"/>
               </rightsmd:Context>

               <rightsmd:Context CONTEXTCLASS="OTHER"
                       OTHERCONTEXTTYPE="COMMERCIAL">
                       <rightsmd:Permissions DISCOVER="true" DISPLAY="true"
                                              COPY="false" MODIFY="false"
                                              DUPLICATE="false" PRINT="false"/>
               </rightsmd:Context>

              </rightsmd:RightsDeclarationMD>
            </xmlData>
        </mdWrap>
     </techMD>
</amdSec>
```

Example 9.8 *Sample METSRights instance*

The **<rightsmd:Context>** element and its subelement **<rightsmd:Permissions>** are the components that allow us to control the rights that we are willing to grant. **<rightsmd:Context>** allows us to specify the category of users to whom we are granting these. This is a closed list, consisting of a narrow range of categories slanted towards the academic sector (ACADEMIC USER, GENERAL PUBLIC, REPOSITORY MGR, MANAGED GRP, INSTITUTIONAL AFFILIATE). It can, however, be extended to define other groups as is done in the second **<rightsmd:Context>** element in Example 9.8, which specifies the limited rights granted to the commercial sector.

The **<rightsmd:Permissions>** element within each **<rightsmd:Context>** specifies the actions for which rights are granted. This is done by a series of attributes, one for each type of act, that are set to 'true' or 'false' accordingly. In Example 9.8 we grant under the terms of the Creative Commons licence an extensive set to members of the general public but a more restricted range (excluding copying, modifying, duplicating and printing) to commercial users. The acts that may be specified are once more a closed list but may be extended using an **OTHERPERMITTYPE** attribute, not shown here.

These attributes with their true/false flags are more precise than their corresponding free-text elements within PREMIS Rights, and so make it easier to manage controls on access to a digital object. For this reason it may be useful to include an additional METS **<rightsMD>** element with at least a skeletal instance of this schema as a supplement to the PREMIS Rights entity. METSRights does include additional elements which allow us to make a simple prose declaration of rights and specify rights holders, but PREMIS does the same with a more extensive set of elements and so is generally to be preferred for these. For this reason, METSRights is best recommended as a supplement to PREMIS, but not as a replacement for it, when this type of access control is required.

9.4 How much administrative metadata do we need?

It must be clear from the preceding discussion that we could potentially fill our records with a huge array of administrative metadata which dwarfs any other type. This is perhaps inevitable, since the administration of a complex (or even relatively simple) digital object requires a much more extensive range of metadata than is needed to put a book, CD or DVD on a library shelf. How much to include is a vexed question, and one for which there is no simple answer.

One overriding consideration will be the extent to which we wish to future-proof our collections and their metadata. Ensuring their long-term preservation requires some degree of guesswork as to their future viability and the metadata that will be needed to support this. Much of the technical metadata recorded in a MIX instance, for example, can be extracted using freely available software tools whose functionality we can reasonably assume will still be available in the future. We may decide, therefore, not to record this for all 500 images that make up a digitised book and to concentrate instead on metadata that cannot be derived in this way, for instance an enumeration of its digital provenance.

However, it is probably best to err on the side of inclusion if we can do so in a way which does not impede the creation and administration of a digital collection. If this metadata can be generated automatically using readily available tools and incorporated into workflows without too much trouble, it is better to include it. Verbosity is not necessarily a bad thing when it comes to metadata, and even a METS file which includes detailed MIX instances for all the images in a digitised book will not exhaust the storage and processing capacities of any viable digital library system. If the size and complexity of such a file does prove unwieldy we can always consider generating two files, one with minimal administrative metadata to support the operations of a working system and another with the full range to act as a preservation copy. Ideally we should generate the cut-down working version from its fully enumerated counterpart, for instance by an XSLT transformation. In this case the latter would stand as the canonical AIP record for the object.

The final decisions on what to include will inevitably depend on a pragmatic appraisal of what is possible within the context of a digital library's operations and resources. This is one area where it is impossible to give a simple answer or recommendation. It may be helpful, as it often is, to see what others have chosen to do. Many make their metadata policies and procedures freely available on the internet and it can be instructive to see what similar operations have implemented. But in the end it will be the individual circumstances of a collection that will be the determining factor.

10

Pathways to Interoperability

10.1 Introduction

This chapter is devoted to the third of the basic principles for a metadata strategy that were outlined in Chapter 3, 'Ensure interoperability'. As was shown there, an ideal state of interoperability would allow metadata to be exchanged with others without requiring any modification or manipulation; this demands more of it than interchange, which does require actions of this kind if it is to be comprehensible to the receiving system. To achieve interoperability requires a degree of congruence between the donor and recipient at two levels: syntactic, a mutually comprehensible encoding format; and semantic, an agreed set of meanings attached to metadata components which allows them to be understood by both parties.

Syntactic interoperability is best assured by the choice of XML as the encoding format for metadata. Its independence from specific software packages, its use of the universally decodable format of text as its foundation and its ability to combine the machine-processable and human-readable should ensure that metadata is comprehensible at a syntactical level when it is ingested into another system. The more demanding challenge is to enable the dialogue between two collections to operate in the semantic sphere as easily as in the syntactic.

We will have already made this easier by applying the other principles that have been followed throughout this book. Using standards whenever possible (Principle 7) is the most obvious of these: employing a metadata standard inevitably entails the adoption of a set of semantics that are known to and applied by others in a community. Controlling metadata content whenever possible (Principle 4) and imposing a logical system of identifiers (Principle 6) also assist here, the former by ensuring the consistent use of shared semantic schemes such as name and subject authorities, the latter by enabling the precise identification (for instance by URIs) of every metadata component. Ensuring software independence (Principle 5) enables metadata to transfer across systems on different platforms and ensuring the integrity of the metadata itself (Principle 8) makes it easier for others to trust its accuracy and authenticity.

The strategy outlined in this book and the principles that underlie it should, therefore, go a long way to rendering any metadata interoperable with others. Unfortunately this is not quite enough to allow us to rest on our laurels and declare a job done: problems will inevitably arise from the complexity of metadata in a digital library, and particularly from the degree of flexibility that must be built into it.

As a general principle the more rigid and controlled metadata is, the easier it is to transfer it to another system without modification. Library catalogue records are readily treated in this way because the MARC standard, despite its seeming complexity to a new learner, has a fixed structure of fields. In addition to this, its contents will conform to cataloguing rules such as AACR2 or RDA and control such components as names and subjects with published authorities and thesauri. These features have allowed the mass sharing of records, co-operative cataloguing and the creation of large union catalogues (such as WorldCat[C3.5]) which combine entries from thousands of libraries.

Digital library metadata does not have this degree of rigidity and so cannot be as unambiguously interpreted as a MARC record. We could perhaps employ this standard (as MARCXML) for descriptive metadata, but in general it is preferable to use a schema such as MODS which allows greater flexibility than a standard library catalogue record allows, so as to meet a potentially more complex set of requirements. The additional schemas needed to accommodate technical, digital provenance, rights and structural metadata all add to the mix and introduce new layers of complexity and variability. All of this makes it increasingly difficult for records to be exchanged and understood as they stand.

If the seamless interoperability of digital library metadata seems difficult to achieve, we can nonetheless alleviate the degree of effort that will be involved for any potential recipient to make a shared record usable.

10.2 Exchanging METS files

As its full name implies, the METS (Metadata Encoding and Transmission Standard) schema is designed to act as a conduit for transferring and exchanging metadata. A METS instance contains all of the relevant metadata for a digital object and may even hold the object itself encoded in Base64. It therefore makes a neat, discrete package which can be moved easily between collections. It is very unlikely, however, that such a file can be ingested directly by the system that receives it without some tinkering.

The problem arises from the degree of latitude built into the METS architecture. All of its top-level sections apart from the Structural Map are optional; this immediately introduces uncertainties as to what one will find when a METS file is received. Every section that is present in an instance offers abundant leeway in the way that it is arranged: this applies to almost everything, from the listing of files and their groupings in the File Section to the disposition of `<div>` elements in the Structural Map. The choice of extension schemas for the Descriptive and Administrative Metadata sections introduces a further layer of complexity, as they themselves are often flexible in the ways that they can be applied. Once these hurdles are overcome, it is also necessary to know what, if any, rules are applied to the content of the metadata itself.

All of this requires the recipient of a METS file to have some guidance as to its contents if they are to make sense of it. This need not necessarily entail much in the way of formality. If they know the overall architecture of METS and the instance is relatively conventional in the way that it is constructed, for instance if it employs only extension schemas authorised by METS, they may be able to interpret it relatively easily with only a little assistance from the donor to iron out any confusions or ambiguities. The first case study in the next chapter successfully uses this approach to share metadata with a union catalogue of similar resources.

However, it may be useful to go beyond ad hoc arrangements of this kind and document a METS application in a more formal manner. A mechanism for doing this exists in the form of what are called **METS Profiles**[C10.7]. These are XML documents conforming to a schema named, unsurprisingly, the METS Profile Schema which document an application of METS in a clear and systematic way. A METS record is said to conform to a given profile if it is constructed following the specifications that it contains.

A profile contains a significant amount of mandatory information, unlike METS itself, in order to make it useful as a medium for facilitating exchange. Its first part consists of the details needed to identify the profile itself, its intended use and its provenance. They include an abstract describing its nature and purpose, contact information for those maintaining it, its relationship to other profiles (if any) and a URI by which it may be uniquely identified. Its main body will then document the extension schemas employed for descriptive and administrative metadata, any cataloguing rules (including name authorities and subject thesauri) that are applied to these, and the overall structure of the METS instance, including the organisation of the Structural Map. Finally, an example METS instance conforming to the profile must be included as an appendix.

Including a METS profile when sharing records conforming to it certainly makes life easier for any recipients. Its rigidly defined format and comprehensive requirements for documenting how METS is applied provide one of the best mechanisms for communicating this important information. However, it does not allow records to be exchanged seamlessly and with no human intervention, something which would be required for full interoperability. They are not, to use the technical term, machine actionable: we cannot give a remote system a METS instance and its corresponding profile and leave it to interpret and ingest it properly. They are merely designed to make it easier for the system administrators and programmers to do their job enabling this to happen.

It is nonetheless a worthwhile exercise to compile a METS profile, particularly to ensure that one's metadata records are comprehensible to future users, and a digital preservation strategy should certainly consider doing this as part of its documentation procedures. It is also recommended to share any profile that we compile with others in the digital library community. The primary mechanism to do this is to deposit it with the Library of Congress, who maintain a publicly accessible register of these on its METS Profiles website[C10.6]. This is done by emailing it to an address provided by the Library, following which it is checked for conformance and added to the register after any required amendments have been made. The website presents the schema in a more human-friendly form than raw XML and also indexes it by such features as its extension schemas, controlled vocabularies and structural arrangement.

As well as a way of sharing the documentation of a METS application and ensuring that it will be accessible to others, the register of profiles can also be an excellent resource to consult when designing an implementation of the standard. It can be very helpful to see how others have done this, which schemas they have used, how they have dealt with any issues and so on. It may save considerable time and effort, particularly in the early stages of getting to know this potentially complex schema. As well as using METS Profiles for guidance of this kind, it is also possible to adopt an existing one in its entirety, should it meet all of our requirements. If we do this, we can record which has been chosen by adding to the **<mets>** root a simple **PROFILE** attribute containing its URI from the Library of Congress website, as shown in Example 10.1.

```
<mets xmlns="http://www.loc.gov/METS/"
      xmlns:xsi="http://www.w3.org/2001/XMLSchema-instance"
      xmlns:mods="http://www.loc.gov/mods/v3"
      xmlns:mix="http://www.loc.gov/standards/mix/v20"
      xsi:schemaLocation="http://www.loc.gov/METS/
          http://www.loc.gov/standards/mets/mets.xsd
          http://www.loc.gov/mods/v3 http://www.loc.gov/standards/mods/v3/
              mods-3-5.xsd
          http://www.loc.gov/standards/mix/v20
          http://www.loc.gov/standards/mix/mix.xsd"
      OBJID="wdl-opl-aaaa"
      PROFILE="http://www.loc.gov/mets/profiles/00000001.xml">
```

Example 10.1 *METS root element (from Example 6.1) with PROFILE attribute*

We can, and indeed should, add this attribute to our own METS instances if we compile and register a profile instead of following someone else's. This will provide an unambiguous linkage between a record and the documentation that explains how it should be interpreted.

10.3 Metadata harvesting

An alternative to supplying METS files directly is to convert them into another format designed specifically for the sharing of metadata. One standard which was conceived for this purpose is the Open Archives Initiative Protocol for Metadata Harvesting (OAI-PMH)[S.21]. As its name implies, it is intended to support the *harvesting* of metadata, the automated retrieval of large numbers of records for ingest into an archive. Many digital repositories make their metadata available through OAI-PMH, including: Europeana[C3.2], an extensive collection of cultural heritage materials from European museums, galleries, libraries and archives; Ethos[C10.5], the British Library's archive of doctoral theses; and arXiv[C10.1], the most extensive open-access repository of preprints in the sciences.

The harvesting of records in OAI-PMH is done automatically by transmitting a request to a repository which sends back an XML instance conforming to the OAI-PMH schema. A very basic record of this type, once more for the oratorio introduced in Chapter 6, would look as shown in Example 10.2.

```
<OAI-PMH>
    <responseDate>2020-09-01T19:20:30Z</responseDate>
    <request metadataPrefix="oai_dc"/>
    <GetRecord>
        <record>
            <header>
                <identifier>http://wdl.warburg.sas.ac.uk/id/wdl/opl/aaaa
                    </identifier>
                <datestamp>2020-09-15</datestamp>
            </header>

            <metadata>
                <oai_dc:dc>
                    <dc:title>Il trionfo della morte per il peccato d'Adamo:
                          oratorio da farsinella chiesa della Confraternità
                          della Morte l'anno 1677
                    </dc:title>
                    <dc:subject>Oratorios</dc:subject>
                    <dc:description>Posto in musica dal p.f. Bonaventura
                           Aleotti da Palermo franciscano organista nella
                           sudetta Chiesa, e dedicato all'illustrissima
                           signora la signora Artemisia Montevecchi
                           Baldeschi</dc:description>
```

```
                <dc:type>Libretti</dc:type>
                <dc:format>Microfilm</dc:format>
                <dc:creator>Aliotti, Bonaventura, approximately 1640-
                     <approximately 1690</dc:creator>
                <dc:date>1677</dc:date>
                <dc:language>Italian</dc:language>
             </oai_dc:dc>
         </metadata>
      </record>
   </GetRecord>
</OAI-PMH>
```

Example 10.2 *Sample OAI-PMH record*

This sample record, which for the sake of clarity omits namespace declarations and schema locations from its root element, represents the minimum metadata that must be present for a viable OAI-PMH record. At its centre is the set nested within the top-level **<GetRecord>** element, which contains the descriptive metadata and identifying information that we wish to share. The descriptive metadata is encoded in Simple DC. OAI-PMH mandates this as the primary schema here, although it is possible to include more extensive metadata in other schemas as supplements to this. Also mandatory are the **<identifier>** element for the object (in this case its URI) and a **<datestamp>** noting when this record was created.

Everything in **<GetRecord>** can be generated from a METS instance. The remaining two elements, **<responseDate>** and **<request>**, are generated by the provider's system when it receives a harvesting request. The first records the date and time that it was received and acted upon, the second any information required by the receiving system to make sense of it (here only the barebones information of the prefix used to identify the descriptive metadata schema).

To share metadata with OAI-PMH requires a system to be in place to receive and despatch harvesting requests; it is not enough simply to run a METS file through an XSLT transformation to generate records conforming to its schema. Many well-known repository systems, including the open-source DSpace[C10.2] and Eprints[C10.4] packages, can handle requests of this kind, so making it relatively easy to share metadata in this way. For those not using a system which offers this facility it will be a judgement call, based on their available resources (financial and otherwise), whether it is worth investing in this approach. However, for organisations maintaining collections on the scale of some of the providers mentioned earlier it may well be a viable option, if they have a suitable software architecture in place, to spread their metadata and contents more widely.

10.4 The Semantic Web

The methodology which has perhaps received the most attention for enhancing the interoperability of both data and metadata is known as the Resource Description Framework (RDF)[C10.10]. This was first devised in the late 1990s by the World Wide Web Consortium as a simple means of recording metadata that is independent of proprietary systems (World Wide Web Consortium 1997) and later found a central role in Tim Berners-Lee's conception of the Semantic Web (Berners-Lee, Hendler, and Lassila 2001). RDF is an abstract model for defining metadata which is independent of any given syntax; it may, however, be expressed in XML, and so is readily generated from METS instances.

The central idea of RDF is very straightforward: it defines semantic linkages between concepts in statements which emulate a simple sentence. In such a statement, a 'subject' is linked to an 'object' by a 'predicate' which articulates the meaning of their relationship. For instance, we could say in relation to the oratorio that 'Il trionfo della morte ...' 'has creator' 'Bonaventura Aliotti', or as represented diagrammatically in Figure 10.1.

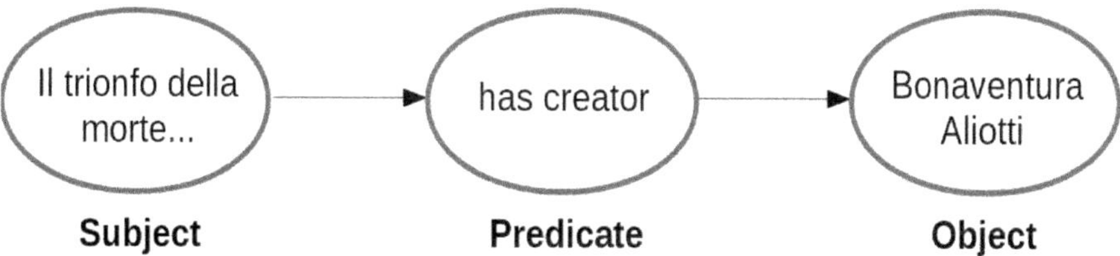

Figure 10.1 *Simple RDF 'triple'*

This tripartite statement is generally known as a 'triple': in it the predicate serves as the semantic linkage between the subject and object, in this case connecting the work to its creator.

A triple of this type is easy for humans to read and decipher but too imprecise to be readily interoperable. What exactly is meant here by 'Il trionfo della morte ...'? Is it this oratorio or another piece with the same name? If it is this one, is it meant in the rather abstract sense as a 'work' or as its rather more concrete digitised version? What exactly does 'has creator' mean and who is 'Bonaventura Aliotti'? The way to get round these issues is to substitute the strings in a triple with URIs (Figure 10.2 on the next page).

Here each component is replaced by a URI which identifies it precisely. The subject is defined by a URI for the version of the oratorio in the digital library, the predicate by one which marks it out as having a 'creator' as defined by DCMI Metadata Terms[S.9] and the object as the Bonaventura Aliotti identified by an entry in LCNAF. What this triple loses in user-

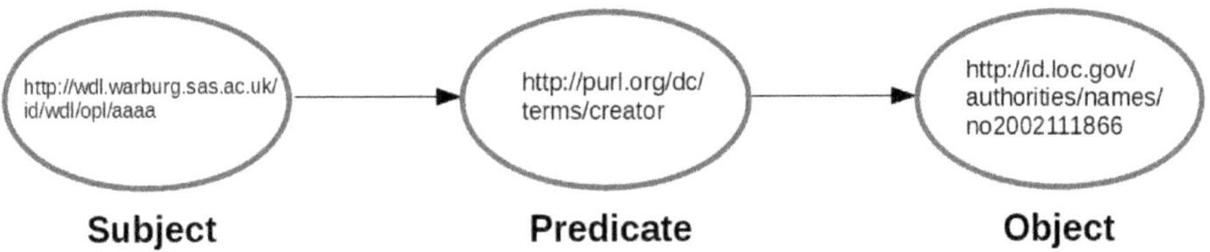

Figure 10.2 *The same RDF 'triple' with URIs for subject, predicate and object*

friendly human readability it gains in the precision with which the content of each part is unambiguously defined.

The idea behind using RDF as the foundation on which the Semantic Web is built is that, by reducing semantic relationships to these small molecules of metadata in which each constituent atom is identified by a unique URI, it should be possible to treat the entire internet as a single dataset. In this way the barriers between silos of information would fade away to create a universal reservoir of data and metadata across which searches could be conducted with ease. An RDF-specific query language, known as the SPARQL Protocol and RDF Query Language (SPARQL)[C10.12], was devised and rapidly adopted as a means of interrogating this all-encompassing web of semantically linked data.

That was the theory behind Berners-Lee's vision. The reality has been less impressive, as he has himself acknowledged (Shadbolt, Hall and Berners-Lee 2006), and the universal dataset has not arisen, for reasons too complex to be gone into here. Nonetheless, there can be some value in considering RDF as a medium for sharing metadata. The simplicity of the conventions that it defines for expressing semantics and its ability to encode metadata that conforms to any scheme ensures that it is readily interchangeable if not seamlessly interoperable. For this reason many major repositories, including the Library of Congress and the British Library, make their metadata available in this way.

There are several options for representing metadata in RDF. One of the simplest, known as N-Triples, lists the three components of a triple separated by spaces. Using this format, we could represent the statement from Figure 10.2 as shown in Example 10.3.

```
<http://wdl.warburg.sas.ac.uk/id/wdl/opl/aaaa>
<http://purl.org/dc/terms/creator>
        <http://id.loc.gov/authorities/names/no2002111866> .
```

Example 10.3 *RDF triple presented in N-Triples, each component represented by a URI*

This example uses a line break for legibility, but in practice the triple would be presented as a single line with a space and full stop (.) to mark the end of the statement. The subject, predicate and object are listed in that order and each is enclosed in angled brackets to indicate that it is defined by a URI. It is also possible to include literal strings in a triple. For instance, if we wish to supply the title in a human-readable form, the N-Triple would include it in inverted commas as shown in Example 10.4.

```
<http://wdl.warburg.sas.ac.uk/id/wdl/opl/aaaa> <http://purl.org/dc/terms/title>
"Il trionfo della morte ..." .
```

Example 10.4 *An N-Triple triple with a string for its object*

A more convenient option, given that our metadata is already encoded in XML, is to furnish its RDF rendition in the same syntax. Fortunately, this is easily managed as a specification exists to represent RDF triples in this way[C10.11]. We could present the DC record from Chapter 7 (Example 7.1) as shown in Example 10.5.

```
<rdf:RDF xmlns:rdf="http://www.w3.org/1999/02/22-rdf-syntax-ns#"
         xmlns:dc="http://purl.org/dc/terms/">
  <rdf:Description rdf:about="http://wdl.warburg.sas.ac.uk/id/wdl/opl/aaaa">
        <dc:title>Il trionfo della morte per il peccato d'Adamo: oratorio da
                farsi nella chiesa della Confraternità  della Morte l'anno
                1677</dc:title>
        <dc:subject>Oratorios</dc:subject>
        <dc:description>Posto in musica dal p.f. Bonaventura Aleotti da Palermo
                        Franciscano organista nella sudetta Chiesa,
                        e dedicato all'illustrissima signora la
                        signora Artemisia Montevecchi
                        Baldeschi</dc:description>
        <dc:type>Libretti</dc:type>
        <dc:format>Microfilm</dc:format>
        <dc:creator>Aliotti, Bonaventura, approximately 1640-approximately
                1690</dc:creator>
        <dc:rights>This copy is licensed under a Creative Commons Attribution-
                             NonCommercial 3.0 Unported License</dc:rights>
        <dc:date>1677</dc:date>
        <dc:identifier>wdl-opl-aaaa</dc:identifier>
        <dc:identifier>https://wdl.warburg.sas.ac.uk/islandora/object/
                islandora%3A3790</dc:identifier>
        <dc:language>Italian</dc:language>
        <dc:publisher>Nella stampa camerale</dc:publisher>
  </rdf:Description>
</rdf:RDF>
```

Example 10.5 *Dublin Core record in RDF/XML*

Although this looks like a standard XML instance, it is in fact a series of triples. All have the same subject ('http://wdl.warburg.sas.ac.uk/id/wdl/opl/aaaa') which is contained in the **rdf:about** attribute of the

<rdf:Description> element. The predicate of each triple is then recorded in the subelements nested within this (**<dc:title>**, **<dc:subject>**, etc.) and its object in the string that forms the content of each of these. The triple from Example 10.4, therefore, is represented by:

```
<rdf:Description
rdf:about="http://wdl.warburg.sas.ac.uk/id/wdl/opl/aaaa">
```

and its first subelement:

```
<dc:title>Il trionfo della morte per il peccato d'Adamo:
oratorio da farsi nella chiesa della Confraternità della
Morte l'anno 1677</dc:title>
```

These subelements use the abbreviation for the DC namespace defined in the **xmlns:dc** attribute of the **<rdf:RDF>** root element. The full URI that this one represents is `http://purl.org/dc/terms/title`, the predicate of Example 10.4.

A metadata record such as this will generally use strings for the content of each triple's object, but it is also possible to replace these with URIs. The syntax in this case is slightly different: if we were to represent the composer by his LCNAF identifier instead of a string, the **<dc:creator>** element would instead take this form:

```
<dc:creator
resource="http://id.loc.gov/authorities/names/no2002111866"/>
```

In all, this short sample of XML contains 12 triples which together make up the full DC record.

If these RDF records are to be interoperable to any extent we have to make sure that the predicates in each triple are readily understood by their intended recipients; they cannot be assigned arbitrarily. The choice of allowable predicates for a given scheme is defined in what is technically known as an *ontology*. This rather grandiose term was defined by the computer scientist Tom Gruber, who first applied it to information science as a 'specification of a conceptualization' (Gruber 1993, 199), a terse way of saying that it is a series of concepts (known technically as 'classes') and their semantic relationships ('properties') which together delineate a subject area. A metadata scheme attempts to do just this, and so is a prime example of an ontology.

Ontologies at their simplest may be no more than a list of concepts with little in the way of interrelationships defined between them; DC is itself a very basic ontology of this kind. Others can be much more complex, introducing dense webs of classes and properties to express fully the nuances of a semantic domain. An XML-based standard known as the Web Ontology Language (OWL)[C10.13] is used to define ontologies in a way which makes them machine readable and interoperable, and sits along RDF as the second foundation on which the Semantic Web is meant to be built.

Many of the metadata schemes mentioned in this book have been published as ontologies, in most cases formally defined in OWL; they include Dublin Core[C10.3], MODS[C10.8], and PREMIS[C10.9]. Getting to grips with these is complex and probably not worth the time and effort involved for the average digital librarian, but in some cases tools exist to generate RDF/XML conforming to them from their corresponding XML instances. The Library of Congress, for instance, has created an XSLT stylesheet to do this for MODS[C10.8]. Using such tools as exist (and more are being developed all the time) can be a relatively straightforward way of exploiting the interoperable potential of RDF.

10.5 Conclusion

It should be clear from the above discussion that achieving interoperability can be a somewhat involved business for metadata of the complexity that is likely to be found in a digital library. Seamless interoperability where metadata can be ingested by a remote system without any modification requires a perfect congruence between the donor's and recipient's syntax and semantics, an even more challenging prospect. If perfection is difficult to achieve, a reasonable degree of interoperability is still feasible, given metadata that follows most of the principles enumerated in the previous chapters.

METS is a safe choice for ensuring a relatively smooth transfer of metadata, despite the caveats mentioned earlier. Its syntactical embedding in XML, one of the most readily exchangeable formats, and its ability to contain all of the metadata (and even data) for the most complex of digital objects in a single, discrete package greatly simplify the mechanics of any exchange. Employing established standards with widely understood semantics within the METS architecture is an important secondary step towards facilitating frictionless transfers, as is the use of content rules, name authorities and subject thesauri.

Any problems that arise from the inherent flexibility of these standards, particularly METS itself, require communication between donor and recipient, either through formal procedures such as METS Profiles or less circumscribed methods of documenting the ways in which they are deployed. Conversion to formats such as OAI-PMH and RDF/XML is also possible when we have the necessary infrastructures to support them. Following this METS-based strategy should, therefore, ensure that our metadata is not confined to silos when we wish it to make its way in the wider world.

11

Implementing the Strategy: Two Case Studies

11.1 Introduction

In this chapter two cases studies are presented to demonstrate this metadata strategy as implemented in a working environment. Both are taken from digital collections based at the Warburg Institute in London, UK. The first of these, the Warburg Digital Library (WDL), is a set of digitised books from the Institute's library. The second, the Warburg's Iconographic Database, is an image archive based on its extensive photographic collection of works of art. These initiatives employ the first two approaches to a metadata strategy outlined in Chapter 4. The Digital Library relies on 'off the shelf' standards (such as MODS), while the Iconographic Database uses an internally designed architecture based on CIDOC-CRM which is then serialised into these; in both cases, METS is used as the overarching architecture within which the metadata is packaged.

The description of practices in these case studies is not intended to certify them as comprehensive exemplars of excellence but, rather as demonstrations of how the standards and methods outlined in this book may be applied in operational repositories. The first of these, while implementing most of the principles discussed here, currently lacks in particular the extensive range of administrative metadata necessary for long-term preservation. The second is a work in progress at the time of publication, to the extent that it has reached the stage of implementing its metadata architecture but the system to deliver it remains under development. Despite these caveats, it is hoped that a discussion of the practical applications of this strategy, particularly the workflows involved in creating metadata that conforms to the standards outlined, will demonstrate that what is proposed here is readily achievable within any digital library.

11.2 The Warburg Digital Library[C11.4]

The Warburg Institute is part of the University of London's School of

Advanced Study, a centre for postgraduate study and research in the humanities which consists of eight member institutes. The Warburg's area of academic activity concentrates on interdisciplinary studies, particularly those concerned with the visual arts. It is named after the art historian Aby Warburg (1866–1929), a German scholar whose primary interest was the influence of the Classical Greek and Roman traditions on later cultures. It was he who founded a library in Hamburg in 1926 which moved to London in 1933 and formed the basis of the current collections of the Warburg Institute.

The WDL is a relatively new initiative which began operations in 2016 as part of a strategic plan to open up the Institute and its work to a wider circle of interested parties than those who can visit it in person. Although in the past some materials from its collections have been scanned and made available as PDFs, the WDL was established to initiate a more coherent approach to raising its digital profile. This plan included a new delivery mechanism and moving its metadata to community-established standards which would allow it to be shared more widely and ensure its longevity.

The platform chosen for the WDL's collections is Islandora[C11.3], an open-source system for the management and delivery of digital resources. This is designed to act as a front-end to the repository system Fedora Commons[C11.1], a bare-bones architecture on which applications of this type may be built. It is readily configurable to fit in with the house style of a digital library's host institution and offers multiple entry points into the collections that it hosts, including browsable indexes, simple and advanced (Boolean) searches and list or grid views for navigating the collections themselves. Figure 11.1 opposite shows the home page of the WDL as configured for the Institute's branding.

Islandora offers a number of 'solution packs', a rather grandiose term for interfaces presenting different types of material. These include packs for still images, newspapers, audio and video. The 'book solution pack', which is used for the WDL collections, allows users to browse through the pages of a book, navigate it by thumbnails or a table of contents, view its catalogue record and download a PDF of the complete volume (Figure 11.2).

Underlying the WDL is a metadata architecture that implements most of the strategy outlined in this book; where it is currently lacking is in its relatively limited set of administrative metadata. This will be rectified in its next stage of development.

At the core of this architecture is the system of identifiers outlined in Chapter 4 and detailed in Figure 4.5.

This hierarchical system of identifiers labels every component of both metadata and data, dictating the Digital Library's directory structure, its file-naming conventions and the internal system of IDs used in its metadata. It

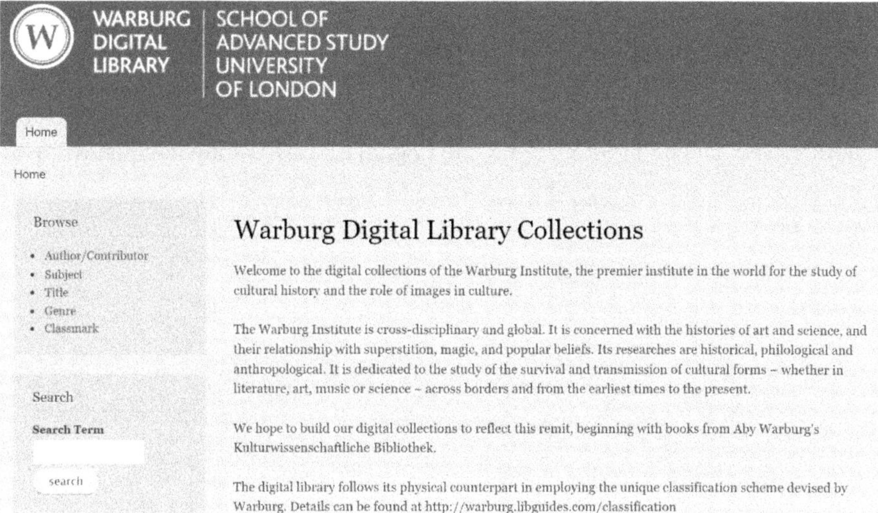

WARBURG DIGITAL LIBRARY
SCHOOL OF ADVANCED STUDY UNIVERSITY OF LONDON
Home
Home
Browse
Author/Contributor
Subject
Title
Genre
Classmark
Search
Search Term
search
Warburg Digital Library Collections
Welcome to the digital collections of the Warburg Institute, the premier institute in the world for the study of cultural history and the role of images in culture.
The Warburg Institute is cross-disciplinary and global. It is concerned with the histories of art and science, and their relationship with superstition, magic, and popular beliefs. Its researches are historical, philological and anthropological. It is dedicated to the study of the survival and transmission of cultural forms – whether in literature, art, music or science – across borders and from the earliest times to the present.
We hope to build our digital collections to reflect this remit, beginning with books from Aby Warburg's Kulturwissenschaftliche Bibliothek.
The digital library follows its physical counterpart in employing the unique classification scheme devised by Warburg. Details can be found at http://warburg.libguides.com/classification

Figure 11.1 *The Warburg Digital Library home page*

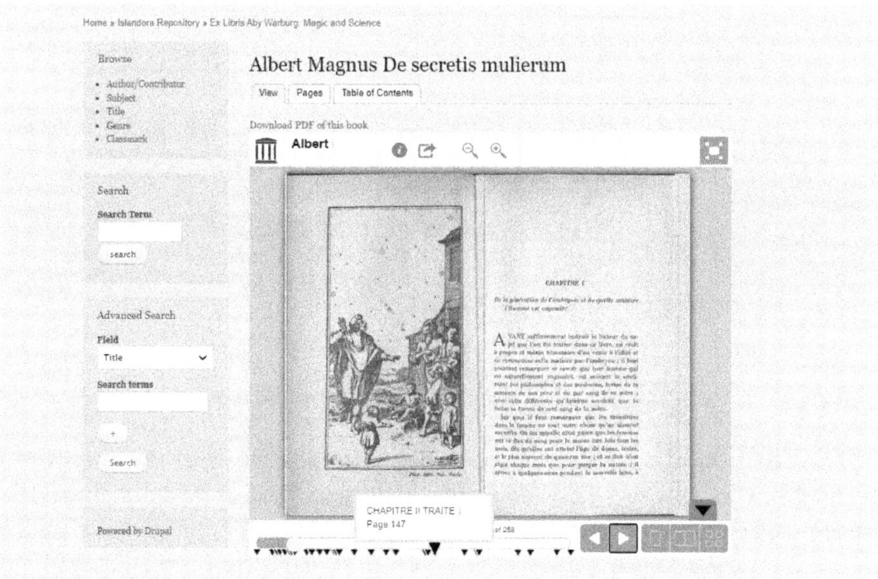

Figure 11.2 *Browsing through a book in the Warburg Digital Library*

ensures that the name of each file is stamped with its place in the overall hierarchy, which alleviates any possibility of it getting lost when, as it inevitably will, it is moved around over the course of its lifetime.

The Digital Library's metadata employs METS as its primary packaging medium and for its structural metadata. MODS is used to record the descriptive metadata for each object: this is embedded within the Descriptive Metadata (**<dmdSec>**) section of its METS instance. This MODS record is itself generated from a MARCXML file, catalogued to the AACR2 or (for more recent works) RDA cataloguing standards. The overall workflow which generates the data and metadata for the Digital Library is shown in Figure 11.3.

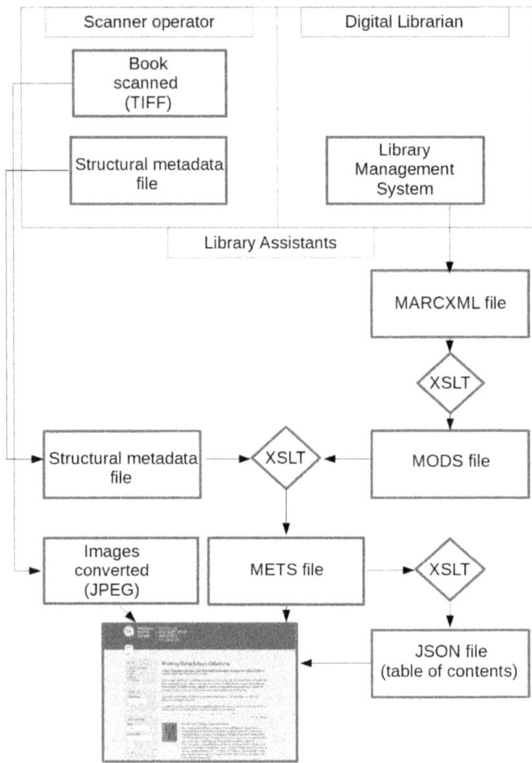

Figure 11.3 *Metadata generation workflow for the Warburg Digital Library*

The creation of a digital object begins with the work of the Institute's scanner operator, who scans a book into high-resolution archival-quality TIFF images. Once the item has been digitised in this way, he/she documents its internal arrangement by creating a record of its structural metadata: this is done by creating a simple XML file, edited from a template, which enumerates its principal sections (usually its chapters) and the page numbers or other designations within each of these (Example 11.1).

```
<structure>
      <div1 LABEL="Cover">
          <div2 LABEL="Front cover"/>
          <div2 LABEL="Endpaper"/>
```

```
        <div2 LABEL="Flyleaf"/>
        <div2 LABEL="Flyleaf"/>
    </div1>

    <div1 LABEL="Front Matter">
        <div2 LABEL="Title page"/>
        <div2 LABEL="[Page 2]"/>
    </div1>

    <div1 LABEL="[Dedication]">
        <div2 LABEL="Page 3"/>
        <div2 LABEL="Page 4"/>
    </div1>

    <div1 LABEL="Cortese Lettore">
        <div2 LABEL="Page 5"/>
    </div1>

    [etc..]

</structure>
```

Example 11.1 *Sample structural metadata file (truncated)*

In this file, which conforms to an in-house XML schema, each section of the work is represented by a top-level **<div1>** element within which a sequence of **<div2>**s is nested, each of which corresponds to a single page image. Each element has a **LABEL** attribute which contains the text that the delivery system will present to the user in a table of contents. This file is created using the XML editing software OxygenXML and validated against the in-house schema.

At this point the work passes to two library assistants who are responsible for the processing and uploading of objects into the Digital Library itself. They run scripts which convert the TIFF images into much-compressed JPEGs for ingest into Islandora. The same scripts also initiate XSLT transformations which produce the METS file for the item as a whole.

Two components feed into this METS record. The first is the structural metadata file produced by the scanner operator. The second is a MARCXML file for the object's descriptive metadata downloaded previously from the Institute's online catalogue[C11.6] by its Digital Librarian. This is initially converted to MODS by an XSLT stylesheet provided for this purpose by the Library of Congress. This MODS file is then integrated with its structural metadata counterpart to produce the METS instance: the first of these is embedded in its Descriptive Metadata section, the second is translated into its Structural Map.

One final XSLT transformation is required to generate the remaining metadata needed to ingest the object into the delivery system. Islandora offers an interactive table of contents function. To enable this requires the information on chapter headings and pages recorded in the METS Structural Map to be converted to JSON (JavaScript Object Notation), a commonly used format for expressing data fields, their values and their hierarchical relationships. A simple XSLT stylesheet generates the required file from the **<div>** elements in the Structural Map (Example 11.2).

```
{
        "table_of_contents": [

        {
            "level": 1,
            "pagenum": "1",
            "title": "Cover",
            "type": "chapter"
            },
                {
                "level": 2,
                "pagenum": "1",
                "title": "Front cover",
                "type": "page"
                },
                    {
                "level": 2,
                "pagenum": "2",
                "title": "Endpaper",
                "type": "page"
                },
                    {
                "level": 2,
                "pagenum": "3",
                "title": "Flyleaf",
                "type": "page"
                },
                    {
                "level": 2,
                "pagenum": "4",
                "title": "Flyleaf",
                "type": "page"
                }
            [etc…]
        ]
}
```

Example 11.2 *Opening of JSON table of contents file generated from METS Structural Map*

At this point all is ready for ingest into Islandora. The JPEG images are put into a ZIP file which is uploaded to the system, the MODS components of the METS file generate the descriptive metadata that it uses for searching and browsing and the JSON file is all that is needed for the table of contents function to operate. Once these files have been uploaded and the new object has been created, all except the METS instance can be deleted and this remaining file is uploaded to the archival storage facility on which the original TIFF images for the object are stored, to act as its canonical metadata record.

At this point two simple operations remain to be carried out. The first is to amend the record for the digitised book on the Library's online catalogue; this is edited to provide a link to the copy on the Digital Library's platform. The second is to invoke the interoperable potential of METS by sharing the metadata record with the Getty Research Portal[C3.3], a union catalogue of digitised resources in art history, architecture and material culture to which the Warburg Institute has been contributing for many years. The METS file for the digital object is uploaded to a shared directory on the Institute's archival storage facility from which it is retrieved by the Getty in a harvesting procedure carried out on a regular basis. This file contains all of the descriptive metadata required for the Portal to create an entry for the object and the location information needed to provide a direct link to it.

As was mentioned earlier in this chapter, these workflows do not include to any great extent the generation of administrative metadata; in particular, technical and digital provenance information on the still images that constitute the digital objects are both missing. These will be introduced into the Digital Library in the next stage of metadata implementation. A retrospective process will generate technical metadata for the images using the open-source utility ImageMagick[C11.2]; this will then be incorporated into the METS records. This useful piece of software can also determine when a file was created or converted from another format, and will enable provenance metadata for each image to be included as well. Workflows for the creation of new objects will also be changed to generate this information on-the-fly and integrate it into METS instances as they are compiled.

This case study shows that the diverse range of metadata required for objects in a digital library can be generated relatively simply. The primary mechanisms that drive most of the transformations required are XSLT and simple command languages such as bash, neither of which requires advanced programming skills to achieve the levels of sophistication demanded by the processes described here. All of the tools needed to handle the processing of metadata and images are open source and free to implement: Saxon[C5.2], a Java-based package, carries out the XSLT transformations and ImageMagick is used to convert the image files from TIFF to JPEG. All of this should demonstrate that implementing an integrated metadata and data environment of this type can be achieved without recourse to proprietary software.

11.3 The Warburg Iconographic Database[C11.5]

The next case study illustrates the second approach to a metadata strategy outlined in Chapter 4, mapping out an architecture and serialising it into existing standards. This is the course undertaken by the Warburg Institute's other substantial digital collection, its Iconographic Database. This is a compilation of over 100,000 images of works of art arranged, almost uniquely for a resource of this kind, by iconographic subject, the content of the image rather than its artist, title or other more commonly used entry points to photographic archives. In adopting this arrangement it emulates its physical counterpart, the Photographic Collection housed within the Institute's building.

This collection was started by Aby Warburg in the 1880s but has been much extended since it moved to London in 1933. It owes much of its shape and form to the ideas and work of the art historian Rudolf Wittkower (1901–71), whose most significant innovation was the creation of an extensive taxonomy of iconographic subjects which forms the basis of the arrangement of both the physical and digital collections. This currently extends to 18,000 terms arranged in up to eight levels of hierarchy, so allowing very detailed descriptions of the iconographic content of each image.

From its inception the database itself and the taxonomy that underlies it have been housed in relational tables in the database management system mySql. They are accessed by two interfaces, the first a public-access entry point for searching, browsing and displaying content and the second a staff-only gateway for creating and editing records. The code that controls these is written in the scripting language PHP (PHP: Hypertext Preprocessor). The database and scripts were all designed in-house by the Deputy Curator of the Photographic Collection.

This platform has accommodated the Database for the ten years since its creation but is problematic for several reasons, the most pertinent of which are its lack of adherence to established metadata standards and its consequently circumscribed potential for interoperability. For these reasons it was decided that the Database's underlying metadata would be revised to rectify these deficiencies in conjunction with a redesign of its platform. This would involve the two stages outlined in Chapter 4: the design of a metadata model encapsulating a new architecture and its serialisation into established standards.

The new architecture was based on CIDOC-CRM[S.4], the conceptual model that has embedded itself firmly within the cultural heritage sector.

Using this as a framework during the mapping out of core facets and their interrelationships clarified thinking and also ensured some degree of interoperability, at the most abstract level, with others who had adopted the same standard. The result of this was a diagrammatic representation of the new metadata architecture (called here a 'Data Model') (Figure 11.4 on the next page).

Each rectangle in this diagram contains a facet (within parentheses) and its associated CIDOC-CRM class (in bold on the line above). Every 'property', the semantic linkage between these facets, is taken from CIDOC-CRM and is shown within an oval between the two that it connects.

At the centre of the diagram are the four core concepts that together encapsulate the metadata for an image in the Database; these are the image itself as an abstract concept, the work of art that it documents, the photograph on which the image is physically recorded and the digital file in which the image is stored when the photo is scanned. CIDOC-CRM helpfully distinguishes the **Symbolic Object** that is the image, the **Man-Made Thing**s that constitute the photograph and work of art and the **Information Object** that is the digital file. This division is useful, as each requires a distinctive set of metadata to enable it to fulfil its descriptive or technical functions in the Database.

The image, a Symbolic Object in CIDOC-CRM, is the core facet to which subject headings from the taxonomy are attached. It is to this abstract component that these terms, which are themselves conceptual rather than substantive, are most appropriately linked. The more concrete Man-Made Thing that is the work of art is correspondingly linked to a more tangible set of metadata concepts which include such features as the artist who created it, key dates in its history and, in cases where the image is taken from a published book, bibliographic details of the volume in which it can be found. The photo, the other Man-Made Thing, is linked to such facets as the photographer who took it, its identifier (such as a negative number) and its copyright owner. The Information Object, the digital file, similarly receives an appropriate set of metadata, including details of any restrictions on how it may be accessed.

CIDOC-CRM proved very useful in differentiating between these central facets and so clarifying the shape of the metadata linkages that stem from them. Preventing these ontologically distinct concepts from becoming blurred ensured that the model has an overall coherence that it might have lacked if drawn up on a blank sheet.

This was only the start to implementing this architecture; the next step was to translate or serialise it to XML. One possibility was to create an in-house schema to represent these facets and interrelationships, a methodology

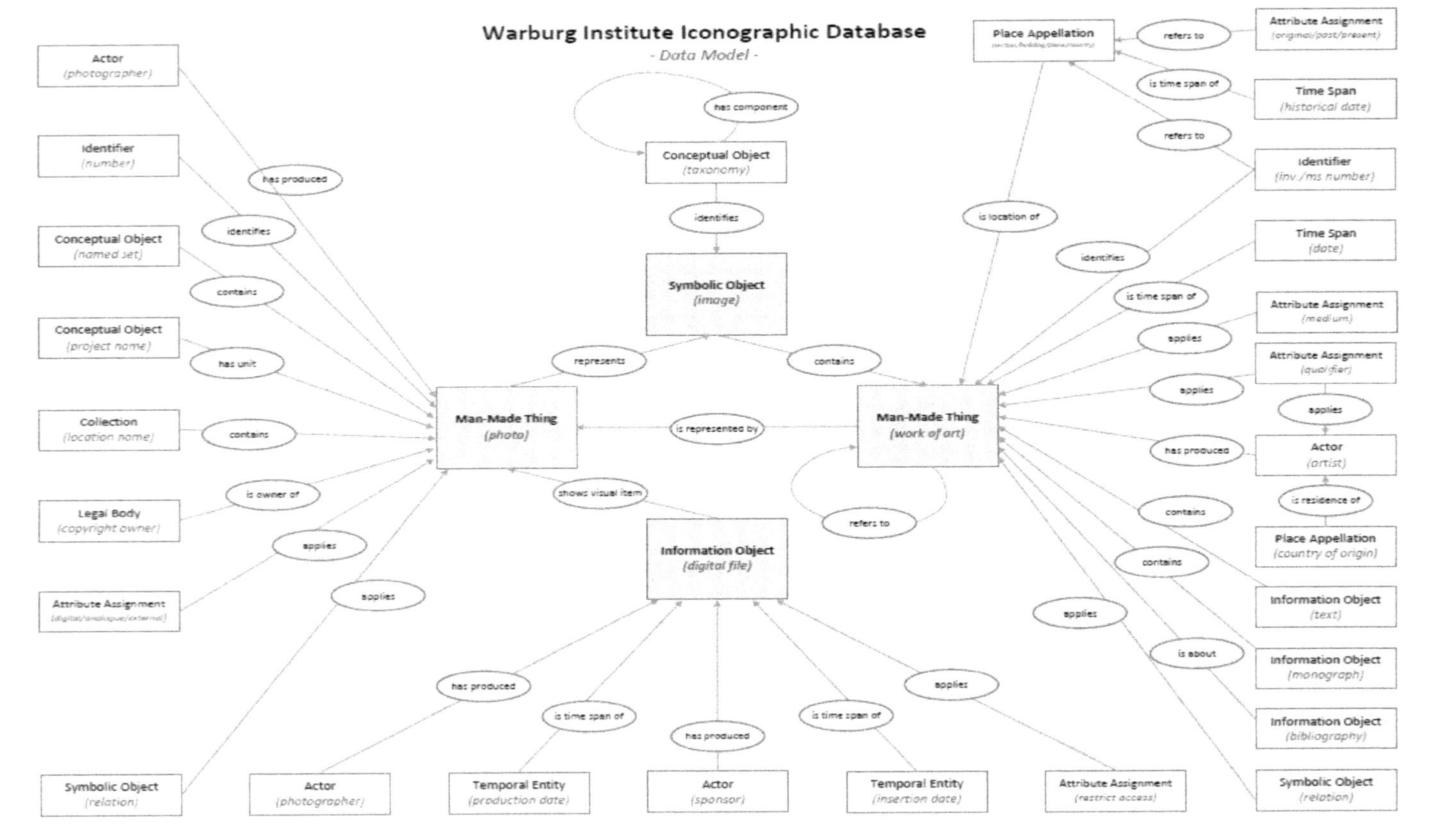

Figure 11.4 *Data model, based on CIDOC-CRM, for the Warburg Iconographic Database*

that was elaborated as the third approach in Chapter 4. This was quickly rejected because of its potential for locking the Database into an isolated silo unable to communicate with others. One of the key rationales for moving it away from mySQL was to enhance its interoperable potential and this would have been counterproductive to this aspiration. It was decided instead to map the model to several of the XML-based standards which have been the subject of this book. Figure 11.5 on the next page illustrates how this was done for its four central concepts.

METS was once again chosen as the overarching architecture for the metadata associated with an image and MODS as the primary vehicle for its descriptive component. Three MODS instances are incorporated into every METS file. The first, which is embedded within the Descriptive Metadata (`<dmdSec>`) section, contains metadata relating to the image itself, particularly its iconographic subjects. The second records the often extensive set associated with the work of art depicted and finds its place in the Source Metadata (`<sourceMD>`) subsection of Administrative Metadata (`<admSec>`). The final MODS instance, which contains information on the photograph, is located within a separate Source Metadata element, its appropriate location as it describes the analogue source from which the digital surrogate is created.

MODS accounts for three of the four core concepts at the centre of the data model; the fourth, the digital file, which is an **Information Object** in the CIDOC-CRM scheme, is accommodated by digital provenance and rights metadata in Administrative Metadata. The first of these, primarily details of the scanning process which created it, is handled by PREMIS Event and Agent objects in Digital Provenance (`<digiprovMD>`). The second, which asserts the Creative Commons licence under which the Institute makes its images available and also restricts access where required by the copyright owner of the photograph, is covered by the METSRights schema, an instance of which is embedded within the Rights (`<rightsMD>`) subsection. Also shown in the diagram is the basic technical metadata that is currently absent; this will be generated using the ImageMagick software package and added as a minimal MIX instance within Technical Metadata (`<techMD>`) as part of the migration to the new platform.

Almost all of the metadata model maps to the MODS element set clearly and unambiguously. Only in the case of a small number of fields from the original mySql tables is it necessary to invoke the schema's extension mechanism. These include a small set to provide the precise location of a work of art within a building (for instance, the room in a gallery where it is exhibited) and an element to record the residency of an artist where this information is relevant to placing their work in context. It is a testament to the viability of

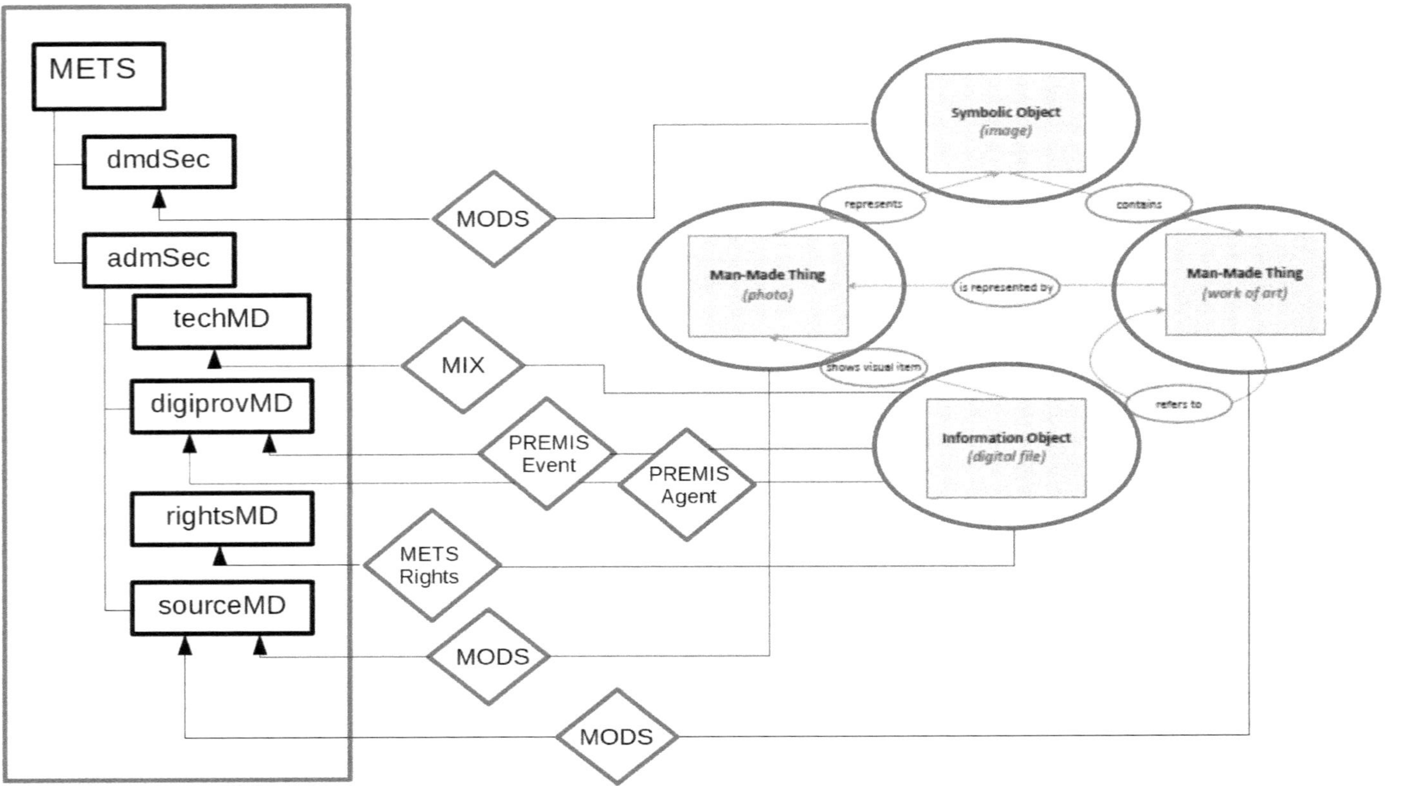

Figure 11.5 *Mapping of central concepts of data model to XML metadata standards*

the MODS schema as a vehicle for descriptive metadata that so few of these extensions are necessary for a complex and detailed model of this type.

The final part of the metadata architecture for the Iconographic Database is the extensive taxonomy which underpins its arrangement by iconographic subject. This also resided in a series of tables in the mySql database and consequently was as limited in its interoperable potential as the metadata for the images themselves. Conversion to an established standard was clearly the appropriate course for this. The obvious candidate was MADS, the schema for authority lists and thesauri that was introduced in Chapter 8.

The hierarchical arrangement of MADS closely mirrors the set of mySql tables in which the taxonomy is stored, and so mapping to this schema proved very straightforward. The taxonomy itself extends to eight levels but this presents no problems for MADS, which allows for chains of broader and narrower terms of any length. Figure 11.6 demonstrates a small sequence of this kind, relating the term 'Apollo and Daphne' to the broader 'Daphne' and then to the top-level 'Gods and Myths'.

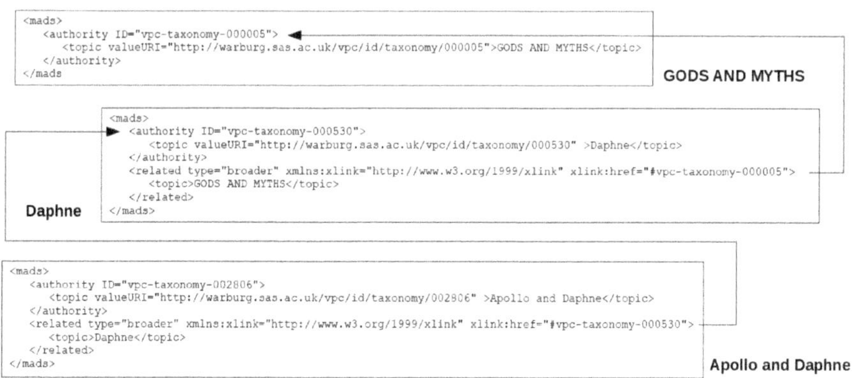

Figure 11.6 *The chain of references that map out the hierarchy for an entry in MADS*

Every entry in this taxonomy receives a URI in the **valueURI** attribute of **`<topic>`** which uniquely identifies it. Each lower-level entry is linked to its broader parent by a **`<related type="broader">`** subelement which uses its **xlink:href** attribute to point to the **ID** of the latter's **`<authority>`** element.

The complex web of relational tables in mySql translates neatly to a discrete XML file in which the whole taxonomy is recorded within a single logical structure that is easy to process and transfer between systems. It is hoped to be able to share this taxonomy with other image archives and so to disseminate the results of the years of scholarly research which have gone into its creation. It will be immeasurably easier to do this in the form of a single file than in the complex web of tables where it formerly resided.

At the time of writing, work on the new system that will deliver the Iconographic Database is only just beginning. A key part of its remit will be the ability to ingest metadata in the form described here, edit it via an interactive interface and export it back to METS or MADS as the 'canonical' formats in which it will be preserved in the long term. It is to be hoped that the new system will have a long operational life, but adopting this approach will ensure that the metadata with which it interacts will still be viable long after it has become obsolete.

11.4 Conclusion

These two case studies demonstrate the feasibility of implementing the strategy outlined in this book in operational digital libraries. They show that the complicated metadata requirements of collections such as these can be met using established standards that have been created and maintained by professional communities of practice. The XML syntax on which this strategy depends renders this metadata highly malleable, allowing it to be transformed in any way needed to interact with the systems used to house digital collections and make them available to users. It also ensures that it can be shared with others, preventing a collection from becoming an isolated silo incapable of communicating with its counterparts.

12

Summary and Conclusions

12.1 Introduction

The work of the librarian has always called for an advanced level of proficiency in metadata. The imperatives of building, developing and managing collections and making their contents accessible have invariably obliged librarians to stay at the forefront of its developments. In the digital library the complexities of handling intangible objects recorded in binary digits on opaque media present new challenges and make additional demands on metadata's role and functions. The particular challenge which the strategy outlined in this book attempts to meet is to reconcile the diverse and complicated metadata needed to accommodate these requirements with the complementary obligation to produce a coherent overall environment which can be easily managed in the present and preserved well into the future.

The first part of this concluding chapter summarises the strategy and its array of interlocking components. The second part draws some general conclusions about metadata and its central place in the digital library.

12.2 The strategy in outline

12.2.1 The basic principles of a metadata strategy (Chapter 3)

The eight fundamental principles which underlie this strategy are the following.

- It should support all stages of the digital curation lifecycle, such as those outlined in the DCC Digital Curation Lifecycle Model[C3.1].
- It should support the long-term preservation of the digital object, preferably within the context of the OAIS model[C3.4], and should aim to create a 'canonical' version of a digital object's metadata, an AIP as defined in the OAIS scheme.
- It should ensure interoperability at both a syntactic and a semantic level.
- Metadata content should be controlled wherever possible by the use of cataloguing rules, name authorities and subject thesauri.

- It should be independent of any given software application, especially a proprietary one.
- It should apply a consistent and logical system of identifiers to ensure that every data and metadata component is unambiguously labelled.
- It should employ standards whenever possible to enhance interoperability and avoid 'reinventing the wheel'.
- It should ensure the integrity of the metadata itself, for instance by recording details of its provenance.

12.2.2 Standards and identifiers (Chapter 4)

Standards should underlie a metadata strategy whenever possible. They can be implemented in three ways.

- They can be taken 'off the shelf' and applied directly. This is particularly appropriate when the contents of a digital library are derived from materials, such as printed books, for which a standard has become widely established or if pre-existing metadata conforming to one of these, for instance in a library catalogue, is readily available.
- A new architecture can be mapped out and then serialised into an existing standard. This may be done by creating a diagram which details the semantic facets required for an application and the linkages that connect them. This initial exercise should, if possible, be based on an established model such as CIDOC-CRM[S.4]. This can then be serialised into a standard such as MODS[S.18], extending its element set if necessary.
- A local metadata scheme may be devised in the case of highly specialised collections for which there is no suitable standard into which an appropriate architecture can be serialised. This should be mapped out in the same way as in the previous approach, preferably employing an underlying model such as CIDOC-CRM, and a data dictionary should be created in which semantic elements, their relationships and any content rules are specified. If possible, an interoperable syntax such as XML should be used and cross-walks provided, as far as practicable, to such schemes as DC[S.13].

A comprehensive set of identifiers should be deployed throughout the digital library architecture.

- The identifiers should be applied to every component, including the directory structure of the file system, the names of every file (data and metadata) and every significant section and subsection of metadata files.

They should be structured to mirror the logical arrangement of the collections, usually hierarchically.
- URIs should be included for every relevant component of the metadata files. These should preferably be generated from the identifiers of their respective elements by translating them into an appropriate format.

12.2.3 Syntax (Chapter 5)

Metadata should be encoded in XML to maximise its potential for interoperability and its viability for long-term preservation.

It should conform to an established schema whenever possible.

12.2.4 Packaging the metadata (Chapter 6)

All of the metadata for a digital object should be packaged into a single, discrete file which can function as an OAIS AIP.

METS[S.17] is the XML schema recommended to perform this function. When employing this standard:

- a comprehensive set of logical identifiers should be used to demarcate every component and enable the links within a METS instance to function;
- descriptive and administrative metadata in extension schemas should usually be embedded in METS rather than held externally and referenced from within it;
- for preservation purposes, consideration could also be given to embedding an object's data files (converted if necessary) within the METS File Section.

12.2.5 Descriptive metadata (Chapter 7)

An established standard for descriptive metadata should be employed within the METS Descriptive Metadata section whenever possible. Multiple Descriptive Metadata sections may be used if one standard cannot meet all requirements.

The standard used should be in the form of an XML schema in order to allow integration with METS.

For most digital collections, MODS[S.18] is recommended for descriptive metadata. When necessary its 83 elements may be supplemented by locally devised additions using its **<extension>** element.

DC[S.13] is generally not recommended as the primary vehicle for descriptive metadata, owing to its broad and imprecise semantics. However, application profiles based on it may be considered for this role. Some potentially useful schemes of this type include DCMI Metadata Terms[S.9] for generic metadata requirements and DC-Libraries[S.8] for bibliographic metadata.

MARCXML[S.15] may act as a useful intermediary between an online library catalogue and MODS.

Other specialised standards may be considered in addition to or instead of MODS:

- VRA Core[S.29] for works of visual culture and images of these;
- Text Encoding Initiative (TEI) P5 Manuscript Description[S.26] for the detailed cataloguing of manuscripts and early printed books;
- Darwin Core[S.6] and Ecological Metadata Language (EML)[S.14] for the biological and ecological sciences;
- Data Documentation Initiative (DDI)[S.7] for the social and health sciences;
- Common European Research Information Format (CERIF)[S.5] for research information management.

12.2.6 Content rules (Chapter 8)

Content rules should be applied wherever possible to ensure the consistency and interoperability of metadata. These should include the implementation of cataloguing rules and the use of controlled vocabularies for metadata content.

Cataloguing rules

- Cataloguing rules should follow standards established within the digital library's professional community if at all possible. Some key examples include:
  - — Anglo-American Cataloging Rules, Second Edition (AACR2)[S.1] and Resource Description and Access (RDA)[S.24] for collections digitised from materials in physical libraries for which catalogue records already exist;
  - — Cataloging Cultural Objects (CCO)[S.3] for works of art, architecture and cultural artefacts;
  - — Describing Archives: A Content Standard (DACS)[S.10] for archival materials;
  - — Descriptive Cataloging of Rare Materials[S.11] for early printed books and manuscripts.
- If no established standard is suitable (for instance, if it is not appropriate to a collection's subject coverage, is too detailed or requires skills and training not available within a library's resources), local guidelines may be devised and implemented.

— If possible, these should be based on existing standards, adapting, simplifying or cutting them down as necessary.
— They should specify:

- the metadata fields to be used, which are mandatory,
- recommended or optional and which are repeatable;
- which controlled vocabularies and subject thesauri should be applied;
- how the metadata content is to be formatted.

Controlled vocabularies

- should be employed for as much metadata content as possible;
- may be supplemented by local vocabularies conforming to the same conventions for the formatting of content;
- should specify a URI for each entry which should then be used to identify it in the appropriate elements and attributes of the descriptive metadata schemas employed.
- Key controlled vocabularies which should be considered include:

— for names, the Virtual International Authority File (VIAF)[C8.14], which integrates 68 name authority lists;
— for subjects, LCSH[C8.9];
— code lists including MARC Relator Codes[C8.11], ISO 639.2 Language Codes[C8.6] and the MARC Code List for Countries[C8.10].

Locally produced authority lists or thesauri, which either supplement established vocabularies or stand on their own, should be encoded in the XML schema MADS[S.16] to enhance their interoperability and longevity.

12.2.7 Administrative and preservation metadata (Chapter 9)

Administrative and preservation metadata should be recorded in the Technical Metadata, Digital Provenance and Rights subdivisions of the METS Administrative Metadata section.

PREMIS[S.23] is recommended as the primary schema for this metadata, and can be supplemented if required by instances of more specific schemas embedded in PREMIS extension elements.

The PREMIS Object entity should be used to record basic technical metadata, including fixity checksums and file formats (preferably as listed in a format registry such as PRONOM)[C9.5]. Additional schemas for this which may supplement PREMIS include:

- MIX[S.20] for still images
- TextMD[S.27] for text
- AudioMD[S.2] for audio
- VideoMD[S.28] for video.

The PREMIS Agent and Event entities should be used in conjunction for digital provenance metadata. A controlled vocabulary for event types should be used if possible.

For rights metadata the PREMIS Rights entity should be used for recording IPR ownership and any licences used for granting access. The METSRights schema may be used in addition to specify more precisely any rights granted.

12.2.8 Enabling interoperability (Chapter 10)

Employing XML as the encoding syntax and standards such as METS, MODS and PREMIS enhances the interoperable potential of a digital library's metadata.

Possible routes to sharing this metadata include:

- supplying METS files directly. Details of the METS application, for instance any extension schemas used, should be fully documented to enable this. If possible, compile a METS Profile[C10.7] and register it with the Library of Congress;
- generating OAI-PMH[S.21] instances from METS using XSLT transformations and providing a gateway for harvesting requests;
- generating RDF XML[C10.11] for ingest into a triple store from METS using XSLT.

12.3 Conclusions

In the opening pages of this book it was emphasised that the approach which it outlines is centred on the digital library as a *library* and so is aimed at the librarians who create, develop, administer and preserve the items in their care. This emphasis is important, as the strategy detailed here is designed to enable curatorship, the librarian's principle concern, to be carried out as effectively for a digital collection as for its physical counterpart. It is important to keep in mind the continuity of practice in librarianship as it has developed over centuries if this is to happen: much of the corpus of knowledge and practice that underlies the profession is as relevant in the digital sphere as in the analogue.

In a digital library we 'select and acquire, we classify, we provide equitable access, and we preserve' as the summation by Shirley Baker in Chapter 1 so succinctly puts it. In this, our 'mission' is the same as for a traditional collection housed on bookshelves. Ranganathan's Five Laws of Library Science, also cited in the first chapter, are just as relevant here if we expand the media cited in them to encompass to something wider than 'books' alone: *resources* are for use, every user his or her *resource*, every *resource* its user, save the time of the user, the digital library must be a growing organism. These remain as pertinent as ever when pointing the way forward for a developing digital library.

Metadata is as central to unlocking the digital library as to its paper-based antecedents. However, some divergence of form and practice becomes necessary when the contents of collections move from the physical to the electronic. The metadata requirements of the opaque contents of a digital library, which require decoding before they can be read, are undoubtedly more complex than those of the printed or written page. This complexity may be daunting when we are faced with the prospect of their implementation in a working environment. Even this chapter's pared-down summary of the strategy outlined in this book runs to 1,500 words, illustrating that it is a far-from-simple matter to devise something which embraces the heterogeneous range of information needed to enable such a library to function and does so in a coherent and logical way which ensures that its metadata (and data) can be managed effectively in the present and future.

One of the principal challenges of a metadata strategy, analogue or digital, is the reconciliation of the opposing imperatives of flexibility and constraint. We need it to be flexible enough to express the individual (even idiosyncratic) descriptive requirements of a collection, but also able to speak to others in ways in which it can be readily understood. The manner in which it is organised needs to be sufficiently adaptable to cope with the complexities of a collection's structure while being controlled enough to construct clear pathways through which it can be navigated by outsiders. In the digital library it also needs to be able to function within the systems that deliver and preserve collections while remaining independent of them. Finally, it needs to address the requirements of the here and now and those of the future, for the latter of which we can make only (hopefully) educated guesses.

One of the primary methods that this book has advocated for reconciling these potentially antagonistic demands is the choice of syntax. XML allows the flexible and the constrained to co-exist in a symbiotic relationship, which makes it a particularly suitable vessel for metadata. The malleability of XML, the mechanisms by which it can be transformed and manipulated, ensures that it can assert its independence from any given platform or software but can readily be converted to accommodate their requirements as and when needed. An XML schema allows metadata to be organised and structured in ways which make it predictable enough to be understood by others while preserving enough flexibility for it not to lose its expressive potential.

The second key to reconciling flexibility and constraint is the packaging of metadata. The digital library is set in a complex metadata landscape, the contents of which must be diverse enough to accommodate the heterogeneous components needed for a digital object to be created, managed, accessed and preserved. Multiple standards are needed to meet the demands of its descriptive, technical, digital provenance, rights, preservation and structural metadata, all of which can be unified syntactically by their shared underpinning in XML.

The logical structures of the METS schema prove invaluable for giving shape to this potential morass of information. The content of the metadata embedded in an instance may be diverse, but navigating it is straightforward and logical. Bringing it together in this way lets us turn a potentially amorphous agglomeration into something discrete and functional, allowing us to create an object that we can justifiably call a 'canonical' statement of the metadata for a digital object. This statement has to be Janus-like in its outlook: it must meet the contemporary demands of working systems which deliver and administer collections but must also have its glance fixed on the future, where its function as a preservation medium will come to the fore.

Metadata will always, therefore, be wrestling with the tensions of reconciling opposites, and so will inevitably be something of a compromise: our aim should be to prevent it becoming an overly messy one. The strategy advocated throughout this book allows us to bring order and shape to what can be a quagmire of information surrounding a digital object. It is important to remember that a metadata strategy should be embedded in the principles of librarianship if it is to achieve this. It is to be hoped that what has been laid out in these chapters allows us to emphasise the 'library' as much as the 'digital' in the digital library and will ensure that we can continue to care for our collections with the curatorial diligence that they deserve long into the future.

Appendix: Sample MODS File Serialised from Data Model

This is a MODS file serialised from the simple data model for the digitised photograph of Michelangelo's *Pietà* in Figure 4.4 (Chapter 4).

```
<?xml version="1.0" encoding="UTF-8"?>
<mods xmlns="http://www.loc.gov/mods/v3"
xmlns:xsi="http://www.w3.org/2001/XMLSchema-instance"
xsi:schemaLocation="http://www.loc.gov/mods/v3
                   http://www.loc.gov/standards/mods/v3/mods-3-7.xsd">

       <location>
         <holdingSimple>
              <copyInformation>
                   <electronicLocator>wxl-0001-0.tif</electronicLocator>
              </copyInformation>
         </holdingSimple>
       </location>

       <relatedItem otherType="workOfArt">
         <titleInfo>
              <title>Pietà</title>
         </titleInfo>

         <name>
              <role>
                   <roleTerm type="code">art</roleTerm>
              </role>
              <namePart>Michelangelo</namePart>
         </name>

         <subject>
              <name type="personal">
                    <namePart>Jesus</namePart>
              </name>
              <name type="personal">
                    <namePart>Mary, Mother of Jesus</namePart>
              </name>
         </subject>
       </relatedItem>
```

```
    <relatedItem otherType="photograph">
      <name>
           <role>
                <roleTerm type="code">pht</roleTerm>
           </role>
           <namePart>Stanislav Traykov</namePart>
      </name>
    </relatedItem>
</mods>
```

The components of the data model are recorded in this file as follows:

- the identifier (filename) for the digital file in the subelements of **<location>**;
- metadata on the work of art depicted in the subelements of **<relatedItem otherType="workOfArt">**. These include:
  - — its title in the subelements of **<titleinfo>**;
  - — the artist who created it in the subelements of **<name>**. Here the **<roleTerm>** element indicates that Michelangelo's role was that of artist (using a code from the MARC Relator Codes[C8.11] list);
  - — the subjects depicted (Jesus and Mary, Mother of Jesus) in the subelements of **<subject>**;
- metadata on the photograph that was digitised in the subelements of **<relatedItem otherType="photograph">**, specifically:
  - — the photographer in the subelements of **<name>**. Here the **<roleTerm>** element indicates his role as a photographer (once again using a code from the MARC Relator Codes list).

Useful Resources

This section lists references to the key metadata standards discussed in this book and supplementary documentation, resources and tools that are relevant to these. The standards themselves are listed at the beginning in an alphabetical sequence with links to their home pages. The supplementary materials are then listed in the order of the chapters to which they primarily relate.

Each resource has a numbered identifier by which it is referenced within the main body of the book; for example, AudioMD[S.2].

The links provided here are correct at the time of writing but may, of course, change over time.

Key metadata standards referenced

S.1 Anglo-American Cataloging Rules (AACR2)
www.aacr2.org/

S.2 AudioMD
www.loc.gov/standards/amdvmd/audiovideoMDschemas.html

S.3 Cataloging Cultural Objects (CCO)
https://vraweb.org/resources/cataloging-cultural-objects/

S.4 CIDOC Conceptual Reference Model (CIDOC-CRM)
www.cidoc-crm.org/

S.5 Common European Research Information Format (CERIF)
www.eurocris.org/services/main-features-cerif

S.6 Darwin Core
https://dwc.tdwg.org/

S.7 Data Documentation Initiative (DDI)
https://ddialliance.org/

S.8 DC-Libraries
www.dublincore.org/specifications/dublin-core/library-application-profile/

S.9 DCMI Metadata Terms
www.dublincore.org/specifications/dublin-core/dcmi-terms/

S.10 Describing Archives: A Content Standard (DACS)
https://saa-ts-dacs.github.io/

S.11 Descriptive Cataloging of Rare Materials (Rare Books and Manuscripts Section, Association of College and Research Libraries)
http://rbms.info/dcrm/
S.12 Digital Item Declaration Language (DIDL)
https://mpeg.chiariglione.org/standards/mpeg-21
S.13 Dublin Core (DC)
http://dublincore.org/
S.14 Ecological Metadata Language (EML)
https://eml.ecoinformatics.org/
S.15 MARCXML
www.loc.gov/standards/marcxml/
S.16 Metadata Authority Description Schema (MADS)
www.loc.gov/standards/mads/
S.17 Metadata Encoding and Transmission Standards (METS)
www.loc.gov/standards/mets/
S.18 Metadata Object Description Schema (MODS)
www.loc.gov/standards/mods/
S.19 METSRights
www.loc.gov/standards/rights/METSRights.xsd (schema only)
https://github.com/mets/METS-Rights-Schema (includes examples)
S.20 NISO Metadata for Images in XML (MIX)
www.niso.org/publications/ansiniso-z3987-2006-r2017-data-dictionary-technical-metadata-digital-still-images
S.21 Open Archives Initiative Protocol for Metadata Harvesting (OAI-PMH)
www.openarchives.org/pmh/
S.22 PBCore
https://pbcore.org/
S.23 PREservation Metadata: Implementation Strategies (PREMIS)
www.loc.gov/standards/premis/
S.24 Resource Description and Access (RDA)
www.rda-rsc.org/
S.25 Text Encoding Initiative
https://tei-c.org/
S.26 Text Encoding Initiative (TEI) P5 Manuscript Description
https://tei-c.org/release/doc/tei-p5-doc/en/html/MS.html
S.27 TextMD
www.loc.gov/standards/textMD/
S.28 VideoMD
www.loc.gov/standards/amdvmd/audiovideoMDschemas.html

S.29 VRA Core
www.loc.gov/standards/vracore/

Supplementary documentation and resources

Chapter 1

No supplementary material.

Chapter 2 (C2)

C2.1 Creative Commons
https://creativecommons.org/
C2.2 MUBI
https://mubi.com/

Chapter 3 (C3)

C3.1 DCC Digital Curation Lifecycle Model
www.dcc.ac.uk/guidance/curation-lifecycle-model
C3.2 Europeana
www.europeana.eu/en
C3.3 Getty Research Portal
https://portal.getty.edu/
C3.4 Reference Model for an Open Archival Information System (OAIS)
https://public.ccsds.org/pubs/650x0m2.pdf
C3.5 WorldCat
www.worldcat.org/

Chapter 4 (C4)

C4.1 Omeka https://omeka.org/

Chapter 5 (C5)

C5.1 Oxygen XML editor
www.oxygenxml.com/
C5.2 Saxon XML converter
www.saxonica.com/documentation/documentation.xml
C5.3 XML Copy Editor
https://sourceforge.net/projects/xml-copy-editor/
C5.4 XML Schema tutorial (W3 Schools)
www.w3schools.com/xml/schema_intro.asp
C5.5 XSLT introduction (W3 Schools)
www.w3schools.com/xml/xsl_intro.asp

Chapter 6 (C6)

C6.1 ISO 8601 Date and Time Format
www.iso.org/iso-8601-date-and-time-format.html (formal definition)
www.w3.org/TR/NOTE-datetime (summary by W3C)

C6.2 METS Primer and Reference Manual
www.loc.gov/standards/mets/METSDocumentationdraft8.30.pdf

Chapter 7 (C7)

C7.1 Dublin Core: qualified DC
www.dublincore.org/specifications/dublin-core/usageguide/qualifiers/

C7.2 Dublin Core: simple DC elements
www.dublincore.org/specifications/dublin-core/usageguide/elements/

C7.3 Dublin Core XML Schemas
www.dublincore.org/schemas/xmls/

C7.4 MarcEdit (software)
https://marcedit.reeset.net/

Chapter 8 (C8)

C8.1 Art and Architecture Thesaurus
www.getty.edu/research/tools/vocabularies/aat/

C8.2 Digital Library Federation/Aquifer Implementation Guidelines for Shareable MODS Records
https://wiki.dlib.indiana.edu/download/attachments/24288/DLFMODS_ImplementationGuidelines.pdf

C8.3 Functional Requirements for Bibliographic Records (FRBR)
www.ifla.org/publications/functional-requirements-for-bibliographic-records

C8.4 International Standard Name Identifier (ISNI)
https://isni.org/

C8.5 ISAD(G): General International Standard Archival Description – Second edition
www.ica.org/en/isadg-general-international-standard-archival-description-second-edition

C8.6 ISO 639.2 Language Codes
www.loc.gov/standards/iso639-2/php/code_list.php

C8.7 Library of Congress Name Authority File
https://id.loc.gov/authorities/names.html

C8.8 Library of Congress Subject Heading and Term Source Codes
https://www.loc.gov/standards/sourcelist/subject.html

C8.9 Library of Congress Subject Headings (LCSH)
https://id.loc.gov/authorities/subjects.html

C8.10 MARC Code List for Countries
www.loc.gov/marc/countries/cou_home.html

C8.11 MARC Relator Codes
www.loc.gov/marc/relators/

C8.12 UMass Amherst Libraries Metadata Guidelines
www.library.umass.edu/assets/Digital-Strategies-Group/Guidelines-Policies/Metadata-Guidelines-v4.pdf

C8.13 Union List of Artist Names (ULAN)
www.getty.edu/research/tools/vocabularies/ulan/

C8.14 Virtual International Authority File
http://viaf.org/

C8.15 W3C Date and Time Formats
www.w3.org/TR/NOTE-datetime-970915

C8.16 Western States Dublin Core Metadata Best Practices, version 1.2
https://digitalcommons.usu.edu/lib_pubs/78/

Chapter 9 (C9)

C9.1 Guidelines for using PREMIS with METS for exchange
www.loc.gov/standards/premis/guidelines2017-premismets.pdf

C9.2 Library of Congress Agent Types
https://id.loc.gov/vocabulary/preservation/agentType.html

C9.3 Library of Congress Event Types
https://id.loc.gov/vocabulary/preservation/eventType.html

C9.4 MIME types
www.iana.org/assignments/media-types/media-types.xhtml

C9.5 PRONOM
www.nationalarchives.gov.uk/PRONOM/Default.aspx

C9.6 TEI Lite
https://tei-c.org/guidelines/customization/lite/

Chapter 10 (C10)

C10.1 arXiv
https://arxiv.org/

C10.2 DSpace
https://duraspace.org/dspace/

C10.3 Dublin Core Ontologies
http://bloody-byte.net/rdf/dc_owl2dl/
C10.4 EPrints
https://github.com/eprints/eprints
C10.5 Ethos (British Library thesis repository)
https://ethos.bl.uk/
C10.6 Library of Congress Register of METS Profiles
www.loc.gov/standards/mets/mets-registered-profiles.html
C10.7 METS Profiles
www.loc.gov/standards/mets/mets-profiles.html
C10.8 MODS/RDF Initiatives (including MODS ontology and MODS RDF stylesheet)
www.loc.gov/standards/mods/modsrdf/
C10.9 PREMIS ontology
www.loc.gov/standards/premis/ontology/
C10.10 Resource Description Framework (RDF)
www.w3.org/RDF/
C10.11 RDF XML Syntax (W3C)
www.w3.org/TR/rdf-syntax-grammar/
C10.12 SPARQL Protocol and RDF Query Language (SPARQL)
www.w3.org/TR/rdf-sparql-query/
C10.13 Web Ontology Language (OWL)
www.w3.org/OWL/

Chapter 11 (C11)

C11.1 Fedora Commons
https://duraspace.org/fedora/
C11.2 ImageMagick (image processing software)
https://imagemagick.org/
C11.3 Islandora
https://islandora.ca/
C11.4 Warburg Digital Library
https://wdl.warburg.sas.ac.uk/
C11.5 Warburg Institute Iconographic Database
https://iconographic.warburg.sas.ac.uk/
C11.6 Warburg Institute Library catalogue
https://catalogue.libraries.london.ac.uk/searchS12/

Chapter 12

No supplementary material.

Further Reading

This section suggests recommended background reading on the topics covered in the preceding chapters.

Chapters 1 and 2

These texts offer general introductions to metadata and its central concepts.

Gartner, Richard. 2016. *Metadata: Shaping Knowledge from Antiquity to the Semantic Web*. Basel: Springer-Verlag.

A beginner's guide to metadata, including accounts of its historical development, ideological underpinning, core features (syntax, semantics and content rules), taxonomy, the Semantic Web, citizen science and folksonomies.

Haynes, David. 2018. *Metadata for Information Management and Retrieval: Understanding Metadata and Its Use*. London: Facet Publishing.

An accessible introduction to metadata and its practical application for librarians and information professionals. It includes detailed advice on the management of metadata as a resource and its application to very large data collections.

Zeng, Lei Marcia and Jian Qin. 2016. *Metadata*. 2nd edn. London: Facet Publishing.

The benchmark textbook on metadata for librarians and information scientists, aimed at the professional metadata specialist or advanced student.

Chapter 3

National Information Standards Organization. 2016. 'A Framework of Guidance for Building Good Digital Collections: Metadata'. http://framework.niso.org/24.html.

A succinct statement of good practice for metadata and digital collections on which most of the principles laid out in this chapter are based.

DCC Curation Lifecycle Model

Higgins, Sarah. 2008. 'The DCC Curation Lifecycle Model'. *International*

Journal of Digital Curation 3 (1): 134–40. www.ijdc.net/article/view/69/48

A very short introduction to the DCC Curation Lifecycle Model and the rationale behind it.

Oliver, Gillian and Ross Harvey. 2016. *Digital Curation*. Chicago: American Library Association.

A key textbook on digital curation which includes a detailed description of the DCC Lifecycle Model and its practical application.

Open Archival Information System

Lavoie, Brian F. 2014. *The Open Archival Information System (OAIS) Reference Model: Introductory Guide*. York: Digital Preservation Coalition. www.dpconline.org/docs/technology-watch-reports/1359-dpctw14-02/file.

A concise (31 pages), non-technical introduction to OAIS and its role in digital preservation, one of a series of introductory reports from the Digital Preservation Coalition (see also Lavoie and Gartner's 'Preservation Metadata', listed under Chapter 9).

Chapter 4

CIDOC-CRM

International Committee for Documentation. 2020. 'Versions of the CIDOC-CRM | CIDOC CRM'. www.cidoc-crm.org/versions-of-the-cidoc-crm.

The official documentation for the current version of CIDOC-CRM is the essential resource for implementing the data model: it runs to around 250 pages but is approachable and clearly explains every class and property.

Oldman, Dominic and CRM Labs. 2014. 'The CIDOC Conceptual Reference Model (CIDOC-CRM): PRIMER'. *CIDOC-CRM Official Web Site*. http://citeseerx.ist.psu.edu/viewdoc/download?doi=10.1.1.642.9493&rep=rep1&type=pdf.

A concise and relatively non-technical introduction to CIDOC-CRM and its application to cultural heritage materials.

Chapter 5

Introductions to XML

Cole, Timothy W., Myung-Ja K. Han and Christine Schwartz. 2018. *Coding with XML for Efficiencies in Cataloguing and Metadata Practical Applications of XSD, XSLT, and XQuery*. London: Facet Publishing.

Aimed at practising librarians, this introduces XML, XSLT and their associated technologies: it includes extensive practical tutorials in their implementation.

w3schools.com. 2020. 'XML Tutorial'. www.w3schools.com/xml/.
One of the best online introductions to XML, which covers all of its basics clearly and with minimal technical jargon.

XSLT

w3schools.com. 2020. 'XSLT Introduction'. www.w3schools.com/xml/xsl_intro.asp.
Another excellent tutorial from W3Schools which introduces the essential features of XSLT: you should be able to write basic transformations after completing this.

w3schools.com. 2020. 'XSLT Reference'. www.w3schools.com/xml/xsl_elementref.asp.
A complement to the 'W3Schools' tutorial, this is a useful reference listing of the XSLT elements and functions needed to write functional transformations.

Chapter 6

Gartner, Richard. 2002. 'METS: Metadata Encoding and Transmission Standard'. JISC Technology and Standards Watch Reports. www.academia.edu/download/6723335/tsw_02-05.pdf.

Gartner, Richard. 2008. 'Metadata for Digital Libraries: State of the Art and Future Directions'. JISC Technology and Standards Watch Reports. www.researchgate.net/profile/Richard_Gartner2/publication/253144337_Metadata_for_digital_libraries_state_of_the_art_and_future_directions/
Two short reports by the current author introducing METS and its application to digital library metadata.

Chapter 7

Dublin Core

Caplan, Priscilla. 2003. 'The Dublin Core'. In *Metadata Fundamentals for All Librarians*, 76–87. Chicago: American Library Association. www.ala.org/aboutala/sites/ala.org.aboutala/files/content/publishing/editions/samplers/caplan_MF.pdf.
The chapter on DC from Caplan's textbook remains an excellent introduction to this standard: it is available online on the American Library Association's website.

MODS: Metadata Object Description Schema

Gartner, Richard. 2003. 'MODS: Metadata Object Description Schema'.

JISC Technology and Standards Watch. JISC. www.academia.edu/download/6723333/10.1.1.112.2714.pdf.
A concise introduction to the MODS standard, its overall architecture and why it is a better option than DC.
McCallum, Sally H. 2004. 'An Introduction to the Metadata Object Description Schema (MODS)'. *Library Hi Tech*, 82–8.
An introduction to MODS which explains specifically the needs that it aims to meet and how it differs from MARC.

Chapter 8

Dextre Clarke, Stella G. 2017. 'Thesaurus (for Information Retrieval)'. In *ISKO Encyclopedia of Knowledge Organization*. ISKO. www.isko.org/cyclo/thesaurus.
An introduction to subject thesauri and their role in knowledge organisation: this is an informative guide for those who wish to understand their theoretical underpinnings.
Lazarinis, Fotis. 2014. *Cataloguing and Classification: An Introduction to AACR2, RDA, DDC, LCC, LCSH and MARC 21 Standards*. Oxford: Chandos Publishing.
A comprehensive textbook covering all of the topics discussed in this chapter (and others elsewhere in this book): they include cataloguing rules (AACR2 and RDA are treated in depth) and subject thesauri.
Miller, Stephen J. 2011. *Metadata for Digital Collections: A How-to-Do-It Manual*. London: Facet Publishing.
Chapter 5 of Miller's book demonstrates the value of controlled vocabularies for enhanced discoverability and provides practical guidance on their implementation (including designing your own if necessary).
Tillett, Barbara. 2003. 'What is FRBR?'. www.loc.gov/cds/downloads/FRBR.PDF.
An approachable introduction to the Functional Requirements for Bibliographic Records (FRBR) model which underlies RDA: it explains very clearly the four levels of description that FRBR prescribes.

Chapter 9

Caplan, Priscilla. 2017. 'Understanding PREMIS: An Overview of the PREMIS Data Dictionary for Preservation Metadata'. Washington, DC: Library of Congress. www.loc.gov/standards/premis/understanding-premis.pdf.
One of the best introductions to the PREMIS standard, an excellent preparation for implementing it in practice.

Digital Preservation Coalition. 2020. 'Digital Preservation Handbook'. www.dpconline.org/handbook.
An authoritative online guide from the UK's primary organisation for digital preservation which places metadata in the context of overall preservation practices.

Lavoie, Brian and Richard Gartner. 2013. 'Preservation Metadata (2nd Edn)'. Digital Preservation Coalition. http://dx.doi.org/10.7207/twr13-03.
The second edition of an introductory guide to preservation metadata (including PREMIS) from the Digital Preservation Coalition. This includes a useful section on tools for creating and administering this type of metadata.

Chapter 10

OAI_PMH (Open Archives Initiative Protocol for Metadata Harvesting)

Breeding, Marshall. 2002. 'Understanding the Protocol for Metadata Harvesting of the Open Archives Initiative'. *Computers in Libraries* 22 (PRESSCUT-2002-213): 24. https://librarytechnology.org/document/9944.
A simple introduction to metadata harvesting and how the OAI-PMH schema facilitates this.

RDF (Resource Description Framework)

Gartner, Richard. 2016. *Metadata: Shaping Knowledge from Antiquity to the Semantic Web*. Basel: Springer-Verlag.
Chapter 8 (pp 87–93) provides a very simple introduction to RDF and the Semantic Web.

w3schools.com. 2020. 'XML RDF'. www.w3schools.com/xml/xml_rdf.asp.
Another excellent tutorial from W3Schools which explains how to implement RDF in XML.

World Wide Web Consortium. 2014. 'RDF 1.1 Primer'. www.w3.org/TR/rdf11-primer/.
The definitive guide to RDF from W3C for those who wish to go into it in more depth.

Chapter 11

Warburg Digital Library

Gartner, Richard, 2021. 'Implementing and Administering a Digital Library: A Case Study of the Warburg Institute'. In *University Development and Administration: Developing and Administering the*

University Library, edited by Fernando F. Padró, Shri Ram and Marlene M. Hurley. London: Springer Nature.
An outline of the design and administration of the Warburg Digital Library, including its place in the Institute's overall strategy, its *Islandora* platform, metadata strategy, digitisation methods and workflows.

Warburg Iconographic Database

Gartner, Richard. 2020. 'The Warburg Iconographic Database: From Relational Tables to Interoperable Metadata'. In *Routledge International Handbook of Research Methods in Digital Humanities*, edited by Kristen Schuster and Stuart Dunn, Chapter 11. New York: Routledge and Kegan Paul.
A detailed account of the metadata strategy for the Warburg Iconographic Database, including its use of the CIDOC-CRM data model and its serialisation into METS and MODS.

Chapter 12

The readings given under Chapters 1 and 2 above are also relevant to the discussion in this concluding chapter.

References

Baca, Murtha, Patricia Harpring, Elisa Lanzi, Linda McRae and Ann Whiteside. 2006. 'Cataloging Cultural Objects: A Guide to Describing Cultural Works and Their Images'. American Library Association. http://vraweb.org/wp-content/uploads/2020/04/CatalogingCulturalObjectsFullv2.pdf.

Bagley, Philip R. 1968. *Extension of Programming Language Concepts*. Philadelphia: University City Science Center.

Bauman, Syd. 2011. 'Interchange vs Interoperability'. In *Balisage: The Markup Conference 2011: Proceedings*. Vol. 7. www.balisage.net/Proceedings/vol7/html/Bauman01/BalisageVol7-Bauman01.html.

Bekaert, Jeroen, Patrick Hochstenbach and Herbert van de Sompel. 2003. 'Using MPEG-21 DIDL to Represent Complex Digital Objects in the Los Alamos National Laboratory Digital Library'. *D-Lib Magazine*; 2003 [9] 11. https://dspace.library.uu.nl/handle/1874/3155.

Berners-Lee, Tim, James Hendler and Ora Lassila. 2001. 'The Semantic Web'. *Scientific American*, January, 29–37.

Caplan, Priscilla. 2003. *Metadata Fundamentals for All Librarians*. Chicago: American Library Association.

Coleman, James and Don Willis. 1997. *SGML as a Framework for Digital Preservation and Access*. Washington, DC: Commission on Preservation and Access, Council on Library and Information Resources. www.clir.org/pubs/reports/pub68.

Foldès, Peter. 1971. *Metadata*. Animation. National Film Board of Canada. www.nfb.ca/film/metadata_en/.

Gartner, Richard. 2004. 'Moves towards the Global Digital Library: Information and International Development'. In *Global Librarianship*, edited by Martin Kesselmann and Irwin Weibtraub, 191–208. New York, NY: Marcel Dekker.

Gruber, Thomas R. 1993. 'A Translation Approach to Portable Ontology Specifications'. *Knowledge Acquisition* 5 (2): 199–220.

Guenther, Rebecca and Leslie Myrick. 2007. 'Archiving Web Sites for Preservation and Access: MODS, METS and MINERVA'. *Journal of Archival Organization* 4 (1–2): 141–66.

International Organization for Standardization. 1986. *Information Processing: Text and Office Systems: Standard Generalized Markup Language (SGML) (ISO 8879:1986)*. Geneva: ISO.

Lavoie, Brian and Richard Gartner. 2013. 'Preservation Metadata (2nd Edn)'. Digital Preservation Coalition. http://dx.doi.org/10.7207/twr13-03.

OED Online. 2020a. 'Semantics, n.' In *OED Online*. Oxford University Press. www.oed.com/view/Entry/345083.

———. 2020b. 'Syntax, n.' In *OED Online*. Oxford University Press. www.oed.com/view/Entry/196559.

———. 2020c. 'Data Dictionary, n.' In *OED Online*. Oxford University Press. www.oed.com/view/Entry/296948.

Ranganathan, S. R. 1931. *The Five Laws of Library Science*. Madras: Madras Library Association.

Rush, Michael, Lynn Holdzkom, Prudence Backman, Daniel Santamaria and Andrea Leigh. 2008. 'Applying DACS to Finding Aids: Case Studies from Three Diverse Repositories'. *The American Archivist* 71 (1): 210–27.

Saffady, William. 1995. 'Digital Library Concepts and Technologies for the Management of Library Collections: An Analysis of Methods and Costs'. *Library Technology Reports* 31 (3): 221–380.

Shadbolt, Nigel, Wendy Hall and Tim Berners-Lee. 2006. 'The Semantic Web Revisited'. *Intelligent Systems, IEEE* 21 (3): 96–101.

Stroeker, Natasha and René Vogels. 2014. 'Survey Report on Digitisation in European Cultural Heritage Institutions 2012'. *ENUMERATE Thematic Network*. https://faro.be/sites/default/files/bijlagen/e-documenten/2014_enumerate.pdf.

Tannenbaum, Andrew. 2003. *Computer Networks*. 2nd edn. Upper Saddle River: Prentice Hall PTR.

Taylor, Arlene G. 2004. *The Organization of Information*. 2nd edn. Westport: Libraries Unlimited.

World Wide Web Consortium. 1997. 'Press Release: W3C Announces RDF'. www.w3.org/Press/RDF.

World Wide Web Consortium. 2008. 'Extensible Markup Language (XML) 1.0 (Fifth Edition)'. www.w3.org/TR/REC-xml/.

Index